AF395536

Stalingrad Survivor

STALINGRAD SURVIVOR
A Memoir of Captivity 1943–1946

WOLFRAM REDLER

Translated by David Brian Lasher

Introduction by Nik Cornish

Greenhill Books

Stalingrad Survivor

Greenhill Books

This edition first published by Greenhill Books, 2026
Greenhill Books, c/o Pen & Sword Books Ltd,
George House, Units 12 & 13, Beevor Street, Off Pontefract Road, Barnsley,
South Yorkshire S71 1HN
For more information on our books, please visit
www.greenhillbooks.com, email contact@greenhillbooks.com
or write to us at the above address.

Originally published in German as *Hände Hoch*, Copyright 1975 by Verlag Josef Egger,
Imst – Tirol. All rights reserved. The original German edition was printed in Austria by
Eggerdruck-Buchdruckerei Gebhard Egger, Imst – Tirol.

English language translation 2025 © David Brian Lasher
Nik Cornish Introduction © Greenhill Books 2025
Illustrations © Heather Hertel & Sarah Heary

The Publisher's authorised representative in the EU for product safety is
Authorised Rep Compliance Ltd.,
Ground Floor, 71 Lower Baggot Street, Dublin D02 P593, Ireland.
www.arccompliance.com

CIP data records for this title are available from the British Library
ISBN 9781805002321
ePub ISBN 9781805002338
PDF ISBN 9781805002345

Typeset by JCS Publishing Partnership
Typeset in Minion Pro 12/14.5

Printed and bound in Great Britain by CPI Group (UK) Ltd, Croydon, CRO 4YY

Contents

Introduction

by Nik Cornish

Wolfram Redler was a born in Feldkirch, in the Austrian province of Vorarlberg, in February 1914. He volunteered for military service in 1933 in an Austrian army mountain unit. In August 1939, having just qualified as a teacher of English and physical education, Redler was conscripted into the German army, which had absorbed the armed forces of Austria as a result of the Anschluss of Austria and Germany in 1938. As a soldier in one of the mountain units he fought in Poland, France and the Balkans. In 1941 he was transferred to the XIII Army Corps for the invasion of the USSR and remained with this formation for the advance on Voronezh in 1942.

The translator, David Brian Lasher, is a retired US naval officer, a student of Redler's in the early 1980s, who wished to bring this work to the English-speaking world. For this I must commend him, as such memories of the hideousness of the Eastern Front during World War II and its aftermath for the ordinary soldier involved are, all too often, overlooked or ignored, whereas those of the senior officers are widely available. Nor should it be forgotten that Austria's involvement in World War II was still, at the time of publication, somewhat contentious – as highlighted by the controversy surrounding the wartime career of Austrian politician Kurt Waldheim, who became president of Austria in July 1986.

Redler published his account of his time as a prisoner of war in the Soviet Union in 1975, when very little was available about such experiences; nor was the horrific, racially motivated treatment of Red Army POWs and the civilian population in the occupied areas of the USSR at the hands of the Axis invaders widely written about outside of the Soviet bloc. Consequently, it is with these factors in mind that the reader of this book must approach these memoirs.

A low-ranking NCO, Redler was in the German Second Army that, during the winter of 1942–43, held a bridgehead over the Don

River in and around the city of Voronezh, several hundred kilometres north-west of Stalingrad itself. Defending the Second Army's right flank were the Hungarian Second Army, the Italian Eighth Army and Romanian Third Army, which were all weak in numbers, poorly prepared for winter and ill-equipped when compared with either the Red or German armies. The left flank of Germany's Second Army was covered by the German Second Panzer Army.

The book opens on New Year's Eve 1942–43, when Redler was on watch with a Russian collaborator and he recalled his awareness that, 'something terribly awful was happening there' (Stalingrad). He had also heard a rumour that 'a division from our sector was pulled out and sent south'.

However, he does not indicate any awareness of the immensity of the Soviet offensives either around Stalingrad or further to the north. In fact the Italian Eighth Army was already in full flight, in Stalingrad General Paulus's Sixth Army was now encircled as the Romanian Third and Fourth armies, guarding its northern and southern flanks respectively, were collapsing rapidly.

The Red Army had, on 9 January 1943, offered the Sixth Army the opportunity to surrender but this had been rejected. This information, as with everything else pertaining to the situation in the Stalingrad *Kessel* (surrounded pocket), was kept hidden from the German public and the armed forces to prevent a decline in morale. During the first winter of fighting on the Eastern Front, Axis units had been cut off but had survived due to Luftwaffe air supply. Consequently, the Sixth Army was ordered to stand fast to allow time for Axis forces to evacuate the Caucasus, and to enable this the Luftwaffe had been ordered to supply it by air – which proved to be an impossible task.

And then, on 13 January 1943, news, more immediately relevant to Redler, broke – the Soviets had attacked the Hungarians and they too were in retreat, exposing the German Second Army's right flank. However, worse was to come when, on 24/25 January, the Soviets launched the Voronezh–Kastornoye operation that struck the German Second Army like a thunderbolt, penetrating 120 kilometres (75 miles) into its rear, threatening the vital rail hub of Kastornoye

90 kilometres (55 miles) west of Voronezh. It was highly likely that the German Second Army would be surrounded due to the speed of the Soviet advance. Had Redler but known it, the recently issued order to retreat westwards towards Kursk was too late.

Then, in late January 1943, Redler's life changed dramatically despite his apparent closeness to 'those with whom I remained, including the general, a few officers and clerks' whom he hoped were 'going to be lucky enough to have time to escape the envelopment'. His vivid description of their intended escape route through the blazing town of Kastornoye is riveting, capturing the sense of utter confusion, chaos, panic – and the primeval desire to survive that came rapidly to the fore.

During the course of the next few days and nights Redler fell in with several groups of German troops. Seeking shelter wherever he could from the winter's bitter cold, speaking barely a word of Russian, with frostbite a constant worry and always the fear of discovering that the German propaganda allegation that the Red Army tortured and killed prisoners was true, Redler staggered westwards towards Kursk. At least Redler had his camouflage suit, a thick padded garment; many of the other troops were dressed in what they had manged to run away in and often lacked a greatcoat or something to reduce the effects of the wind.

Then one day, when Redler emerged from his hiding place near a farm, he was to discover whether or not Goebbels had lied when he fell into the hands of a Red Army patrol. It was 31 January 1943. His captors were combing the countryside for Axis stragglers and Redler was assigned to a group of POWs who were being organised by nationality.

This process was nothing unique as the Soviet regime strove to break the Axis forces' sense of unity in this way, by treating the nationalities differently and giving the non-German, less enthusiastic allies an underdog, the Germans, to blame for their misfortune. Interestingly one *Hiwi* (the term for former Red Army POWs or Russian collaborators who, for various reasons, worked and fought for the Axis) told his NKVD interrogators that the Austrians treated them worse than the Germans did. The

Hungarians also enjoyed a similar reputation for their treatment of POWs and civilians and were thus targets for retribution by soldiers and civilians alike. Redler also discovered that POWs would receive no more consideration than the ordinary Red Army soldier when it came to rations and hygiene.

The next phase of his captivity was the seemingly endless march across the snowy wastes through war-ravaged, barren countryside. Here they met with mixed receptions from local civilians and guards, many of whom expressed their loathing for the invaders by more than words. Redler's column also encountered common humanity from both civilians and military personnel. He notes that, 'Each day we covered approximately 30 kilometres.' Inevitably, in their wake they left a pitiful trail of dead compatriots who had died from hunger, disease, untreated wounds or simply been shot. In many cases the latter casualties were often shot to put them out of their misery or just because of the guard's desire for vengeance.

Eventually Redler and his fellows reached a holding camp where he discovered how well the Soviets were carrying out their policy of dividing and ruling the international hordes of POWs and how they would all be expected to work for their captors. Redler also got a shave and discovered what he described as, 'For us Central Europeans, this ceremony was truly the hallmark of the barbarity of being held captive in the east.' In fact, shaving was a standard method of reducing the risk of lice-borne typhus, which was to prove such a scourge to POWs on both sides of the front.

When 'postcards' to home are mentioned I believe Redler means the Red Cross/Red Crescent type that were sent from POWs to their families. Goebbels had foreseen this happening in December 1942 and had ordered that such be intercepted before arrival to prevent any decline in civilian morale. This order was not rescinded until the war ended.

The monotony and horror of this march destroyed all sense of time and it is unlikely that any of the POWs would have been aware of the Sixth Army's surrender at Stalingrad on 2 February 1943. Redler's description of life during the next three years makes for hard reading.

Finally, on 31 August 1946 Redler was released from captivity, returning to Austria where he eventually resumed his life as a teacher of English, Russian and physical education. His skiing prowess led to his working with the Austrian skiing team and eventually to his part-time teaching post at Wagner College in Bregenz in his native province, where he met David Brian Lasher.

The conduct of the war on the Eastern Front was brutal and the treatment of POWs, by both sides, horrific. Neither the Soviet nor the Nazi regimes placed much value on human life and Redler's account demonstrates one side of that coin to great effect. But at least he survived and returned home.

In early January 1943 Red Army intelligence had estimated that the troops facing them in the Stalingrad *Kessel* numbered 86,000 and they were simply unprepared for the number of POWs they captured; this mirrored the Axis' situation during 1941. The chaotic conditions that ensued during the reduction of the *Kessel* in January 1943 saw Soviet POW figures reach some 120,000 by the end of that month. However, there is no breakdown of where in the region they were captured or their nationality. Naturally, this figure does not include those immediately executed for collaboration, including *Hiwis*, of whom there were some 19,000 in the *Kessel* alone.

As with all memoirs of the Eastern Front, this is a very useful work, particularly, as noted earlier, the time when it was written. Therefore, I would suggest it is an informative addition to this genre.

Nik Cornish

Translator's Introduction

Stalingrad Survivor is a story of survival. First published in German in 1975 with the title *Hände Hoch* (РУКИ НАВЕРХ) – 'Hands Up!', it is the true account of Wolfram Redler, an Austrian corporal captured in the vicinity of Stalingrad in early 1943. Exact numbers are difficult to come by, but of the approximate 300,000 soldiers who were captured during those winter months, less than 10 per cent lived to be repatriated after the war. More than three years later, Wolfram Redler was one of those men.

I met Wolfram in September 1981 while studying at the Wagner College campus in Bregenz, Austria. 'Wolfie', as we affectionately called him, was truly a joy to be around. He was an adjunct professor and he accompanied us on our various visits, including to Vienna and on skiing trips. During class, he would sometimes relate stories from his experience. I purchased his book, hoping not only to read it but to translate it for others one day. This work is the fulfilment of that hope.

Admittedly, it was a difficult challenge. Although I studied German and spent a year and a half of my life in Austria and Germany, my German was rusty and German idioms can be rather tricky. Nevertheless, this was a labour of love.

From time to time, Wolfram uses phonetic spelling to convey the dialects of some of the people. In one example, a Hungarian Jew spoke a blend of Yiddish and German, and I did my best to place it into context. In another, Wolfram met a comrade from Vienna who used a local dialect with words that have no equivalent in High German. In this instance, I was fortunate to be assisted by my friend Derek Golembeski and his colleague Eva Kuttenberg, a professor of German and native of Vienna, who helped me through the translation of that dialogue. I would also like to thank Tatiana Bogatova, a native Russian, who helped me on occasion with some of the Russian translations.

Furthermore, I appreciate that Heather Hertel, an art professor at Slippery Rock University, and one of her students, Sarah Heary, provided illustrations for the story. These sketches help bring the story to life.

Last, but not least, I owe a debt of gratitude to my wife, Julie, who endured countless hours over the past two-plus years as I worked on this translation.

In addition to numerous idioms, which sometimes proved difficult to translate, there were occasionally complex sentences, which I have broken down into simpler parts. While there are undoubtedly errors in translation, and some liberties taken in expressing things in a way that is more in keeping with the English language, I have been careful to structure sentences as close to their original wording as possible, and to portray events as Wolfram described them. I believe it remains true to his story, and that Wolfie would approve. The reader should bear in mind that Redler wrote his book in the 1970s and therefore it does contain some stereotyping and language that is uncomfortable and less acceptable today, but which I felt were part of his storytelling.

The spelling of words, especially Russian ones, was tricky. When there is a clear English equivalent – as in the names of cities or proper names – I have used the English spelling. Where Wolfram's German spelling of a Russian word used 'w' to convey a 'v' sound, I have spelled it with a 'v', to help the English reader pronounce it. For example, Chapter 26 uses 'Alexandrov' instead of 'Alexandrew'. When there was no equivalent, I have used the German spelling used by the author.

One deliberate change I have made is to use the past tense to describe the story, rather than the present tense Wolfram employs throughout the book. While the present tense does help the reader experience the events as they occurred, it seemed more appropriate to tell his story as he related events to us. His book was published in 1975, approximately thirty years after the fact, and it is my hope that this translation brings equal authenticity to the account.

Furthermore, the original work has an index of Russian words and the German equivalent. Rather than duplicate this, I have used square brackets [ ] to provide the English equivalent the first time the word is used. I also used these to add information to explain the meaning or historical context. If a word is used several times, it is included in the Glossary at the back of the book. In contrast, the use of parentheses ( ), albeit infrequent, echoes the use by the author to explain certain words.

Wolfie was a great storyteller. He told us that, before the war, he worked with the Austrian ski team. He recalled one time in March 1938 when the team went up into the Arlberg region to practise. When they came back down to the village, a Nazi greeted them and demanded the Hitler salute. The Anschluss had occurred while the team was up in the mountains, and no one had any idea what had happened. When Wolfie refused, the man took the butt of the rifle and struck him across the face. That is who Wolfie was: honest, tough and principled.

As I read this book, I recalled some accounts that Wolfie relayed to us. I specifically remember him telling us he learned to chew fish bones. It is a graphic example of how desperate the prisoners' hunger became. In another example, he said there was one time he collected the bread ration given to his neighbour, even though his neighbour was dead. We see this on the train to Siberia. Wolfie figured it didn't matter because the bread was of no use to the other man, and Wolfie was just trying to survive. He repeatedly asks the reader to consider what it says about humanity that prisoners were reluctant to report someone was dead for fear of losing out on food. It serves as a painful reminder of the moral depravity each of us could face when our basic instinct for survival is laid bare.

Since the story ends with Wolfie walking through the streets of Vienna, we do not find out what happened to his family or his house. However, I remember him saying he found it very difficult to verify his identity. Government officials apparently had listed him among the presumed dead, and he had a huge struggle to prove that he was, in fact, who he said he was. When you read his account, you will understand why officials thought it highly unlikely that he could survive capture on the Russian front and more than three years as a prisoner of war in Siberia.

One of the things Wolfie used to have us do in class was to memorise phrases, or to repeat in our own words stories he told us. In particular, he told us a fable which he wanted us to repeat as best we could in German. It was about two frogs who found themselves in a dairy. Both of them fell into a can filled with milk, and then realised they couldn't get out. On and on they struggled, but it was to no avail. After some time, one said to the other, 'I can't go on any more. There is no way to get out of here.' He gave up, and drowned in the milk. The second one kept fighting. Late into the evening and throughout the night he continued his struggle. Finally, in the morning, he found himself sitting on a large clump of butter. Jumping as hard as he could, he was able to reach the rim, and so was saved. '*So lange Leben ist, ist Hoffnung,*' Wolfie said. 'As long as there's life, there's hope.' That was his motto, and that is the story of *Stalingrad Survivor*.

Upon returning to Bregenz in the mid-1990s, I was told that Wolfram Redler had passed away, apparently from a heart attack. The man was a survivor, but in the end we all meet the same fate. We are all mortal. The great lesson of life, and of this book, is not how we die, but how we live. Wolfie was a man who showed everyone around him how to live.

This translation is dedicated to him and to all those who knew him.

David Brian Lasher

The Last Race

It was *Silvesternacht* [New Year's Eve]. The detachment's sergeant major came into our bunker to assign the night watches. I felt it subconsciously: this time it's your turn. It could have been worse; I was accompanied by a Russian Hiwi [deserter] who, in contrast to me, was having to go on an empty stomach. In the wilderness of the southern sector of the Russian front, the only joy to be found this *Silvester* was with alcohol.

The icy cold encircled me and my 'Russki'. He was attentive to every noise, while I dreamily dozed off. What was I thinking about? Going home, naturally. How much longer would it be? My firearm had been hanging on my shoulder for three days now; moreover, it was my second winter in Russia.

The uncanny silence on the front soon made me sober and at the same time suspicious. It was incomprehensible to me that nothing was stirring, when in the previous winter the Russians would have taken the opportunity to attack. From the standpoint of a simple infantryman at the command post along the front lines standing watch, all I saw was a perfectly stationary belt that began in the vicinity of Orel [380 kilometres south-south-west of Moscow (see the metric conversion table at the end of this book; keep in mind that measurements Redler gives were likely very rough estimates, especially after capture)] and extended southwards to a bridgehead that ended in Voronezh [470 kilometres south of Moscow]. I knew from our prisoner that an entire Russian brigade or even a division had withdrawn from their lines. There was certainly something afoot when those forces could be called up at any moment. Or perhaps it was true, as some of our company patrols had been saying for days, that all available Russian forces were needed for action in and around Stalingrad.

As I listened in the darkness, my thoughts turned to the southern tip of our armed forces that were located in Stalingrad. Although news had not yet reached us, I had no doubt that something terribly awful was happening there. And although the watch was uneventful, the overwhelming feeling I had persisted.

The following days passed without incident. Then, suddenly, the news arrived: 'There is a breach in the lines near Millerovo [770 kilometres south of Moscow and 390 kilometres west of Stalingrad]! Germans and Italians to retreat in two major directions: one set of forces towards Rostov, the other towards Kharkiv. The front along the Don has been pierced. Stalingrad is in peril.'

Now it was clear: the Paulusarmee [forces of Field Marshal Friedrich Paulus, commander of the Sixth Army during the Battle of Stalingrad] was incapable of mounting an operation without assistance. A division from our sector was pulled out and sent south. We never heard their fate.

Early in the morning the commander sent for me. His facial expression betrayed an ominous look that did not bode well. An attack on the neighbouring military sector of Hungarian troops had overrun their lines. The general staff's map showed a breakthrough of 20 to 30 kilometres in the main lines of the Hungarian army, which my commander said resulted from a massive artillery barrage that included *Stalinorgeln* [Stalin's 'organs' or instruments – Katyusha 13mm multiple rocket launchers, capable of firing as many as four dozen rockets more than 10 kilometres in a ten-second burst].

With a single blow our awareness of the military threat doubled. At the same time the Russians were advancing rapidly in the south towards Stari-Oskol [610 kilometres south of Moscow]; reconnaissance of the enemy to the north near Livny [370 kilometres south of Moscow] indicated military units were preparing to attack.

How did our side respond to this extremely critical situation? We did nothing! It is truly unbelievable that not a single command was given that could have had a decisive effect on the situation. Our comrades in the advanced outposts had no idea how to proceed.

Then we received a new report: Stari-Oskol had fallen to the enemy, and Soviet light tank forces were already at Kastornoye [the site where Soviet troops broke through German and Hungarian lines along the Don River front on 28 January 1943, thereby encircling the Second German Army. The author uses 'Kastoronje', which is the German name for the same city].

With this, our army was encircled in the vicinity of Voronezh. Only then did we receive a *Führerbefehl* [a command coming from the Führer's headquarters], directing the rear echelon to withdraw from the bridgehead it held at Voronezh in a direction towards Kursk, where our forces had had success the previous summer.

It was too late! The Russians had already pierced the *HKL* [*Hauptkampflinie* – main front lines] from the north in order to unite with the approaching southern troops to close the pocket.

The movement to encircle our forces advanced quickly and we were forced to act in haste. There was no longer talk of a staged withdrawal with specific targets and timetables. Troops that were still engaged in the city knew nothing of any commands and everything was in a state of confusion. The planned retreat became a flight.

What unfolded over the next several hours is difficult to describe in words. The only avenue of escape was a small corridor through the city of Kastornoye, but within two hours Russian T-34 tanks, from both the north and the south, closed that route. Unimaginable panic ensued, soldiers began throwing their weapons away and plundering the food supplies, and even officers who kept their weapons were unable to reform lines or stop the chaos. There was a total dissolution of order, and each looked to his own for survival. Because the only route of escape had been closed, and the one remaining bridge over the river was under heavy bombardment, our troops destroyed their supplies and vehicles, and they tossed away anything that might slow them down.

The personnel at the headquarters who were familiar with Hitler's directive to withdraw began heading westwards. But were those with whom I remained, including the general, a few officers and clerks, going to be lucky enough to have time to escape the envelopment?

The 'K' [Kastornoye] railway hub was in utter confusion. Ammunition stores exploded, making a tremendous roar. The train station and houses caught fire, creating an orgy of destruction. In an instant, an inestimable amount of goods and materials were consumed by fire. Personal belongings, including the clothes we were carrying, as well as secret maps, burned at the hastily constructed command post, and the remaining vehicles were destroyed. They had to be kept from falling into enemy hands. The only way to move through the deep snow was on foot or by sled, as the one remaining street was completely blocked.

As the last remaining units tried to protect the army's withdrawal through the city, an order reached us, the last one I was to receive from the German Wehrmacht. It directed us to disengage independently. The radio message only pronounced what was already the reality, and further transmissions were now impossible.

A lieutenant who served as the Russian translator and who possessed local knowledge led our small group through the western part of the city at night. The 'K' railway hub was already occupied by the enemy, and it was no easy task to get through. The blazing conflagration, fuelled by hay, straw and supply trains loaded with gasoline, illuminated the winter landscape with burning buildings all around us. The inferno only increased the chaos.

The commander's vehicle zoomed by, followed by a vehicle with an anti-tank gun. I could not keep up the pace on foot. Alone among the mass of retreating troops, I used the sea of flames to steer myself towards the only way through to the west. I don't know how I did it. Panic, fear and flight took hold of me. Suddenly I found myself completely alone. Then, an anti-tank vehicle passed by. Some soldiers were hanging onto the gun like a bunch of grapes; one fell, screaming, 'Take me with you, take me with you!' – without success.

In this moment, in a split second, I recognised the situation. With one leap I sprang onto the gun barrel, wrapping both my arms around it in total desperation, hanging on for dear life while dangling my feet in the air. It was a wild ride as we escaped through the narrow pass.

By the skin of our teeth we reached the railway beyond the edge of the city. From there we were instructed to continue our westward march. I met up again with our company commander, who in the meantime had lost a number of men.

We trudged through the snow, following the railway tracks, while taking cover among the parked railcars. The enemy fire increased in intensity, but when the railway embankment became flat, we lost our cover. From there on, the remaining cars had been abandoned. We could no longer continue along the railway tracks because they had been captured by the enemy. We found a *panje* [small Polish or Russian draughthorse], with which we could traverse through the knee-deep snow on a sled. Luckily, the sky was starlit, and the North Star guided our direction.

At dawn we found a good place to rest that was well camouflaged, taking cover from the Ratas [Polikarpov I-16, a Russian fighter plane used during the Spanish Civil War and World War II; during the Spanish Civil War the Nationalists nicknamed it the '*Rata*', or 'rat'].

The last rations were consumed and we did not expect any further provisions. I was sent to the nearest village to see if there were any enemy forces there. I had scarcely left the village when Ivan moved in from the opposite side.

Much to my surprise, when I returned to our rest area no one was there. There was nothing left for me to do but follow the tracks in the snow. I had been unable to catch up with the group when night began to fall; it was the third or fourth night in a row that I spent without sleeping. Then I encountered a group of young soldiers. The cold and other hardships had defeated them. Unable to continue, several of them simply stayed where they fell in the snow. Neither encouragement nor threats were of any use. Their fate was to freeze to death, to be shot in the back of the neck, or in the best case – and I had to ask myself whether it really was the best case – become prisoners.

A few kilometres further I found a horse-drawn wagon. Lying on it were the wounded. They cried out, 'Comrade, help us!' I grabbed the horse's reins, but it would not take a single step. With no way through the deep snow and no feed for the animal, the situation was hopeless. None of the wounded could go any further, partly because of exhaustion and partly because of their wounds.

For the first time I experienced tragedy which I, myself, could not escape. My instinct for survival prevailed and I continued on.

Even though I knew there was nothing I could do to help them, the decision to move on with those who were able, while leaving those who could not behind, demonstrated to me the inhumanity in abandoning them.

Slowly, my doubts began to intensify. Could I make it or not? I had enough strength, I wasn't wounded, but the distance to the new front lines had to be at least 100 kilometres. I also could not imagine how any resistance to the Russian onslaught could be mounted amid all this confusion.

Such thoughts overwhelmed me as I trudged along through the night. In a nearby village we heard a few shots ring out from one of the first houses. 'Frozen like snot' – in the beautiful army lingo – I lay in the snow. As the shots became louder, we responded indiscriminately. Orders were shouted from somewhere, but no one felt obliged to do anything. As a stream of those near me started to flee, I no longer had any idea who was around me.

I tried to avoid the village by going round a hill to the right. I was successful. After about two hours I ran into a loner who spoke half Russian, half German. He was friendly, and he shared his last bit of canned meat with me. I continued the march. It became lighter. We found a haystack and we both tried to get a little sleep. After some time we were awakened by a noise. The remaining infantrymen had followed our tracks and found us, but fatigue forced us to rest a little longer. Then we continued, as with the setting sun, always westward.

The next village which we scouted was, by the grace of God, unoccupied. The locals did not give us any problems; just the opposite, they gave us cooked potatoes, cabbage soup and a piece of bread to strengthen us for our continued trek. I fell to the ground like a sack. I didn't care what happened to me during my sleep. I only wanted to close my eyes and rest, and not think of anything.

Early the next morning we pulled ourselves together and pushed ahead. Ever forward! Just don't get caught! Our motley crew consisted of around forty troops. Each of us was worried we might be left behind, or somehow find ourselves alone. The officers and men stood on a plateau, each of us experiencing hunger and thirst. The cold spared no one. Filthy and unshaven for days, lice-ridden for weeks, we were in despair, both physically and mentally. We found we had gone to the dogs. Nevertheless, I wanted to save my own skin, in so far as I was capable of doing so.

As the crimson sun rose, it radiated its beams across the wide, snow-covered land. A white mist, superimposed on the hoarfrost, covered the cabins and alder trees which occasionally dotted the horizon. Suddenly, enemy artillery ruptured the silence. It became clear that the Russians were moving closer and closer, encircling us as the explosions came from several directions. In one moment, the sounds of battle were ahead of us, in the next moment behind us, and then on either side. After a few hours we realised we were lost; we saw we were simply looking at the same village from the other side. We were going in circles. Our maps had failed us – the scale was too small to be of any assistance. The existence of occasional houses helped in terms of orientation, but on its own that was not much help.

As we continued across the country for about an hour, we saw a small wood, and to the left a typical one-street Russian village. Naturally, we avoided the open field – we saw the contrails of planes overhead – striving forward to find cover in the small wood.

Instead of cover, we were greeted with a murderous rain of bullets stemming from machine guns located about 100 metres inside the edge of the wood. At the same time, mortars were exploding in heaps around us. We attempted to put up a resistance, but despite it being well intentioned, it was of little avail. We were lying in the open, our adversary in the protected woods. All we possessed were some *Karabiner* [German bolt-action Mauser rifles], while the enemy was fully equipped. Tak-tak – even tank shells began to strike us. The wounded stayed lying in the field, while the rest of us, without leadership, incapable of concerted action, took care to save our own lives.

In spite of the heavy bombardment there was nothing left to do but get up and run towards the nearest cabin. Of those who made it, I was the first to arrive, while others died attempting to seek cover. Completely out of breath, I found cover in a frozen riverbed next to the house. After a short breather, I continued moving through the stream. I broke through the ice, and my felt boots became saturated with water. Almost instantly, I had huge clumps of snow on my feet. Traction became increasingly difficult and, above all, moving onwards was exhausting. I tried using my hands to remove the clumps from my frostbitten feet, but this, too, was impossible.

Full of despair and rage at the bad luck that had befallen me, the noise of battle intensifying overhead, I tossed everything that was hindering me into the snow: my jacket, map case, ammo pouch, two grenades, etc. Then, using my bayonet, I was able to apply enough weight and pressure to hack loose the clumps of snow from my feet.

What should I do now? I took out a cigarette and lit it. I knew I could not leave my present position. I figured since it was already the afternoon I would stay until I could make my way through the village under the cover of darkness. Mind you, I had no idea whether there were any Russians in the village, and if so, how many. I thought I heard the voice of an occasional commando, but I wasn't sure.

If they captured me, what would they do? Would they make me a prisoner or would they kill me? Was Goebbels' propaganda true or not? In the past few days, several of my fellow comrades had used their own pistols to end their agony. Despite their examples and all my doubts and everything weighing on my mind, I was unwilling to do that. I would not seize the chance to throw my life away.

I did not have very long to ponder the situation. A Russian civilian came up over the bank with two pails to fetch some water. Using an iron pick, he made a small hole in the ice and scooped water into the bucket. Lying motionless in the snow and covered by my piece of winter camouflage, I held my breath. This went on for a few dreadful minutes. Finally, he finished filling the buckets and he began climbing the embankment. Then he slipped and rolled down the embankment with his buckets. Then he saw me. I jumped to my feet and tried to hold onto him so he wouldn't give me away. He screamed with all his might and he was able to escape from my grasp. In vain I tried to catch him. As soon as I popped my head over the embankment, I realised it was over now. A pack of Russians were coming towards me with MPs [*Militarpolizei* – military police]. I only understood the words they bellowed at me: '*Ruki verch*! [pronounced roo-kie v-verk] – Hands up!' Even without that command I had no choice but to surrender.

2

Ruki Verch! – Hands Up!

As I was standing there, unable to make sense of the thoughts racing through my mind, ten hands began searching my body and rummaging through my clothes. Before I knew it, my watch was gone. They tore off my 'winter medal' and my sports badge and threw them both in my face. Two Russians ended up on the ground fighting over who would get my fountain pen and mechanical pencil. My wedding ring – was not taken. '*Nix gut Material!*' This was true. It was not real gold, so it remained on my finger. As another ransacked through my military pay book, a third ripped out a page from it and began to roll a *tschik* [smoke]. I was completely robbed of all my cigarettes. One acted nobly and returned my cigarette pack, as well as a handkerchief. They particularly enjoyed having fun with my silver, mother-of-pearl lighter, but with their rough, rather large hands, they were not able to use it. One of them put it back in my hand; I think it was the sergeant. '*Ne rabotaet* – don't do that!' he said. I took the lighter in my hand and lit a cigarette, which was passed around to the others.

Then came a pause. Each one of them held a piece of something they had taken from me in their hand as they smoked. What now? Was this the moment …?

'No, comrade, Hitler is *kaput!*' he said and everyone laughed. I made a pleasant grin in return. Then, leaving me standing there, they turned away. Immediately, a partisan came and began to take me in the direction of the woods which I had wished to enter earlier.

Until now I had been spared. I began to stagger away, with my guard in front of me. Since I was behind him, I could easily have slipped away. But that seemed pointless, because it would only be a matter of time before I was captured again. Was he taking me into the woods to kill me? As I followed him I could feel the tension, but after marching for more than half an hour through the woods, nothing happened, except that I noticed that the noise of battle was moving to the west.

On reaching a clearing we came upon some cabins and a collection of people at a Russian command post. That's where I was gathered with the other prisoners, and a guard assigned us into groups based upon nationality.

Now was the first time it really hit me that I was a prisoner. Here we stood before Ivan, despondent, broken spirited and physically exhausted. No one said a word. Everyone felt the gravity of the past few days in our bones.

In the distance Russian infantry marched towards us. They swore at us wildly as they approached, and threatened us by pointing their machine guns at us as if they meant to kill us right there. We did not react at all. We had no idea what they were saying, but their gestures were clear. We accepted our fate with a sense of complete apathy. Perhaps it was luck, but they had to continue their march and they had no time for us.

Then a young officer, bearing a chest full of medals, emerged from a thatched-roof cabin. His great stature and non-threatening attitude was not something I was accustomed to from someone with Asiatic features. He called each group by nationality. First, the Finns! He did not seem to take kindly to them. Then came the Austrians and he ordered me inside.

It was a decrepit cabin, similar to any one of the millions that one would find in Russia. It had a low doorway that opened into a narrow anteroom. It was probably used to milk a cow or goat when there was one. At the present time it was empty, except for some clutter that lay on the floor. The musty air saturated the small space. The only ventilation was a slightly open single pane, one-sixth of the window. It was a flies' paradise in both summer and winter. The 'living room' was full of prisoners. After greeting them silently with a nod, I squatted down in the corner.

While the Russian commander and the interpreter interrogated two Austrian officers, I looked around the room. The feeling that I was currently out of mortal danger gave me a moment of calm. My glance fell upon two civilians who appeared to be humble *kolkhozniki* [the original spells it *kolcholsniki*], or collective farm workers. There was no place for them at the crudely constructed table, so they sat upon the stove that provided heat for the sleeping place above it. Only a weak light could penetrate from outside and a kerosene lamp flickered within. The walls were simple whitewash, showing the filth. Cobwebs were throughout. On one wall was a simple photo that had turned yellow with age.

'Comrade, come here,' said the interpreter, a Jewish emigrant. 'Are you now convinced the Germans have lost the war?'

I shrugged my shoulders: 'Perhaps, I don't know.'

'What is your rank?'

'Corporal.'

'You lie,' he screamed. 'You are an officer.'

That was not the impression I wanted to give, so I removed my camouflage jacket and showed him my two stripes. He was satisfied and smiled. Nevertheless, I had the feeling he did not trust me. Then the commanding officer mumbled something into the interpreter's ear. The interpreter turned and asked, 'How many Russians have you shot in this war?'

I was not really prepared for this question. 'I never counted,' was the first thing that came out of my mouth. Not wanting to make an unpredictable situation worse, I continued, 'I don't think I ever killed anyone.'

'Yes, so say they all,' he replied, with a satirical laugh.

Upon my enquiring if I could ask a question, he said, '*Gut, los!*' [Go ahead!]

'I am hungry!' Without any inhibition I asked if I could have something to eat. Although the commander and the interpreter were initially a little taken aback by my presumptuous question, they gave me a handful of potatoes from the pan that was sitting on the table. I had no idea when the next time would be that I might have any food tossed to me. Greedily, I devoured all the potatoes.

With that, the interrogation ended.

By evening the number of prisoners had increased considerably. We squatted outside in the snow. Two German Focke-Wulf machines [Fw 190 fighter-bomber aircraft] circled over the command post. For me, and perhaps the others, there was a strange feeling. What I would give to have the power to get out of here! But that is in the past, for ever in the past! Then, any remaining hope I had was ripped away. '*Nitschevo* – they don't matter,' shouted the Russian.

By now, the main front lines must have moved well to the west, because Ivan was continuously filing past. Ski troops, *Stalinorgeln*, mortar brigades, motorised units, light artillery, heavy artillery, tanks, assault guns – and what truly astonished us – a large amount of brand-new American military equipment.

Finally, we were formed into four rows and prepared to march off to an unknown location.

Suddenly an MP barked at our ranks. One of the men marching past had emptied his magazine and fired wildly at us. Is the prisoner simply wild game? Loud screams and chaos ensued. I was not hit, and simply stood there looking stupid. Some casualties, wearing Hungarian uniforms, were carried off from our ranks. After the episode, calm returned.

An hour passed. Despite the cold we were not permitted to keep moving, so we simply flailed and crossed our arms to protect ourselves from freezing.

3

'Davai!' – Moving on into the Russian Hinterland

The guards finally arrived. The procession of the disarmed soldiers, the *Faschisti*, as the guards called us, set itself in motion.

In the meantime it became pitch black. We continued marching for a while. Automatically, I moved one foot in front of the other along the slippery, hard-frozen road that fortunately was free from troops moving towards the front.

At a minimum, under these circumstances, one is afraid of becoming an arbitrary sacrifice. The snow crunched with the monotonous sound of the march. The silence was only occasionally interrupted by the guards: *'Davai, davai!* [the original has *dawai* throughout] – Move on, move on!' *Davai* – for the physically exhausted and injured! I could regularly hear the sound of shots being fired, sometimes in front of me, sometimes behind me. I asked my neighbour what that might mean. Most likely, they were bullets to the back of the head for those who could not go any further. In short order, this gruesome assumption proved to be correct. We passed close by one of our fellow prisoners who lay motionless on the ground. He has gone to rest, I thought. Who knows what he might have been spared?

'Halt, company, about face!' What was this nonsense? Back in the direction we had been marching from for hours? Back to where we had been? Yes, precisely, as the guards had lost their way. After some to and fro, we went in another direction. Were we really going to march all night? Personally, I had had enough of this hell. I had been on the run long enough. Now, as a prisoner, I had to continue marching and marching? I didn't know how much more of this I could take.

Around midnight – exactly when I could not say, as no one had a watch – we entered a village. The loam huts had been cleared out, and sixty to seventy men were crammed into a room that was no more than 20 square metres. This is something one has to experience for oneself! When I spent the night in a barn back home, at least I was able to stretch out. When nature called, I could relieve myself without the risk of being killed. I would not be robbed of my last remaining effects. And how is it here? No place was left, not even a small spot; we were crammed so tightly together that we spent the night standing upright. We were dead tired. There was no light. Then the door ripped open. Five or six soldiers were taken out. About five minutes later they returned.

'What is it?'

'They stripped us of our skivvies and undershirts.'

'Why?'

The guards who accompanied us did not have anything to eat either. They used the undergarments they took from us to barter with local civilians for some bread, potatoes and milk. We did not get anything, but we did not expect anything. I mentally prepared myself to go hungry for a rather long period of time.

Once again the door was opened. This time, two officers were removed. They had lambskin boots with leather soles. They returned with rags in their hands instead of shoes. Thereupon, I pulled my cammies over my boots so no one would see them.

The night passed very slowly. I stood close to the stove and I was able to stretch my hamstrings, alternating one and then the other.

Dead tired, I lay my torso upon the opening to the oven, with part of my body inside. I tried to close my eyes. I could feel the lice moving about me. By now, there must be quite a number crawling around, I thought.

Anytime someone had to relieve himself, it created a huge fuss. Whatever calmness existed was swept away by the agitation. Then we began to notice that those who did so were not returning. Time and again shots were heard. Once morning came we saw it: the guard, dead drunk with vodka, had killed each one who went outside to answer nature's call. 'A carefree state,' I thought to myself.

Without food, without washing, at daybreak we continued onwards.

Unlike the day before, the sky was overcast. It began to snow. A light east wind blew in the white, soft flakes, swirling as they passed by. I really wasn't very cold, but then I had become somewhat accustomed to it. In addition, I was happy to be moving again. The conditions of the previous night had made us all rather stiff.

One thing made me very depressed. I lost one of my gloves. I didn't know whether someone had taken it from me, or whether I had simply lost it. In all probability, someone else was wearing it. There was nothing left for me to do, but to put my bare hand under the armpit of my other arm. My pants pockets were way too cold. Another source of misery was my runny nose. With the constant discharge, my single handkerchief was no longer of any use; instead of behaving like a Central European, I had to deal with it just like a good Russian … The handkerchief was anything but presentable. It was impossible to wash.

Speaking of washing! My skin was already itching, and my face was probably layered with filth. I saw it on my hands, which had cracks forming in some places. Perhaps the grime was keeping them warm. That would be okay. One time I tried to use snow to clean off the dirt, but it only ended up smearing it.

'*Davai, davai*! Comrade!' That was the first word I learned and it is solidly impressed in my memory. We had been underway for nearly forty-eight hours and still we had not received any rations. We already knew that there wouldn't be any to come until we arrived at the camp. But where was the camp? '*Skora budjet* – we will be there soon,' is all they said, a small hope for us to hang on to. Slowly, however, we began to feel hunger pangs. The hunger was accompanied by thirst, proof that our trouble was becoming serious. Some of my comrades continually reached to the ground to put snow in their mouth. I warned them it was useless, but it became increasingly difficult for me to resist the temptation as well. My tongue clung to the roof of my mouth, and my throat was parched.

Far and wide, there was no house visible, only an occasional protruding bush or shrub across the white plain, like silent ghosts accompanying us. No animal, not even a bird, was to be seen or heard; only the footprints of the defeated column in this vast emptiness.

Beside me was one of the two Austrian officers whom I knew from the interrogation. He was struggling to drag himself along. His dialect sounded anything but Austrian. He told me that he had claimed he was from 'Austriez' because he thought his fate would better. I felt sorry for him. Had his boots not been taken from him the day before, he would be wearing lambskin instead of shredded rags torn from his coat that were wrapped around his feet. He was already struggling to breathe, and he was older than most. We alternated trying to shore him up. We couldn't let him fall behind. We knew he had a wife and children. He had to live! To die as a prisoner? What crime did he commit? For doing his duty as was required by his position? These questions gnawed at me, but I was too worn out to ponder the answers. After a while, the officer fell further behind and I eventually lost sight of him. There was nothing more anyone could do for him. What a pity.

But I made an oath, for me alone: they would not break me! I would return home.

Finally, a village came into view! Perhaps there might be something to eat and drink. A few among us could speak Polish or Croatian. We sent them to the guards with our request.

'How many of our countryfolk did you allow to starve to death?' we heard in reply. You won't believe me when I tell you. They threw all of them into a pond – yes, it's true.

For the most part, the village was burned to the ground. Only an occasional chimney remained. Was it possible that our own troops had done this? If so, it did not bode well for what we might expect.

And so it was. Hardly had we been discovered when the inhabitants began running towards us, the children following closely behind. They screamed at us in unison: '*Fritzi, Fritzi, jaizi, gusi, moloka, njema?*'

These words were like a slap across the ears and face. 'Eggs, hens, milk – none' – how often had we demanded them when we moved in to occupy a village? This chorus accompanied us for a while. Some spat on us, others threw snowballs at us, ridiculed us or scolded us for the sorrows we had heaped upon them. A wizened old lady tore the glasses off the face of one of us, threw them to the ground, and then danced in joy on them. Now she had her victor's trophy!

Despite all the scorn and contempt, a few of us begged for some bread. It was like expecting food from a stone. But that's not what happened: suddenly a few scraps of dry bread were hurled onto the snow. Like vultures, ten to twenty prisoners plunged towards the pieces. Most of them had not eaten for days prior to being taken captive. The guards fired warning shots in response, once near the civilians to drive them away, the other towards the heap of prisoners to restore order. They did not intend to cause harm.

I, however, had a little luck. A few steps further on, an elder slipped me two or three sugar beets. Furtively, I placed them into my jacket. The beets were like manna from Heaven to me!

In the next village we stopped to rest for the night. The accommodation was a little better. There was more space, but it was colder.

In the middle of the night there was a changing of the guard. This meant we would be searched again. Who had a knife, a lighter, or any kind of cutlery, like a spoon or fork? German cookware is especially sharp. Anyone who did not hand these over would be shot. Each man, in turn, was searched. Anyone caught trying to conceal something was promptly removed. This was a very lengthy procedure. When they came to me, my wallet only contained photos, letters and a few worthless German Marks. Any expensive memorabilia was torn from me. Finally, we tried to fall asleep again.

So things went day after day. Each day we covered approximately 30 kilometres. They repeated the body searches, interrogations continued, and in every village we met with derision and mockery. That was understandable, since we had been complicit in the misery and destruction that had been inflicted upon them.

Our march travelled over familiar terrain. It had once been the former German *HKL*, with trenches, bunkers and command post completely obliterated by the bombings. Nowhere could a body be seen; the corpses lay under the white mantle of snow. Who would have thought that I would see this place again under such conditions and circumstances?

I was so thirsty. The feeling of hunger had passed. Not even a drop of water the entire day. A narrow path led through a minefield. We recognised that from the clearly marked stakes. Then I saw immediately to the right of me a champagne bottle sticking in the snow. I dared to jump to the side. With one tug I was able to retrieve it. Hurray! Something to drink. I ripped out what remained of the cork and poured the liquid into my mouth. Ugh, damn it! It was petrol. I hurled the bottle away, leaving a revolting taste in my mouth that only made me even more thirsty.

The column came to a sudden stop. The guard pointed to two or three Russian workhorses frozen in the snow. Without knives, however, we could do nothing. The guard gave us his bayonet. Using it, we carved up one of the horses. To soften the hard frozen pieces we had to use our own body heat, so we stuck them under our jackets. How our faces shone with joy! For the first time we had something of substance to eat. We could not wait for the meat to thaw. To keep my right hand from freezing, the one which was missing a glove, I had to lick the meat constantly. Like a dog, I locked my jaws to break off a chunk, although I would have preferred to gobble down the entire piece of meat all at once.

We spent the night staying in our old positions. That seemed rather odd to us. I recalled that on the days fighting did not take place, we would pass the time trying to amuse ourselves in the dwellings we had built. Now, though, the situation was entirely different. One could clearly see how hastily we had abandoned our fighting position, and how the pursuing Russian troops had rummaged through what remained. Things were lying all over the place. Nevertheless, we hoped to find some deck chairs that might have been left behind, as well as anything edible. But since it was pitch black and we did not have any lights, we wandered about clumsily. We finally settled down in any spot that was reasonably comfortable. For the first time, the guards were not concerned about us. It was probably because they went looking for food. Marching rations, as they were called by those in the rear supply lines, were nowhere to be found. It was also unlikely that any 'Fritzi' would attempt to run away from our 'convoy', simply because we were too exhausted to try, and the distance to our lines had become far too great. Who could overcome those odds without the prospect of any shelter or food?

We lay close together because it was bitterly cold. This time, thank God, we were spared the unpleasant searches and accompanying commandeering of our belongings that had become customary. That was how I had recently lost my trousers, leaving me only with camouflage pants. In the extreme cold of the night, that was hard to ignore.

Due to diarrhoea and our inability to wash ourselves, ailments were terribly widespread. Many of us developed sores between our legs and the aches and pains began to intensify. Unfortunately, the effects of continually eating snow were taking their toll. Underwear was so filthy it had turned black, and it had become a hotbed for lice.

My hope lay in getting to the camp. I imagined we would find conditions to be at least somewhat humane. Every day the promise was repeated: '*Tolko drizet kilometer* – only 30 kilometres more to go!' It soon became clear, however, that this was only the column's daily goal. After a while, despondency started to set in. New prisoners began to join us at specific meeting points. They didn't know our final destination either. Although there was a constant influx, the column did not grow. Casualties along the way depleted our ranks at about the same rate that new prisoners were brought in, so our numbers remained roughly balanced.

Once again we approached the dreaded paved road. It was here that one had to always consider encountering replacements being sent to the front. It had been my experience that the reinforcements were always worse than the front-line troops. Then we came upon a military unit that was approaching at high tempo. It was a mess. I couldn't believe my eyes. Were two tanks actually driving through the middle of our column? Those of us who were far enough away ran wildly into the snow. Then, just a few steps away, I heard the screams of comrades being crushed. The shrieks pierced the sky. Were they mad? To mow down defenceless prisoners in this way? Accompanying this was an orgy of shooting, as if they were hunting rabbits. The mounted infantry started using us as target practice. Our guards cursed at them to stop, but it was to no avail. They themselves were in danger. Shaking, I lay in the snow, trying to play dead. Surely, they had to consider what they were doing. Or did they simply want all of us dead? As I peeked out over the snow, I saw two jeeps driving like bats out of hell towards the chaos. Officers jumped out of their vehicles and began waving their pistols around and shouting orders. Finally, order was restored. We slowly began to fall in, and once again we continued our march along the road. A few wounded and a number of motionless corpses remained in the snow behind us. What was one to think? There was nothing to contemplate – words could not describe it.

It was a difficult existence, running for cover on the open roads. Until now I felt I had been spared from the worst. Despite the deprivation and strain – more than ten days had already passed – in comparison to the others I was still good on my feet. When something went wrong, I could run, jump to the side, quickly take cover, lie on my stomach. This was something many of my comrades could not do, and they began to give up. I knew, however, that surrendering to these conditions meant the beginning of the end.

Deep in thought, I trudged along. The column had torn itself apart, and I was all alone in the middle. That was always dangerous; one became an easy target.

What then occurred took place in a matter of seconds. An *LKW* [*Lastkraftwagen* – supply truck] convoy with five trucks came around the bend. I ran as fast as I could to catch up with the others.

To my horror, I saw someone lift a rifle to shoot at me, I heard a shot ring out, and I went crashing to the ground. The rear wheel brushed my sleeve and ran over part of my jacket. Despite the short range, somehow he had missed. 'Lucky bastard,' I thought to myself. 'If that didn't get me, nothing will.'

In no time I caught up with the formation. Once there, I began to appreciate how near to death I was. My neighbours remained silent when I told them. Then one said to me, 'Don't you think it might have been better had you not escaped? At least then, you would have had peace.'

No, no, not that. I did not want to perish in Russia. I swore to myself that I would survive.

Gradually, the guards began to see that using the road was a problem. We diverted off the paved road, moving roughly in a parallel direction. The guards were almost exclusively Asian, and from their rash demeanour we expected them to be rather wicked. On the contrary, they proved to be good natured and really helpful people. They had been accompanying us for three days already without relief.

The long march had finally brought us deep into the Russian hinterland, far from the front with absolutely no trace of the war. We expected to see a different picture of the villages and their inhabitants. To our surprise, conditions were no different and did not improve, at all. The homes and the people were dark and gloomy, except for the covering of snow. One village looked just like another. To the left and right of the shovelled and sometimes well-trodden streets were small, thatched, loam huts that were roughly the same size and placed in an irregular pattern. Here and there they were occasionally whitewashed. Otherwise, neither the doors nor the windows showed any sign of paint. The wood appeared used and weather-beaten and looked as if it came directly from the forest. Outside the village stood the collective farms and barns, which were built entirely of wood and constantly guarded.

In an elevated area or well-defined point, at times a village church was visible. However, instead of fulfilling their original purpose, they now served as a garage for agricultural equipment, tractors, trucks, etc. Over the entrance were three capital letters: MTC – Motor Tractor Station. The church crosses had been replaced by these markings, and their locations were known to me from the Russian military maps.

Even in the *ploschad* [the village square], where all important events took place, there was a larger-than-life plaster of Paris statue, most often either Father Stalin or the Great Proletarian Lenin – the great proletarian on account of the peculiar portrayal: the shabby clothes, unshaven, the ragged look strongly emphasised, so as to accentuate the model of the spiritual proletarian. Two or three small, faded, red flags, as well as a banner with some kind of slogan fluttered in the wind. A board was hanging from a pole with the names of all the best workers, letters framed in gold. An iron rod, crossbar or some other metal object dangled from a pole, which would sound when struck. The *starost* [district administrator] or the village elder would use it every morning to call the people to work and to admonish them in the evening of their duty to work. It could also be used to sound the alarm for outbreaks of fire or bombing raids. One other thing in the *ploschad*: a loudspeaker served as the single village radio that was tuned in to the daily broadcast. Every Soviet citizen had the possibility of hearing the daily programme broadcast directly from Moscow. Such a device was quite handy; no one had to purchase their own, just like in paradise.

A rumour began to circulate within our ranks: there will be bread today! Yes, indeed. Bread from a collective farm. However, it would be another 17 kilometres before we got there, so we heard. Just the thought of bread alone made us attentive, and we picked up the pace. We hoped it was not one of the notorious *Scheisshausparolen* [shit-house rumours]! How often we had been disappointed, yet again and again we grasped onto any hope to keep pushing forwards, even if it was faint.

In the afternoon we reached the aforesaid village, which brought us to a halt. It was actually another 3 to 4 kilometres further than we had been led to believe, but that was of no consequence to us. We were then divided into a few groups, with some of us being placed in abandoned homes. The people here were not quite as spiteful.

Nevertheless, from their eyes one could see what they were thinking: there are the 'Fritzi', the fascists, the monsters, who brought this war upon us. Old men and women or children stared at us. Nothing of use remained in their homes. Nevertheless, they did not utter a word. Yes, of course, these were the 'Fritzi', but this time they were not dangerous. The last few days had taken care of that.

On that day I began to feel very sick. My tonsils hurt so badly I could not even swallow my saliva. Along with it came a blizzard so fierce that one would not dare even to take a dog out. A few of us had entered a small place, where I found enough space to lie down. It was not nearly as cramped as before. It was nice to be able to stretch out my legs. My entire head was hurting. For the first time, I was truly sick. I felt so hot that I must have been running a very high fever. It must not have been too bad, because I still felt hungry and thirsty. Poldl, who was one of the prisoners whom I had befriended, got permission from the guards to heat up some water in a rusty tin can. Never in my life had hot water tasted so good. It was simply priceless. With my one glove I was able to hold the scorching tin can and I eagerly brought it to my mouth. I sipped the steamy water, which nearly burned my mouth. But I expected it to alleviate my sore throat.

Bread was distributed! Indeed! Even the guards were in a cheerful mood. Two from our convoy waited in the room. In the meantime it became dark. A kerosene lamp flickered dimly in the hands of one, while the other took a bag from his back and laid it on the floor. The bread was in the bag. We were spellbound. Dear Lord, finally something to eat. My heart rejoiced. For a moment I forgot everything, all my misery was gone. The only thing I could not do was stand; if I did, I would lose my place. And it was important for me to rest during the night, otherwise my condition would not improve. And what about the next day?

One Russian then gave a short speech. I could sense what he said [the translator then confirmed this in his translation].

'For the first time you German fascists are receiving bread, produced by Russian workers. This is because our leader Stalin has compassion on you. He does not let anyone starve, not even you, our great enemy, who have wronged us. We, your guards, see how hungry you are. For this reason we consulted a wealthy collective, who have given you something to eat.'

He emphasised one loaf would be divided among every four of us.

'*Spasiba, spasiba*,' we repeated one after the other. This Russian 'thank you' flowed easily from our lips. My friend Poldl received a heavy 2-kilogram loaf for me, him, and two other comrades. But how were we to divide it? Given our hunger, a few among us were already fighting over how the bread was broken. A good many deliberately divided their loaf into unequal portions. No one had a knife.

Then, an idea came to me. I had not thrown away my dog tags; they still hung on a chain under my shirt. I quickly removed them. I laid the cord, on which the lice hung, aside. With the edge of the elliptically shaped dog tags, we first cut the bread into four equal pieces. Then began the difficult task of cutting it up into smaller pieces. This we managed to do, and we were satisfied with the just portions. My dog tags were then passed around, while Poldl watched to make sure they did not disappear.

Thus began a sacred ceremony. With a silent prayer we enjoyed bite after bite, trying as hard as we could to make it last as long as possible; with ravenous hunger we devoured piece after piece, with several laying their field caps on their lap so as not to miss any crumbs that might fall.

Strangely, during all these days I was not thinking of home. Now, seeing that I wasn't going to starve, I was overwhelmed. In an instant, my homeland, wife, mother, children, all of them occupied my thoughts. I wanted to cry. But no, I shouted at myself, I could not lose heart. I was alive, not lying shot or dead in some field. I was going to return.

Once I returned to my senses, and I consumed my last crumb, I was overcome by an unbridled desire to sleep. I fell fast asleep until someone awakened me.

Probably never before was it so difficult for me to continue the march. My legs felt extremely weak. Beads of sweat ran down my forehead. Once we got outside things improved. I was refreshed by the stiff east wind. '*Davai*, let's go …'

There were two, however, who could not continue. Their feet were severely frostbitten. Regretfully, we looked upon them. Not long thereafter, we heard two or three shots ring out. They had gone to soldier heaven, they were redeemed, I thought.

This time, however, I was deceived, and probably the others as well. The interpreter and the guard exchanged words with one another. Thereupon the two men lying in the snow were prompted to get back on their feet. With Ivan supporting them, they hobbled to the nearest house, where the guard handed them over to one of the village elders. We shook our heads in disbelief. It is not easy to truly understand a Russian. Their soul is rather capricious. I had the feeling that both goodness and evil coexisted within them, transitioning from one to the other without any moderation. The incident gave us the courage to persevere.

Overnight at least half a metre of snow had fallen from the sky. That made movement far more difficult. It took a while, longer than usual, before I was able to adjust to the pace. My good friend Poldl continually waited for me as I fell further behind. He said to me, 'You are like a sick horse.' It was some consolation for me to know I wasn't the last one. There still remained several men behind me, who probably had it worse than me. I felt that I had tonsillitis. Under normal circumstances one would stay in bed. When I thought about where my bed was, it brought a bitter smile to my face.

The guards announced that we would reach the camp the next day, although we were never sure if it was true. Fine. This 'zavtra' – tomorrow – we had heard all too often. What was left for us, though, other than to have a reason, any reason, to hope? One thing was certain: if this 'excursion' were to continue much longer we would all be dead. Day after day we marched 30 to 40 kilometres, in wind and weather, almost without any food or accommodation – by that I do not mean a cooked meal, but at most a piece of bread, a few beets or a handful of potatoes. That was all we had been given over the past fifteen days. That would bring down even the strongest man. On top of that was the emotional burden of knowing that at any moment our life hung by a thread. For those of us who remained, we had reached the extreme limits of what was humanly possible to endure.

That very evening, I swapped my wedding ring, the last precious gem I possessed. With a heavy heart I parted with the only thing remaining that connected me to home. But I was hungry, truly starving. A Russian partisan who was involved in the action offered me bread in exchange. I gave him the ring without any real assurance he would keep his word. After approximately twenty minutes I began to lose hope. Then, I could hardly believe my eyes, he showed up with a loaf of bread under his arm. There and then I devoured two-thirds of the loaf, with the continual fear that the partisan would discover that the ring was an imitation and would, as a result, take away this treasure I needed to sustain myself. The remaining piece I stuck in my sack for Poldl.

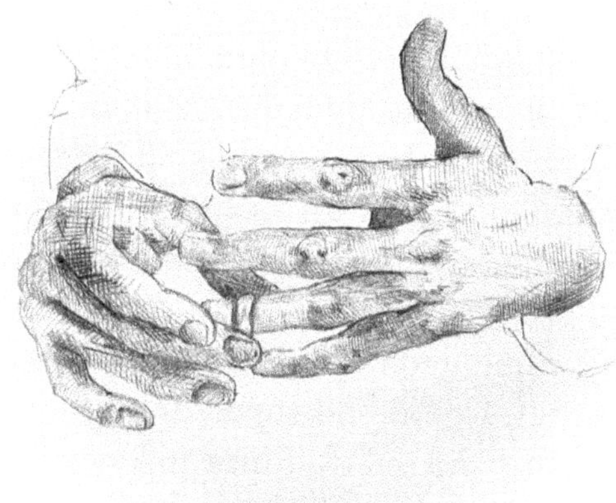

I looked for him, but I could not find him. Then I saw him standing in the corner of the barn where we had bivouacked, speaking to a pair of Russians. He was bargaining and he came to me, beaming with delight.

'What do you say, I was able to exchange a winter coat for an entire loaf of bread!'

'Where did you get the coat from? You're still wearing yours!' I asked.

'Yes,' he said with a smile, 'I have – I found it.'

I yelled at him: 'You did not find it. You stole it from someone!'

One word led to another, and then we found ourselves clobbering each other like juveniles. It was truly bizarre, to have two half-cripples slugging it out. We looked at one another and then gave up the fight. A second later we were even laughing. Nevertheless, it did not sit well with me. I said to Poldl, 'Look, you can't take the only thing remaining from someone to exchange it for bread for yourself, when the need is great for all of us.'

Those were my views, but it was done. Poldl tried to account for his actions by claiming that when it comes to starvation, mankind forgets his moral compass. He becomes angrier than an animal, and his most basic instincts are aroused. Perhaps he was correct. It had already cost me far too much mental exertion, and it was time to let it go.

Thank God it slowly became dark; with it, my concerns of a reappearance of my trading partner faded away. Furthermore, in one more night – assuming it was true – we would be in the camp.

By the next day I had begun to recover. I could observe this by the length of my stride. It was quickly returning to normal. I concluded that Russian bread must be nutritious. It probably contained unimagined vitamins mixed in with the grain. That one could live off carbohydrates alone for an extended period of time was something new to me.

Continuing, we came upon a railway embankment. There were quite a few gearboxes, troops and supply transports. They were of no danger, because they did not have time to identify us as prisoners by the time they began passing by. In addition, we were careful to take cover near the wall of the embankment. This line was likely headed to a major city. After about 20 kilometres we began to see smokestacks and houses. An hour later we arrived at the edge of the city. Upon reaching a Red Cross station, i.e., a field hospital, we gathered and waited. We had already learned all about waiting, and we no longer found it difficult to do.

The weather turned. It became very warm, and water from the melting snow went right through our boots. Things would improve when we got to the camp, we thought.

A couple of Russian women came to us and distributed little

packages, explaining we could use them to make *kasha*, a type of porridge. '*Karascho, karascho*' ['Good, good'], they said, meaning it was something good to eat. We were supposed to dissolve the gruel and then cook it. But how was this possible under these conditions? I carefully removed the paper, which was very greasy. I broke off a piece and tried it. Oh, it was marvellous! *Kasha* was a mixture of ground sorghum, fat and salt. Russian soldiers carried it as an emergency supply. Damn, I could not control myself and I picked up the packet and devoured it, just as it was. I was upset with myself over my inability to wait until conditions permitted me to prepare it properly. But I was not the only one to do so.

We travelled through the streets of a city that was nearly deserted. Apart from keeping our eyes on the person in front of us, we looked eagerly for signs of the camp. We passed right through the city, leaving the last houses behind us, but nothing was evident. Once again, our doubts resurfaced; would we ever reach it? Then one of the guards reported that it was just another 4 kilometres to the camp. That we could manage. The sky was heavily overcast and it began to rain. That was all we needed. Was this really happening? A rain shower in the middle of the deep Russian winter? One thing was for certain: we still had not experienced the finer points of a prisoner transport.

Not too far from us a building appeared through the mist. As we came closer, we recognised barracks surrounding a factory. That could be it, I thought. The guards then confirmed that we had reached our destination. We could discern figures moving back and forth in the factory site. They were captured soldiers. This sight did not encourage us. We would wait and see what was in store for us.

There was no barbed wire to hold us in, neither was the site separated by a fence. Well, not quite. What kind of a sign was that? '*Sapretnaja zona* – prohibited area!' At each of the corners of the site, watches were posted. We just stood there waiting for entrance to the camp. But it was not so simple, as we first had to be counted. One, two, three times they counted us, each time coming up with a slightly different number. And then the guard would start over again from the beginning: *Ras, twa, tri* … It wasn't so easy to number 260 men accurately. This time it had to be exact, as custody was to be consigned to the camp from the transport.

Meanwhile, I began to feel dampness through my cammies, the rain was falling increasingly harder, and then it started to snow again. Perhaps, surely, I thought, we could dry our clothing inside. The building, and my impression of it, did not give me a lot of confidence.

Finally, we entered the *zona*. Our column moved through the main building. My God, you should have seen it! Gazing down upon us were filthy, tattered, unshaven, gaunt prisoners. 'Where are you from? What unit did you belong to? Where were you captured?' And so it went. Each of them was looking for a familiar face or someone who belonged to their company. In vain they searched, among this motley throng.

We simply asked: Is there something to eat, will we be able to sleep, what kind of work must we do? To these questions there were no answers. That was odd.

We had been deceived into thinking this would lead to a protective roof over our heads. A rumour then spread through our ranks: there was no space for us. What, go back outside again? The rain began to lighten, only to be replaced by heavy snow, the dampness oozing continually through our clothes.

Davai! – they began splitting us up. Seventy of us entered through a dark passageway, up the stairs to the third floor. A door was opened and we entered a large room. There was no table, no bench, no oven, not to mention any bunks. All four walls were whitewashed and the ceiling was supported in the middle by two large pillars.

After the experiences of the last few days, I really didn't expect much different. Nevertheless, deep down I had still had some hope of a cot or something similar to lie upon. Definitely no such luck.

The interpreter announced to us that we would remain here a while. He said not to worry, that more would be joining us. That would also make the room warmer. Warmer would have been nice, as it was still freezing cold inside because the windows could not be shut tightly. The wind whistled methodically through the holes. That was a bitter disappointment. We were all completely soaked. And there was no possibility our clothes would dry given the sparse heat emanating from our bodies.

Poldl and I looked for a place we could settle down. Lying on the hard floor, I was able to close my eyes for a moment. Honestly, I was overcome by despair. Lord, what had I done that things were going so 'well' for me? But despondency was something I could not allow, not when my fate depended upon it. At least my throat was better, and in comparison to others I was in pretty good shape.

Now would have been a good time to have something to smoke. A Johnny or a Memphis – but, what was I thinking? Any kind of a cigarette or tobacco or even tea. When I asked Poldl if he had anything to smoke, he put his hand into his pocket and pulled out some newspaper scraps, then reaching into his pocket again, he held in his fingertips some peculiar-looking tobacco.

'What is that?' I asked.

'Oh, it is something exquisite, you're not familiar with it. It's called *machorka*, genuine Siberian fine-cut tobacco.'

I laughed and thought to myself, Okay, that might taste good. The main thing, though, is if it can be smoked. With sophistication, Poldl rolled the tobacco, clenching an edge in the thick paper and chewing it to make it stick – and *voilà*, the *papirossi* [a filterless Russian cigarette] was finished. It tends to more closely resemble a cigar. The chopped tobacco stems were coarse, and rolling the paper was not easy.

A new problem arose. Fire. Where were we supposed to get something to light it with? We had long since lost access to matches or a lighter. Wait. There was a glimmer across the way. We were there instantly, asking if our comrades would give us a light. I was very careful during this ceremony to ensure the cigarette didn't fall apart as it was passed over. The stuff didn't taste that bad; I had actually imagined it would be worse. And the cigarette's inky newspaper gave off a particular aroma.

We inhaled the foul smoke into our lungs, Poldl taking a few drags, followed again by me. Some people claim that smoking alleviates hunger. Not in this case. Would there be something to eat? We heard the camp had a kitchen. It was supposed to be staffed by Romanians.

Once a day there was supposed to be soup. On our first day we were too late and we missed it. I rummaged through my bread sack, looking for any remaining crumbs or remnants from my cigarette case. I gathered all of them together and put them in my mouth; admittedly, not everything I ate was bread.

It became dark. There was no light, at all. Sprawled out on the floor, we awaited the night. We lay close to one another in order to keep warm. I kept my eyes open for a long time, staring at the ceiling. I wanted to think, but that was going nowhere. The worries I had about my meagre existence were too great.

Suddenly, the door was flung open. It startled me, a light appeared, and a Russian spoke to us. We didn't understand a single word. An interpreter, whose mother-tongue was anything but German, translated for us:

'No one is permitted to cross into the prohibited area, do not go anywhere near it, otherwise you will be shot. If you go outside at night, you should not go further than sixty paces from the main building; otherwise, you run the risk of being killed by the guards. *Spakojne notsch* – goodnight.'

That was all they had to say to us, so I thought. I turned onto the other side and tried to fall asleep. Confound it; the wooden floor was so hard. And it was not as though I was getting any fatter. It felt as if I were lying on bones. As I fumbled around to try to make things more comfortable, I noticed my hips had become much smaller. I would have been glad to place anything underneath. But I needed my field cap as a pillow. There is no doubt that necessity is the mother of invention. I took off one of my wet boots and laid it under my right hip. That was a little better. It was certainly not a solution, because it caused one foot to freeze. Moreover, the continual upstairs, downstairs movement interrupted any sleep. All night long people were coming and going, caused by the constant urge to urinate. Many also struggled with diarrhoea. A few times I had to go myself. On the occasions I got up, I found myself also needing to stop and rest. My legs were really worn out.

In this state of exhaustion, I was able to sleep. Such were conditions at the camp, the goal we had longed for, our hope that had maintained us throughout this hunger march. I was still unable to get an accurate picture of the situation. Perhaps it was my first impressions that disappointed and depressed me. Incapable of seeing things clearly, I hoped a lucky star would provide me a way out.

4

In the Death Camp

I woke up. It took me a while to come to. It must have been a very deep sleep, something I had not experienced in a long time. Everyone was lying close together. Poldl had been so kind, taking a piece of his coat and draping it over me to protect me from the cold. Outside it had become bitterly cold, with patterns of frost covering the window panes. Snow crystals blew through the gaps, swirling as they entered. A restless feeling overcame me. 'Davai. Davai,' still rang in my head. Marching continually had become habit. But no, I could stay, I could rest, I didn't have to expose myself to the wind and the weather. The march was over. To be honest, I wasn't even sure how long it had taken. Was it sixteen days or more? As if anyone knew. Was it Sunday or Tuesday? Was there anyone who kept track? Indeed, we had no idea how much time had passed or what day of the month it was. Was our memory failing us, too?

The stomach, however, does not care about the date. It growled in agony. Some decided to have an animated discussion about a good, home-cooked breakfast. They looked to an illusion for a sense of well-being: steamed coffee, clean-shaven and showered, sitting at the table surrounded by family. One had to wonder, what kind of epicurean life some of them must have lived: smoked pork, eggs and bacon for some of them; others adored rolled oats, soup or something similar; one swore by milk, another told of his favourite breakfast recipe. What poor braggarts, I thought. But hunger deceives you into believing these things.

Family – how long would it take before they heard of my fate, before they received the missing persons report? Hadn't the OKW [Oberkommando der Wehrmacht, the High Command of the German Armed Forces] always told us the Russians did not take prisoners? It was possible they heard nothing at all, or perhaps 'killed in action for Grossdeutschland' [Grossdeutschland – Greater Germany – was the Nazis' informal name for the Reich, adopted after the annexation of Austria in 1938]? There had to be a way to communicate with home, even if it was only these words: I am alive.

We wondered if the Russians maintained an International Red Cross, or whether the Geneva Conventions even applied here. As if anyone would know this …

Everyone, get up! *Proverka* – roll call. Once again we were counted. We asked the interpreter: would we get something to eat today? Yes, yes, was the answer, and then he recited the familiar menu: one serving of soup, in the amount of a German field drinking cup, three to four hundred grams of bread and a teaspoonful of reddish, unrefined sugar. All the same. I tried to estimate how much longer someone could live on these daily rations. Assuming there was no change, I didn't think I would last more than three to four months. Naturally, that depended upon whether the soup consisted of just water or if it had some fat, and if something like noodles or vegetables were added. The interpreter explained that since we were the last to arrive, we would be last to be fed. In other words, it would be after noon.

It started to turn light outside, and I decided to go downstairs to find somewhere to wash. I assumed that here, in the camp, there would have to be a place for us to wash ourselves.

As soon as I'd descended two or three steps, I heard loud, strange voices coming out of the room below us. Should I, should I not? And so, I stepped through the door. 'Get out, get out!'

However, I stood very still. At the same moment, one of them came after me and bellowed: 'What are you doing, comrade? Get out, only Hungarians and Romanians are here, no Germans are allowed!'

'I'm from Vienna,' I calmly replied. The bouncer's face softened and he explained to his comrades that I was from Pecz [Vienna]. He couldn't actually invite me to stay, because the room was already overflowing with a motley group. It was a wild and crazy collection of men, who plagued the air with clouds of smoke. Many claimed they were freezing, but some were probably exaggerating, I thought.

Nevertheless, it was warmer here than it was upstairs … Then, among the crowd, I saw a few civilians.

'You, wearing civilian clothes,' I asked, 'where did you get them?'

One of them appeared to be wearing a genuine Ulster [a Victorian-era overcoat] that seemed none the worse for wear.

'Well, you see, to a large extent we are Jewish,' was the Hungarian's reply.

'Jews? How did you end up here in captivity?'

'Oh, that is very simple. Sit down and I will tell you.' We sat right next to the door, and he began his story.

'During 1941–42, we spent most of our time in a Hungarian concentration camp. One day, all those able to work were examined by a medical committee, and we were placed on a rail transport to an unknown location. We ended up somewhere in the vicinity of Kursk and we were sent to a road to construct an emplacement. After the July offensive, we advanced with the Hungarian army to the Don, where they used us to build winter emplacements. Life was very hard for all of us. It should be said, the Germans – at least those with whom we interacted – were far more decent to us than our own countrymen. And, as you yourself are aware, one day all hell broke loose, the Russians ripped through our front lines, and on the spur of the moment we were driven back along with the Hungarians. Each of us looked only to our own survival. We were alone. The majority of us went over to the Russians full of hope, seeing them as our liberators. What a great disappointment! The Russians overran us as well. They treated us the same as they did the fascists. It was really bad luck that we had on civilian clothes, because Ivan took us to be partisans, and we had difficultly convincing them that we were Hebrews. '*Nitschevo* – Whatever!' First, we had to hand over our civilian clothes. They were very keen to have those. My brother was wearing a fur-lined coat. Because he refused to hand his coat over, they shot him on the spot, no questions asked – my good Stephan!'

With tears in his eyes, the man could not continue his story further. I did not pursue any more details, because I could envision the rest. I asked if it was somehow better for him than for us. 'Not at all. Our hunger is just as great, we are just as lice-ridden as all the others. Every day a few die of either dysentery or typhus.'

When I heard the word typhus, I listened attentively. Yes, certainly, when one is ridden with lice, there is always the danger of becoming infected with this perilous disease. How is one supposed to defend against it? I heard there was no delousing performed here. The more lice you squash, the more you end up having.

I said goodbye. I actually wanted to relate a story to him, but I found that very difficult. I left and went down the stairs in search of some water.

By coincidence, below me was a group of prisoners pulling a sled through the snow. On it were two large barrels, from which water was splashing to and fro. As they passed by I held out my rusty cup and asked if I could have some water.

'Don't be a fool, the water is for the kitchen.'

Aha. 'Where did you get it?'

'Down by the river, but you're not allowed to go there!'

'Thank you.'

Thus, no water, no chance to wash myself. So I reached down and grabbed some snow, rubbing it into my eyes and hands. If only I had some soap; that would be nice. The scabby filth would not come off. So I stood against the wall and looked once to the left and once to the right. I quickly lowered my pants, and I attempted at some length to remove the lice from my underwear. I was horrified. It was no wonder these creatures would give me no peace. I was literally riddled with them. Open sores had developed in some areas of the skin. The best thing I could have done was to throw the pants away. But I didn't do that because I would freeze without them. I cleaned them as best as I could. After a while I couldn't bear it any longer because of the cold.

'Hello,' someone was calling, 'are you from the third floor? Go there at once; the Russians want something from all of you!'

What could they possibly want, I thought to myself, as I put my clothes on and climbed the stairs?

Halfway up I had to stop, because two lifeless bodies were being carried down the stairs … both dead.

When I reached the top, a Russian pointed me towards a corner with the others. I understood. The usual search for more belongings was already underway. You poor devils, I thought, you think you are going to find something on those who are even poorer than you? As I stood there observing Ivan's impulses, I actually felt sorry for them. The Russians must have become very fond of the spoils of war, having the opportunity to advance towards Germany, finally being able to collect enough watches, rings, lighters, wallets, pins, thimbles and things of that kind to satisfy their urges – these poor people! Anyone in that situation would lack good manners. At the same time we heard: 'This is *nemetzkaj kultura* [German culture], you grimy pigs?' It must have meant something to them to make this clear. As we dwelled on the floor, coughing and spitting where we were, their remarks did not really bother us.

Lord, let this cup pass us by. A few worthless objects they had taken from us lay on the floor. I found it rather harsh that these poor devils were taking even spoons away from prisoners. With what were we then supposed to eat? our hands? The only things they left us with were battered, rusty tins in which to eat our food. Looking at the Russian faces, I could see they were obviously disappointed over their gain. They had certainly hoped for something more valuable. If only they had known how many hands had ransacked us since we had been taken captive.

They took their spoons and collection of other little treasures, threw them into a sack, and took them away. Then one of them came back and yelled:

'*Petnazet tschelovek – na vodikatschka* – fifteen men to carry water!'

I was not nearby, and I would not do anything of my own free will, at least not while I did not receive anything to eat. The fifteen who were selected certainly hoped that they would.

Strange, I thought, that a factory would not have running water. What I had just witnessed below, however, did not make the water collection exactly appealing.

Noon finally came. 'Six men to receive rations!' Wonderful! We eagerly looked forward to how good the soup would taste. Soon we detected some clatter coming up the staircase. Four men were carrying two *potschki* – wooden barrels with a pole sticking through two handles on the top of each barrel. On such a narrow staircase these were anything but easy to carry. As such, much of this precious liquid was spilled. The two behind them carried a strip of canvas with bread, and the interpreter, a man from our group, held a Hungarian mess tin full of sugar. Directly behind him was a Russian whom we had seen on previous occasions. He was probably the *natschalnik* – the commandant. He appointed the interpreter to the position of *starschina* – the 'senior soldier in the room' – and asked if anyone was able to speak Russian. Four or five immediately volunteered, but only one was given the honour of being the deputy to the senior man. These two were given authority over us, so to speak, and responsibility for a fair distribution of the rations.

One loaf was divided among every six men.

The soup was served with an improvised ladle, made of a stick with a drinking cup fastened to it. This worried the newly appointed *starschina*, because all of our thoughts revolved around this moment, hoping at a minimum that our hunger would be partially satisfied. The thin tin cup became so hot from the concoction that I had to place it on the floor immediately. Using my orphaned glove, I was able to hold it. Cabbage soup … it tasted good, even though it consisted of chopped-up, somewhat salted cabbage leaves, cooked without any fat. With no spoon, I slowly savoured my first camp soup.

In the meantime, Poldl grabbed a loaf for six of us and began to divide it up. In workmanlike fashion, he skilfully used dog tags to cut the wet *kljeb* [also spelled *chleb* – bread]. But some men quickly decided that the quantities were not equal. Then one of us came up with a good idea: draw a number for each piece of bread. So that is what we did. Each one of us received a number, one through six, for each piece of bread. One of us would turn around. Another would point to a specific piece of bread. The one whose back was towards the bread would then say a number. The one who had that number would receive the randomly selected piece of bread. And so it went. This system proved satisfactory to each of us.

As I swallowed bite after bite, I became convinced that all life was relative. Under normal circumstances I would never have eaten a piece of wet, rancid bread, but today it tasted to me like cake. In my tin container on the floor were the remnants of the cabbage soup. I fished them up with my fingers and carefully laid them upon the bread – what a spread!

There was even dessert – a level teaspoon of sugar poured into our hands.

Even such meagre portions conjured visions of some of my favourite dishes. Poldl was grinning. He had news to share.

'I heard that, for a portion of bread, the Hungarians would give us a shave. What do you think?'

A piece of bread. I had to think about it. Without this serving I would not have made it through the day; nevertheless, I considered what was more important, some bread to put in my stomach or the filthy, matted, lice-ridden hair covering my face. Both were of vital concern, but I had to prioritise. If I didn't eat, I would not survive; but lice were not necessarily infectious, even though my face was covered with them. So I decided to remain unshorn. One thing, though, nagged at me. I had been soaking wet and extremely cold, yet I had not come down with a cold or cough. The only thing that bothered me was that my legs were feeble.

Well, what do you know, our numbers began to grow. It was amazing how many they brought in. More bodies could certainly make things more comfortable at night. The proverb proved to be true, the more the merrier. For me, personally, the room was already full enough. Poldl called towards the door: 'There are a few hundred coming, enough to fill the entire planet.'

That meant 150 would be joining us. To lie down or to stretch out was no longer possible. A few soldiers began yelling at one another, and in an instant a huge brawl ensued. Things got completely out of control. And there was no one present who could command peace. By himself, our *starschina* was powerless. 'People, calm down,' he said. 'When the Russians say so many people must fit in this place, then that is how it needs to be.' Wehrmacht rank no longer mattered. Actually, just the opposite was true. Those ranking from sergeant on up were being taunted, and this was especially the case among soldiers who had experienced Prussian bullying and demands for submission, simply for the sake of demonstrating their authority. The rigorous training was a thing of the past, and under these circumstances one would do well to forget about his rank.

Slowly, it was agreed that we would sit in rows, back-to-back, so our feet would not be touching. As it became dark, each of us sought a place where our legs were placed opposite one another in order to have enough room to lie down. I was fortunate that the man opposite me had legs that were comparatively not as long, and so I did not end up with any boots in my face. Poldl grumbled like a workhorse. Apparently, he had less luck. The darker it got, the more unbearable this position of half-lying down, half-sitting became. As our bones pressed against the floor, we tried to turn over, but there was no room. What was going on? Someone started to climb over those who were lying down. Oh dear, something hit me in the eye. It was understandable that when a comrade had diarrhoea, he had to go outside. Some were very sick. But trying to walk through the ranks in the dark when there was no walkway was no way to do it.

'My feet, my feet,' one of them piteously cried out. He probably had frostbite. It is not pleasant to walk with it. It was a horrible night, and I was glad when daylight broke, even though I had hardly slept.

After roll call, Poldl took me by the arm and we went looking for another place to sleep. We could not endure staying there for an extended period. 'Do you mean to say we will find it better elsewhere?' I considered out loud. 'When we return we may find there is nothing for us to eat.'

'Let's take a look to see what we can find. We'll be back long before they bring something to eat. Come on.'

In the other rooms of the factory, we found they were just as full, if not even worse. So we went downstairs to peek around. Further back in the same wing was an entrance. We headed for it. Upon entering, with some difficulty, we climbed a steep staircase.

Without being seen, we reached a half-open door … Looking inside, we couldn't believe what we saw. The concrete floor was covered with straw. Curiously, no one was stirring. A great silence prevailed in the room. Then someone wearing a Red Cross armband approached us. 'What are you looking for? This is an infirmary for those who are seriously ill. It is best if you leave. Everyone who is brought here is going to die.'

'What do they have?' I asked.

'The same as you, comrade. Hunger; in addition, dysentery and typhus.'

We let the medic know that we would promptly disappear. That reassured him, and he turned away. Silently, we took a moment to look around the room at those lying down. When we saw we weren't being observed, we grabbed an armful each of the coveted straw, and hightailed it out of there.

Just near the exit, when we were out in the open, I saw a hole in the wall next to the stairs. I threw down the straw and disappeared into the opening. It led to a small, pitch-black room, which was not high enough to stand in, but at least we could lie down. Hurray! We found night quarters for both of us. There was no room, however, for anyone else. We quickly gathered the straw inside, spread it out and cheerfully looked at one another … One thing was certain: the next night we would be able to sleep more comfortably. Only one thing bothered us: with any luck, no one would discover us and take away our bedchamber.

Around noon we left our den so that we were not too late to get our 'meal'.

So, the days passed by, one like the others. We were relatively comfortable and no one disturbed us.

What a disappointment it was when one day we found our little den bolted shut! How selfish and cruel to not even permit this! There was nothing left to do other than to return to the mass accommodation.

We became afraid, and an unpleasant feeling overcame us. We really didn't know what or why.

Then we received a promise: today was shaving day! We were really looking forward to see what would happen. Was it that the Russians found us so unpresentable, or did they fear an epidemic?

A few Romanians, who considered themselves among the better class of prisoner, came in with shaving brushes! Lo and behold, that was something! Well, wouldn't you know? They came from enclaves within our homeland. Regardless, we were looking forward to a shave. Two of them were armed with clippers, which they would use to cut our hair. But they appeared to have been newly opened and cleaned for us.

And so it started. While one was lathering with soft soap, the other was removing the hair. One would not call this a trim. Entire heaps were taken off. Oases of hair remained. As soon as the first was done, laughter burst out at the sorrowful appearance.

'A Stalin haircut,' said one.

'If your old man could see you now,' said another.

But the laughter died away as the number of those being sheared increased. We looked like dishevelled hedgehogs.

But then, it was my turn. The shave proceeded as follows: I removed the field cap, and with the broadside of the razor they quickly removed the hair. Would the blade be sharp? I felt tense as they scraped, or more accurately, uprooted my hair. I instinctively tried to communicate to the *Wasserpolak* [*Wasserpolak* – 'Water Polack' – referred to Slavic people living in Silesia in the seventeenth century. During World War II it was a derogatory term used to describe the Slavic people living in German border areas] that he should leave my moustache, because I could not bear to have the

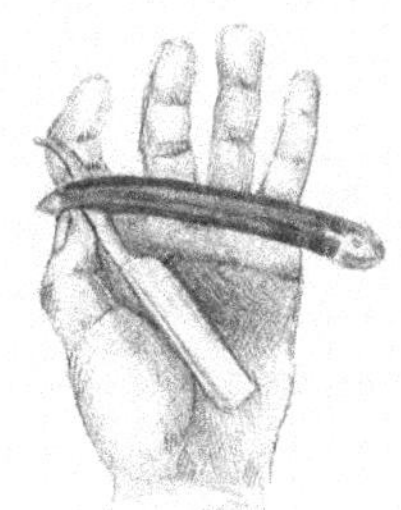

razor used below my nose. However, he did not understand me and scrape, scratch, it was done, and along with my hair came some skin and blood from my face. In any case, praise the Lord for the good will bestowed by this cultural deed! I had certainly atoned for some of my sins.

The irony of my thoughts vanished when I looked into the faces and saw the heads of my disfigured comrades. It was good that there were no mirrors on hand, so that each of us would not be frightened by what we saw. Using sleeves or a rag, a few of us wiped our faces dry.

For us Central Europeans, this ceremony was truly the hallmark of the barbarity of being held captive in the east.

Daily life in the camp changed relatively little. We, the inhabitants of this bleak structure, continued to lose strength day after day. We even found it difficult to do light work in the camp, and we each tried, as best we could, to avoid being assigned to a work detail. For myself, it took everything I had simply to venture up to the roof. I had to go outside, I had to have fresh air, I couldn't simply remain lying on the ground and let myself go, even when it brought me to the point of exhaustion. I found exercising just as important as nourishment. A half-hour each day, sometimes as much as an hour, I 'trained' in the open air; I could not do any more than that because my feet couldn't take it.

What I would have given for even the smallest of comforts! Even they were gone. There was literally nothing here to make do with. No bench – oh, how nice it would have been to be able to sit in a chair, to improvise a bed, to have a table – but these were ridiculous thoughts. Wood? For the last two days, not even the kitchen had firewood. For this reason, there was no warm soup. Instead, believe it or not, there was raw, frozen cabbage, chopped up in barrels, then carved out and placed in our hands. It was time to sink or swim! But I didn't eat it, because it would needlessly agitate my stomach and bowels. How many here among us were getting no rest due to diarrhoea? How destitute some were, although a few of them were to blame for their own physical condition. Senselessly, and lacking any self-discipline, they sucked down dirty, cold water, in an attempt to quench their consuming thirst. This icy water meant death! Frequently they took the water directly out of the storage barrels that were provided in every room in the event of fire.

This terrible affliction destroyed the last bit of sincere camaraderie between us. Among us were the 'business-minded', who viewed those who became sick from drinking the water as a way of increasing their own share of the bread ration, which they wanted – and received. A few even feigned being 'helpful'. They would offer to distribute bread to the sick, get them soup when it might be available, grab some sugar – always making sure to keep a little for themselves; then, when the sick were no longer aware of what was going on, the false Samaritan would reap the benefits.

To have to watch all of this was dreadful. What kind of human beings were they? Simply to prolong their own life, they deliberately shortened the life of another. But as I said, here hunger knew no bounds. Men became like animals. Under these circumstances, the mask that each of us wears comes off completely.

The conditions became ever more wretched. Theft held sway. Each man stole from another, whether it was simply a sock, a part of a handkerchief, a mitten or something similar; one could exchange it for bread or *machorka*. Soon, the sugar would be gone. Soon, there would not be enough bread to go around, because one or another of us had stolen a loaf. It was during this turmoil that the first typhus fever epidemic broke out. And what did the Russians do? They grumbled about the '*Nemetzki svini*' [German swine], counted our dead each day and the number of survivors, and distributed propaganda pamphlets about Stalin, Lenin or whatever the name might be. We acknowledged their magnanimity, in that we tore off pieces to roll our cigarettes. This was all done surreptitiously in order not to be seen. Only after the lecture, when the leaflets were collected, did they notice some were missing, and then there would be a terrible fuss. But who would they hold responsible? Personally, politics didn't interest me. Being in such desperate straits, we blamed it on the great stupidity of the prison camp storekeeper.

The time passed, the days and weeks trickled away, and I continued to ask myself: What are the Russians really planning to do with us? Did they want to preserve us as a workforce for the Soviet

Union? Or had they simply not thought things through, leaving us here to waste away until we were all dead? Or were we, perhaps, to be re-educated? I heard there was something like the Antifascists [Antifa, or Antifaschisten, was an international Marxist–Leninist antifascist movement; the German Communist Party adopted it in 1932 in response to the rise of the Nazis, and both used similar tactics]. Apparently, they were prisoners who had been held in Russia for some time, and who had become antifascist. One day one of them came and gave a lecture about the cultural and socialist progress that had been made in the USSR since the October Revolution. We listened in silence. As soon as he had finished, one of us said:

'Now I find it much easier to die. Should I somehow make it home, I will be sure to tell them of all the progress you have made.'

This touched off a fierce debate, which ended just as quickly. 'It makes no sense, it is pointless to argue,' said one of the soldiers. 'It is better simply to agree with them; just play along.' They made it known to the evangelist that they had become convinced, that there was only one land in the world that had a future, the Soviet Union. The antifascist, enchanted by his own words, received an extra piece of bread for his work – no one noticed the irony.

In no way did my captivity produce a political bias. I like to be objective in my thinking. Up to that point, however, I had not seen anything that would inspire me. Hence, I would wait.

I never expected that a prisoner of war, especially a German, would be welcomed with open arms. We had inflicted far too many calamities on Russian land. Nevertheless, one could still insist on a degree of humanity in the twentieth century. After all, we were soldiers, not criminals; we had to fight, that is what soldiers are supposed to do. Why not just stand us up against the wall? If they hesitated to shoot us in the front, why not make a hunt out of it and shoot us in the back?

These were the thoughts that continually went through my mind. There was only one thing I could do – endure! Perhaps one day the soup would be more filling.

Death of a Friend

5

Poldl concerned me. He stopped eating unexpectedly, and he would just lie on the cold, filthy floor, refusing to go outside even for a little bit, except when his bowels plagued him. He told me his stools were very watery, mixed with blood and mucus. Understanding what that meant, I tried to console him and I forbade him from consuming any liquids. I was sorry there was so little I could do to help. Helpless and powerless, I had to watch as he moved ever closer towards his demise. He was no longer able to swallow any bread; he dreaded it and found it revolting. But what if someone brought him a slice of toast? I recalled that on the opposite side of the yard, there was something like a smithy. One time I saw a fire there. Perhaps there was a makeshift hot plate on which I could toast the soggy bread.

After we received our rations, I immediately set off to go there. I looked inside carefully through the icy, small windows. I could not discount the possibility that someone was there. All I saw was the glow of the fire. Oh, it would certainly be warm in there. I waited for a little bit. *Oy vey*, I thought, a Russian came out of the door. There was nothing I could do. Fortunately, he continued further without noticing me. I looked inside through the small crack in the door and I saw two civilians. I was certain they were Hungarian Jews. Cheerfully, I went inside.

'My dear fellow, there is nothing here for you,' was one man's response.

'But look, my friend is seriously ill, and I wanted to toast some bread for him,' I answered.

His expression revealed that he sensed a deal. 'Okay, I will allow it, but only if I receive one-third of the bread.'

'And so you shall,' I said, although it disturbed me that I would be handing over my friend's portion that did not belong to me. But I thought this was the only chance I would have to make the bread palatable for Poldl.

'Say, how will we slice the bread?' I asked.

'Come, come,' said the Jew obligingly, 'there is a knife – it's improvised.' With these words he handed me a broken spoon handle; on one side the iron was sharpened, and on the other the metal had been wrapped around to form a handle. It was a curiosity, something I had never seen before, nor would I have been able to imagine it.

'Hurry, before the Russian returns. He is a savage!'

I quickly cut the bread into small pieces and I divided them, placing them on the furnace plate. 'Listen, you will get your piece first,' I said as a precaution.

'Of course, I am not going to cheat you, what are you thinking?'

In the course of the grilling I learned that the Jew was a nice chap. The warmth had softened me, and we both began to chat. He told me about Budapest, and I talked about Vienna.

'Earlier, comrade, I used to visit Vienna regularly, when Sárosi [György Sárosi, a Hungarian footballer] played centre-forward for our national team, leading us against Vienna at the Prater [a public park in Vienna]. Oh, mama! There was nothing like it. The Austrians with Sindi [Matthias Sindelar, an Austrian footballer known as the 'Mozart of Football'] as striker were our greatest competition.'

For a moment, the good man became so preoccupied he forgot where he was. He felt as though he were at home. He knew practically every one of Vienna's league clubs. I also showed that I was familiar with many of the Hungarian teams through the Mitropa Cup. We were both enthusiastic and enraptured by the conversation.

The toast was then finished. Spontaneously, he gave me a hug.

'Take all your bread with you, I will not accept anything.'

With delight and full of gratitude I shook his hand and promised now and then to visit. 'Yes, just come, I would enjoy that, but only after rations have been distributed. That way, the Russian will not be here.'

Happily, I hastened across the yard to Poldl. He would certainly be waiting for me. Within a few steps, I stood by him and passed him the still damp, but steaming, brown toasted, savoury bread. Appearing absolutely forlorn, he looked up towards the ceiling. I bent down to him.

'Poldl, what is with you, what is wrong with you? Look, I have good bread for you.'

With the sweep of the hand, he gestured dismissively that he didn't want it. Oh, I smelled a nasty odour emanating from him.

'Poldl, is there something in your pants?'

He nodded a silent yes. I could not let him lie like that.

'Poldl, listen to me … don't you want to go home any more? … Do you want to die in this miserable land? … Poldl, I implore you, don't let this happen – God willing, you won't. Pull yourself together!'

I lifted him up and shook his head intensely in order to make him responsive. 'Remove your pants, I will try to clean them in the yard.'

All the encouragement was futile. I grabbed his pants and pulled them off. I was overcome with disgust as I saw his emaciated legs and I was confronted with the terrible stench. I covered him with his coat. While I carried his clothes outside, my stomach wanted to heave. In the cold, dry snow, it was extremely difficult to clean his things; I was freezing and I had so little strength. I struggled to clean off his pants as best I could. I went back upstairs and put them on, even though they were cold and rigid. But it made absolutely no difference to him, my dear, poor fellow. He barely reacted. Who knew when it would it be my turn? This damn never-ending snow during the march to the camp had killed so many of us. No medical help, no shelter from the cold, no soft bed, not even medicine, it was a miserable fare.

After a few days Poldl no longer opened his eyes. We carried him outside, rigid and stiff, weighing hardly anything. There remained nothing of his personal effects that could be taken to his home, were I ever to make it there. The only thing I knew was his home address. I hoped I didn't forget that, as I had nothing on which to write it down. The four of us carried him into a large, vaulted cellar.

After seeing this gruesome morgue, we returned, horrified. Were there really entire mountains of former soldiers, men, completely naked, emaciated skeletons, frozen by the cold? It was terrifying to look at. I had experienced some of this during various campaigns, but a mass grave of corpses, or it would be better to say skeletons, was something I saw now for the first time.

The Russian accompanying us commanded us to take off Poldl's clothes and to place them in their respective piles. A few soldiers from different nationalities took the body and threw him onto the pile of corpses. I asked the German who was near me: 'Why aren't you burying the dead?'

He replied, 'We are not permitted to do so during the day, that leaves only the night. We don't bury them, instead we stuff the bodies through holes we made in the ice by the river. Now, however, the Russians have forbidden that. In the next few days you will be digging mass graves. That, however, is going to be rather difficult, because the ground is frozen to a minimum of 50 to 70 centimetres.'

I didn't need to hear any more. Trembling, I turned away. We were going to dig our own graves. The Russians are an amazing people. Have they always been so, or did they only become so because of the war? Was this normal for them, or were they unable to act differently due to current circumstances? There was no reason for conditions to be so dreadful, or so I thought.

Even though I found myself back in this damned room full of men, I felt terribly alone and abandoned. But now was the time to stand on my own two feet; I wanted to hold my ground in this cruel world.

A few days later some of us had to go out into the open, approximately a hundred metres away from the building, and clear away the snow. We used ice-axes and pickaxes to dig graves in the rock-hard ground that would serve as a resting place for our dead. The strength which I at one time had possessed had long deserted me; nevertheless, I worked doggedly, I was as tough as nails, going out each day. It was certainly better to keep busy than to lie around in these stifling quarters and descend into melancholy.

6
Typhus Epidemic

One day, all of a sudden, I felt crippled. Despite the icy cold, I had thick beads of sweat running down my forehead. The guard looked at me as though my time was up. He dismissed me back to the camp. In the meantime, a crude barbed-wire fence had been erected around the complex, and it appeared just as wretched and as miserable as those who existed behind it. In the few weeks since our arrival in this death zone, a 'watchtower' had even been erected. With difficulty, I dragged myself back towards the barracks; I could barely manage the stairs. I lay down in the place that had become mine. I sensed something very odd, although my stools were fine. I felt very hot; I was certain I had a very high fever. I spent the night restless and full of worries, not being able to sleep.

The bread which I received didn't taste good any more. I mixed it in with a little soup, which helped it go down better. Incidentally, the soup was new, no longer containing cabbage, but instead a pearl barley mix; not much, mind you, but I was content with it, nonetheless.

I was not the only one who felt ill. Many of us complained about a fever.

During the next morning's *proverka* [roll call], two Russian women in uniform came in. Well, I never expected that. I wondered why they were there. Then they took our temperature. My temperature showed 39.6°C. Did I have typhus? We removed our clothes from our upper bodies, and the two female medical officers, or whatever they were, examined each of us individually. Like many of my comrades I was marked with an 'X' in indelible ink on the back of my hand. So, yes, I had caught it, now I knew for certain.

At lunchtime the interpreter came and asked all of those with an 'X' on their hands to get up – and take everything with us! Our small group of around thirty was led to a deserted barracks – with each of us helping to hold and support someone else. I had no sense what to make of this gathering, or what a casual observer from our homeland would think.

In the anteroom a Russian snapped at us, 'Strip off everything!' I felt so sick and weak that I was unable to stand as I removed my clothes, so I placed my forehead against the wall, which helped. Why were they doing this? For what purpose?

Each of us was assigned a black iron ring. 'It's used to hang something,' someone said. No, no, only clothes were to be hung. Then it became clear, we were going to be deloused! The garments were left on the rings, we kept only our boots or the rags on our feet. We were frozen to the bone. The anteroom was not heated, and the door did not close all the way. They signalled to the first ten of us and led us into the next room. Thank God, I was one of them. An oven stood in the corner that radiated some heat. Emaciated, we gravitated towards it as if it was a magnet. Three barbers pointed us towards a bench and the painful hair removal from all parts of our body began. First came a little soap, and then Romanians, who were given this 'business', began their work, and not without a little sadism. If only the knives were a little sharper! When they were finished, my chest was gashed with open sores.

After each of us survived this extraordinary ordeal, we waited by the stove. 'Everyone shaved,' called a Russian. '*Davai!*' Into the *bania* [bath]. Wash up! Every third man was given a small wooden bucket full of water – I couldn't believe my eyes – tiny pieces of soap were lying on a board. The Russians handed them out. My neighbour apparently didn't understand he was being handed soap. He instinctively put it into his mouth, but instead of spitting it out he ate it. As I watched him, his only reaction was to twitch his shoulders. Would I also become so desperate that I would eat soap instead of bread?

We took turns washing each other, as best we could. In the water were white things, probably dead lice. It had been a long time since I had seen my body without clothes. It frightened me to see how little meat was on my bones, the ribs were clearly visible, the pelvis sticking out of my side, the knee joints protruding forward. What doctors call subcutaneous fatty tissue didn't exist; not only that, even the most basic muscle groups, the ability to sit still, had shrunk to a minimum. Was this the precursor to the heap of corpses I recently saw in the cellar?

After our bath we shivered as we waited for our clothes. The fever and this procedure wore us out, leaving us extremely enfeebled. The door tore open, and the Russian threw us the steaming clothes. Oh, the warm air was a blessing! Then we began the search through the messy bundle on the floor. Where possible, each of us wanted our own clothes back, and we had to be careful because it was very easy to mix them up, especially when someone else's appeared better than one's own. Thank God, I found my bundle, and I put on my malodorous but warm shirt. Although the filth remained, the lice were all dead. This was apparent because little white particles were strewn all over the clothes. My sweater had become completely grey, so there must have been millions of them inside.

One by one, I slowly put my clothes on. I suddenly felt faint, becoming weak at the knees and then I lost consciousness. When I woke up, I felt so hot. Where was I? Oh, still in the *bania*, but outside by the barbers and fully dressed. I was only out for a little bit. I thanked my comrades.

Our little group then left, led by a guard, gratified to be rid of the lice that had been covering our bodies. We were not taken to our old quarters, but rather to a different barracks about 100 steps away. Aha, isolation! Perhaps the accommodation was better there? It seemed to take a rather long time for me to come to my senses, but eventually I was cured of any such illusions.

The place we were taken was again nothing more than four bare walls and a floor as our bed, only the rooms were a lot smaller. However, there were far fewer of us, so it was possible to move a little.

During the change in our accommodation, I completely forgot that we had not received our daily rations – had we been cheated? I was not eager for bread, but I craved some soup or something warm to drink.

My concerns, however, were misplaced. Late in the evening the door opened, and with the aid of a gas-lit flame we received our soup. Oh, it was a type of grain soup, like semolina! It tasted so good to me, and because a few were unable to eat and so declined their portion, we could even have a little extra. I could not have been that sick if the soup still tasted good. Satisfied, I lay down, holding onto this belief even if it meant I were grasping at straws. Grain soup. If I were to receive this on occasion, then perhaps I would make it … With these thoughts I fell asleep.

I was tormented, however, with wild dreams. My neighbour pushed me.

'Stop your endless singing. You're not letting us get any rest.'

Well, I hadn't known I was singing. I only had the feeling I was staying in a bunker, chasing after some bottles of wine; they were lying in front of me, but I could not reach them. Then I wanted to get into my hammock. The hammock was hanging at home between the foyer and the kitchen. It then occurred to me I was not at home. Suddenly, I was standing in the delousing station in Brest-Litovsk, about to go on leave, and I was getting ready to check in for the train to Warsaw … the train was right in front of me … I kept calling, 'Stop, stop!'

Then I woke up. I felt so hot. My tongue was glued to the roof of my mouth. What I would give for a sip of water … but water meant death. I wanted to drink like a fish, a bucketful, an entire kettle, I could have emptied a well.

But no one came; all that could be heard was snoring, groans, and from time to time, shrieks from my comrades.

Early in the morning our temperatures were taken again … over 39°C … We started receiving soup twice a day, in the morning and evening, bread at noon. It stuck in my throat, I couldn't eat any more, not for anything in the world. It was as though my throat had been laced up. I was afraid to go to the toilet. My stools had changed significantly over the past twenty-four hours, they had become very loose. Only by summoning up every last bit of strength was I able to pick myself up. There was no more walking about, I swayed to and fro, needing to use my hands on the wall to remain upright. It felt to me as if I had a case of vertigo. Hans, what have they done to you – a total wreck!

Death happened there rather quietly – one simply fell asleep. Our *starschina* also fell ill. Even though he was one of the largest and strongest among us, he had to fight with everything he had against death. Death came especially hard for him. One morning, he went insane. He jumped up, raving like a lunatic, drooling from the mouth. He said something, he jumped over his colleagues on the floor, and then he ran with all his might headfirst into the wall, collapsing to the floor; he didn't get up again.

Later he was dragged out. No one was able to carry him. Every morning a Russian would come and call out, '*Skolka kaput* [How many dead]?' Then the dead would be counted. Their empty spaces would be taken by new cases that arrived.

I didn't think about dying. I didn't want to, I refused to. I focused my thoughts on the semolina soup; it would help me get back on my feet, it would nourish me, I would survive. The bread accumulated. I used it as a cushion. Nobody wanted it. A Hungarian tried to exchange it for *machorka*. I gave him the bread. If he brought something back, fine, if not, at least he had tried. But Istvan did not disappoint me. '*Ăs jö toback*' ['The tobacco is coming']. He gave me a handful of tobacco and I took it, loose as it was, and stuck it in my pocket. '*Kösyenem sepen*' [Thank you very much'], I said, and the Magyar grinned from ear to ear. It was probably a good deal for him. I looked for paper in my pants pocket, and I still had what was left of the brochure on Lenin's writings we had received. 'Long live the Soviet Union' was printed on one side.

Many of those with whom I had lived during the past few weeks were no longer with us. One after another had been carried out. My appetite still had not improved. At a minimum I tried to eat the crust of the bread, because it was not as sour; I sprinkled the little bit of sugar we received each day on the crust. I knew I had to eat the bread, even when it tasted awful, because apart from the grain soup it was the most important part of my nutrition. Again and again, I struggled to pick myself up, overcoming headaches and daily temperatures ranging from 38°C to 39°C. Would I be able to get through this long period of fever? That was the question that weighed heavily upon me, so long as I was capable of thinking.

There was barely a word spoken in our room. Most were very near death; they either slept or they were delirious. Interruptions only occurred when the Russians came in to count the dead, to take our temperature, and when distributing soup and bread. Due to the very high fever, the feeling of hunger was almost completely gone. In place of it we were plagued by thirst. I constantly craved something to drink. Was it supposed to be a consolation to me that it was the same for the others? Was it luck that I was too weak to be able to go outside to find anything that might be potable? Actually, it was, because along with the fever my dysentery was considerably acute. Instinctively, I knew that the intake of fluids, especially cold water that had not been previously boiled, would only worsen my condition. Of course, I often had the urge to try to go to the latrine but I tried to restrain myself, and with a conscious effort I was able to do that. Although it was not very far, it was torture for anyone who tried to get there. Often the walk was in vain, because it was simply cramps causing this urge.

This one time, however, I could not hold back. I had to go outside. I crawled over my comrades towards the door. Once I reached the corner, I used the walls to try slowly to lift myself up. I was unsteady. Like a drunkard, I staggered along the narrow passageway, scraping against the left side and then the right. That day I was especially run-down. I had to stop and rest. A Russian who passed by said: '*Na, ti, Faschist, skora kaput budjesch* … Here, you, fascist, are you soon doomed?' That much Russian I already understood. I didn't respond because, after all, my fate was not yet sealed.

What a mess I saw outside! A flood of excrement, filth and water, a stench that defied description. One had to wade ankle-deep through refuse just to get to the latrine. I tried to walk with my heels along the boards, so as not to sink into the mire. With one hand I balanced myself against the wall, while I slid sideways across the board. Alas, I was truly dismayed. I came to a point where I was not even capable of stepping up 25 centimetres onto a board! I stood there helpless. I asked a comrade if he could help me. He only shrugged his shoulders, he couldn't. Once again, I tried to pull myself together. I attempted one more time. I nearly made it, but then both knees gave in and I fell backwards into the excrement.

I called for help; my voice, however, was barely audible. Two 'foreigners' – Romanian or Hungarian – wanted to pull me out. But they were themselves sick and could not manage it. There I lay, incapable of standing up. I did not want to turn over onto my stomach, because then I would have faeces smeared on all sides. If anything, I wept in distress.

The on-duty Russian showed up. 'You pig,' he blared, and with one pull he dragged me out. Then he chose two prisoners to carry me into the snow and clean me off the best they could. They were not very gentle, which was understandable given the drudgery of what they were doing. While they removed my cammie jacket and pants, I crouched down with my shirt and sweater, but I was otherwise naked with my 39°C temperature. Using my hands and boots, I also cleaned myself off. I was grateful that I received any assistance at all, for up until this point I had not seen anything helpful from the other side. Then they helped me up to my feet. I thanked them. They led me back to the barracks to the place where I had been lying. Exhausted, I lay down and went to sleep.

My neighbour shoved me in my side. He didn't understand my language, he was no compatriot. Holding his thumb and index finger to his nose, he made it clear to me that some foul odour was emanating from my body. What was I supposed to do? There was nothing I could do to change the situation. I nodded silently and then turned my back to him.

This was the life of a dog, and what I am saying is no exaggeration; in fact, a dog's life back home would be better than this. Even when a dog is not in the house, at least he has a little dog's house with a bed to lie upon, at the very least one made with straw; he is given something to eat daily, enough to give him strength to stand; neither is he in fear for his life, and he is content with his existence. This may be true, but the dog wasn't engaged in misconduct; he didn't start a war. As a result, we were left to languish, to lead an existence below that of an animal.

I heard a fuss in the hallway. The interpreter came and led us to believe that those remaining would get bunks to sleep on ... Wonderful! Then again, there was a bitter pill to accompany this; yes, we would get bunks, but no straw. An advantage, nonetheless, because each man would have his own place to sleep, and we would be off the floor. We were thus relocated. We were not burdened with moving any baggage, we had enough to do, just to move ourselves, to lift ourselves off the floor, and to haul ourselves along. This 'room' was located in the same barracks. Many of us had to crawl on all fours to get there.

The bunks were arranged in a small place, one stacked on top of the other. The so-called weak were to take the ones on the lower level. I counted myself among them, because the latrine episode demonstrated that I was hardly capable of using the bar to climb up to the upper level.

In my new place I was seated next to an Ottakringer [a person from the Ottakring district in the western part of Vienna]. He complained continually. I had to calm him down again and again, trying to persuade him that in his condition, any agitation only served to make things worse; our nerves were frayed enough, and we could not endure this burden any further. He seemed to make light of this, saying [in his dialect]: 'Listen, the situation is this. They think with Stalin they might have a paradise. Let them try to come to Vienna with their *kultura* [culture]. The Viennese don't give a damn. Why? Art is the religion in Vienna! ...'

I calmed him down and replied: 'Look, the Russians have nothing to do with this, that we live in this filth, like dirty pigs, helpless, crude, and needy. They are barely surviving themselves, and they are supposed to assist us? You can't demand that. The main thing is they give us some soup and bread each day – we will recover from this.'

Otherwise, I tried to convince him that it was best for him and for me if we simply tried to console one another.

In the meantime, my cammie jacket dried, but the smell continued to cling to it. Indeed, we all smelled equally ripe, it was hard to tell the difference, except in the most drastic cases. A good many could no longer summon the energy to go outside. So they performed the call of nature where they were, into their undergarments, in a way one can only imagine – it was beneath human dignity – only to eventually perish.

One saw all of this, and there was nothing you could do to change it. These kinds of incidents no longer attracted attention, each of us was too busy dealing with our own situation. It also happened to those lying in the upper bunks, either because they could not make it out in time or because they were no longer conscious; the mess began to seep through the bunks and filter down below. What did the man below do about it? He looked apathetically at the bunk above, rolled as close as he could to one side, and then waited for the medic to come and wipe it up.

Yes, we even had medics assigned to us – prisoners who volunteered to undertake this service in return for a little more food. However, they were more likely to be collectors of cadavers than orderlies for the sick. For a few days they were able to receive greater rations to keep them on their feet, but then the fever would overcome them, as well.

Then oedemas started to appear. The feet, the hands, the face, even the genital areas would swell. Although for many it would simply come and go, for others the water would collect in the abdominal cavities and even ascend into the heart. Once this happened, death would soon follow.

I also had swelling in my left hand. My fingers looked like *Knackwurst* [sausages]. This concerned me, but eventually it went away.

One day the Russians brought us raw potatoes – they were supposed to help with the oedema. I ate one of them, but I was unable to stomach a second. Still, we received another surprise: the grain soup tasted like fish! I even found remnants of fish meat in my tin can and a few fish bones. I placed the bones to the side for dessert. We soon learned to crush the bones and to chew them, the bony substance seemed to be important for our body. Our survival instinct led us to believe these things, even though they may have bordered on lunacy.

One day the soup tasted especially good. Damn it, if only I could toast the bread, then I could eat that, as well.

Pepsch, who was the one from Ottakring, assured me he could find a way to toast it. He claimed that in another part of the barracks there were Russian casualties, and they had fire. He cut the bread into pieces.

'Pepsch, where did you get that knife?' I asked in amazement.

'Psst, be quiet, you idiot!'

'Yes, of course.'

So I didn't say anything more. He placed the slices into a rag which had once served as lining to a military jacket, crept to the door, taking a little time to be able to stand. He winked at me and disappeared as he wobbled through the door.

I lay back down and waited. I had to lie on my back. It hurt to be on my side, because both hip bone areas had bedsores. I also had a terrible itch in my left foot, especially in the toes, that gave me no rest at night. Did my toes have frostbite? I had to look. I pulled my boot off; my socks had been missing for some time. I used rags to cover my feet. Oh dear, I saw the one toe had turned black, and the surrounding toes were slightly frostbitten on the ends. What should I do? Alternating hot and cold baths would have been good. Ointment, a protective dressing … but where could I get them? I again wrapped the foot with the rag, pulled on the boot, and then left the toes to their fate. I was looking forward to Pepsch's return. I had a good feeling I would be able to eat bread today.

Finally, he stumbled back through the door. Without saying a word, he sat down on the board beside me.

'What is it, Pepsch? What happened to you?'

'I'm done,' he said after an extended pause. 'When I was half-done toasting the bread, suddenly a Russian soldier came in, and he decided there was something about me he didn't like. He became fiercely angry, grabbed me by the collar, and threw me out of the door. I lay there a while, gathering the crumbs he threw at me. Here, take them, I don't want them.'

The poor man was physically and emotionally broken by this treatment. I wanted to console him, but he rejected it. I tried to show him just how good the bread was, but he did not share my delight.

It became apparent I had overcome the worst of my illness. Now that I began to feel better, I had the strong desire to clean myself up a little. As my beard showed, time had not stood still, and the thickness and texture of my hair had begun to grow back. At least that was how it felt when I ran my hand over the top of my head. A shave and a haircut were necessary. A dirty and matted beard is a suitable playground and breeding ground for lice.

Although the previous delousing and shearing was a depressing memory, I would much prefer that procedure than to have to deal with trying to squash the lice, which was not at all effective in dealing with these repugnant creatures. The best example I can give is that it was like trying to squash a newly christened T-34 [Russian tank] by shooting at it.

Together we brought our request to the interpreter, and we were eventually able to persuade the Russian that we had to be deloused again. In fact, the next morning we were asked to take our clothes in our arms and to line up in the hall. If only it were so simple. I had expected to be able to do more, but I found I was barely able to stay on my feet. For a moment, I became dizzy and almost blacked out. I used both hands to prop myself up against the wall. I could not afford to fall over. It didn't go much better for Pepsch, and so we held onto each other, arm in arm. 'Let's go, take me with you,' cried another. 'Okay, come here, it will be better with three.' The third was a Burgenländer [from the Austrian state bordering Hungary]. So the three of us held and supported each other, staggering forwards until we were out in the open.

The fresh air was obviously good for me. We were, however, so weak. We could not even have withstood a sudden gust, it would have knocked all three of us down. But what was I saying, all three? The remainder of the group gave the impression they would rather dig graves than go through the process of 'bathing' again. On several occasions we had to stop and rest. The guard who accompanied us understood this completely and seemed relaxed as he looked around the area; he knew, there was not a chance someone was going to try to run away.

When we arrived at the *bania* we had to wait. *Oy vey*, more waiting! Something like that was always bad. One didn't have the strength to stand for very long, especially outdoors. A few of us then sat down in the snow. That was certainly not good, but I couldn't bear it much longer either, so I sat likewise.

As I considered this soft, white snow, a thought came to me: you see, there was a time in your life that snow, whether powder or corn snow, brought great joy. Today, you look at it indifferently, almost with hatred, it only means the cold, freezing – a long winter.

After waiting nearly an hour, we were led into the anteroom. We took off our clothes, as before, received our 'haircut', shave, a little washing up, delousing of our clothes, and then we went through the difficulty of finding our own clothes and putting them back on after they had all been mixed up.

There were a few pigs in our midst who had every intention of stealing a sweater, a shirt, or anything else in order to swap it later for something to smoke. As a result of the heating in the disinfection chambers, our clothes stank in such a way that it was disgusting to slip back into them. A few of us were unable to tolerate this stench, coupled with the stuffy air, and they ended up falling flat onto the ground. Two died during the process. It was probably because their hearts gave out. Once we departed the *bania*, they were just left lying outside, naked and motionless in the snow. We were not surprised; they were critically ill and emaciated, just like us. Whether sooner or later, it would happen to each one of us.

Silently and heads shaking, the three of us hung onto each other as we went past our comrades. This bath had so drained us that it took great effort to make headway. Men over eighty years old could walk faster than us. Moreover, a strong breeze had picked up and that further hampered our movement.

When we arrived at the barracks and stepped into the room, we saw four or five naked figures shivering, either squatting or lying on the wooden platforms. One of them, a German, explained they had not been able to join us because their fevers were too high. At first the Russians tried to make them go, but when they realised that under the circumstances their temperatures were too high, they left them behind, telling them to take their clothes off so they could be sent for delousing. These poor devils had to wait three to four hours naked in this cold room. We had already been back for an hour when someone brought their clothes back on a stretcher. Naturally, nobody received back the same clothes they once wore.

This short excursion was good for us, in spite of the hardships. I made up my mind that from now on, each day I would go outside for a little while. I had this certain feeling that since it was now spring, as the warm rays of the sun shone upon our miserable bodies, my health would return, provided that the Russians did not let us starve to death. But they weren't going to let us starve, at least not intentionally, that much they had made clear. It was probable that the meagre rations received by prisoners was due to some organisational shortcoming. Pepsch found out that in an adjoining building where wounded Russians were lying, they were likewise limited to fish-and-grain soup and bread. When I compared how the Germans cared for and treated their wounded, I found this almost unbelievable. But it appeared correct; the Russians were accustomed to a humble lifestyle, and they had proven that their strength should not be underestimated; mind you, at a certain cost! A life of austerity has no pleasures!

I had become preoccupied with doubt and conjectures about the Russian character. Is he perhaps … not as bad as I thought? I don't really know exactly how to word it. At the same time, we received quite a surprise: a cup of *machorka* was given to us along with cigarette paper. That was a source of great delight for us. I had barely thought about it because of my stomach and bowels. Nicotine effects the intestinal walls and irritates them considerably. The temptation, however, was too great to resist, so I clumsily managed to roll the cigarette. A light! Yes, of course, *spitschki* [matches] and a striking surface had also been provided. Our spirits were raised considerably. It was truly a pleasure to light a homemade cigarette in such a refined manner. Hmm! This was harsh stuff. It burned my tongue. Despite everything, despite sickness and fever, in an instant the room was a den of smoke. I knew I had to give up smoking again. It made me dizzy.

After several days I could sense that things were looking up for me. My bread ration had become too little for me. That was a good sign. My fever had also broken; the only thing that concerned me was my bowel movements … as thin as water. While this condition did not improve, it remained very difficult for me to stand on my feet.

Interestingly enough, we were left completely alone. This was only interrupted once, when a Russki wrote our first and last name in Cyrillic script on our lower leg with an indelible pencil.

The interpreter explained that if someone died – which unfortunately occurred all too often – at least they would know the name of the deceased. He said it was probably an attempt to create a register of all the dead in the event someone wanted to conduct a search. This did not make any sense to me, because no attempt had been previously made to identify those placed in a mass grave. And trying to notify relatives under the current circumstances did not seem feasible. The most likely reason appeared to be that it was an order, and when a command comes down from on high it is best to obey.

It was only another six or seven days since the last delousing before we became plagued again with lice. It was no wonder, since some of the newly ill were being placed with us without having had a *bania*. To protest this was not even thinkable, and besides, the lice were multiplying at an incredible rate. They were biting us and feeding upon our defenceless sores.

One day looked like it would be beautiful. No, really, except for the cold and snow, there was also sun. Its powerful rays radiated warmth through the two gloomy windows in our room. I watched them a long time as the light streaked along the dirty, grey walls. Through the windows I could see a cloudless, blue sky. I said to myself that I had to go outside, and I began to make my way towards the exit. As I was going, I called to Pepsch and told him he should join me. But he didn't want to. Lying around, nothing but lying in place, was certainly not good. How often had I resolved myself to go outside into the fresh air? It was certainly my intent to do so. But bodily weakness also brought with it a weakness in willpower. You could not do anything unless you really set your mind to it.

I finally got as far as the door, and I just stood there. It was truly magnificent. The snow glistened white, and the sun felt so pleasant. I leaned against the door and simply enjoyed breathing in the winter air, which was mixed with a little bit of spring. I was certain it was already springtime at home, and my best estimate was that it was late March – although I did not know for sure.

Along the side of the barracks sat a few figures who used the wall as a back rest. They sat on the ground where the snow had already melted, exposing themselves to the warmth of the sun. It did not take me very long to consider doing likewise, so I joined them, supporting myself against the wall. How good it felt!

What does a prisoner think, when he has a minute to imagine he has been given a second lease of life? He thinks about going home, he devises plans for the future. There is so much he wants to do, so many things he wants to change: to build himself a new life, to better himself, to learn something new, to work for himself and his family, he wants to enjoy life, to not let the little things bother him, to appreciate and be content with the small things in life.

These and many other random thoughts crossed my mind. I slowly closed my eyes, so I could concentrate on the soft gleam of the sun that surrounded me. Then I began to dream of my beautiful Austrian homeland, the lakes, the Alpine meadows, the cities and the villages, and the many pleasant people who lived there.

Then, it suddenly struck me: was it possible to be happy in the middle of this terrible war? With all the deprivation and suffering, any sense of joy, serenity or zest for life seemed like a betrayal. In spite of all this, I called out loud enough for everyone to hear: be content that you may make this place your home, where we are far away from Stalin's 'Wonderland'.

Lost in thought and untroubled by anything, I sat there a while. There was not a cloud in the sky, so the sun was able to radiate its full warmth. Looking around, I saw a couple of us were able to find something quite useful to do with this time. One removed his jacket and the other his sweater, and they were removing those irksome pests from their clothes. I did likewise. Here, in the light of day, I could really see how they became nestled in my coat in the area around my neck and my armpits. Gleefully, I kept squashing them.

However, I found this process of crushing them too laborious and it was taking too long. So I took a handful of snow and made a snowball. Then I used my finger to make a hole in the snowball, and I began flicking all the little creatures into the hole. May this little ice box agree with them, I thought. Once enough had been gathered, I took the ball and threw it into the white field.

My method met with the approval of my comrades, because it allowed us to reach our goal more quickly. It reached a point where I could not see any more in my sweater. I could no longer tell the difference between a live nit and the lice that had shrivelled up. In all my eagerness in this battle against lice, I removed my shirt and cleaned it carefully as well. If only I were able to obtain a new shirt. It had been almost three months that I had been wearing this same shirt. Fortunately, it was a dark colour, so the grime did not show as badly. With regards to my underpants, I won't dare to speak.

As the time passed, I failed to notice how low the sun had fallen. I began to shiver. I quickly slipped into my clothes. Using the wall to support my head, I found it difficult to get up off the ground. Without help or support, I do not think I could have done so. My thighs no longer had any trace of muscle on them. They were as meagre as a fence post, completely devoid of any strength. One more time I took a deep breath and I disappeared back into the barracks.

Pepsch welcomed me back enthusiastically with a thickly rolled *papirossi* sticking out of the corner of his mouth.

'I don't understand why you never go outside into the fresh air,' I said. 'It is the best medicine for us.'

He didn't react at all. So, I lay down again on the boards and began to roll a cigarette myself. Somehow, the stogie relieved hunger or boredom. Smoking helped pass the time.

As soup was being passed out in the evening, I developed an acute pressure in my bladder and an excruciating pain in the area of my kidneys. I endeavoured to go outside. I had no idea what was wrong with me, I screamed as I urinated. I thought I might be developing a chill. I was a real fool. Admittedly, I had stayed too long outside sitting on the damp ground without any support. Now I was paying for it.

As soon as I finished the rest of the soup, I felt the pressure again to go and relieve myself. And so it went, I had to constantly go outside. Then, suddenly, I was unable to move. An intolerable pain forced me to writhe on the boards. Pepsch threw me someone's old boot and told me that if I had to take a leak, I should use it.

That night was sheer agony. I didn't get a minute of sleep, turning from one side to the other. My good friend chastised me: 'You see, you and your fresh air!'

He was right. But what was I supposed to do now? I was completely helpless.

The next day I did not move, I ate not one bite; I burst into tears from the pain. My neighbours had already given up on me. I heard exactly what they were saying to one another: 'Well, he won't be with us much longer.'

In that moment I actually wished to be delivered from this life so all this pain would go away; it was too much. I looked towards Heaven and prayed to be heard: Lord God, if you are listening, please put an end to this pitiful life …

It was the first time during my prisoner's existence that I had given up.

I must have been asleep or unconscious for a long time. I felt like I had been transferred back into reality from another world. I was still alive! Instinctively, I reached around to the area around my kidneys and I felt no pain. It was gone. Was it possible? I did not trust myself to try and stand, but everything seemed to be fine, and whatever pain existed was very slight. I could only shake my head. The attack had simply gone away of its own accord. I no longer wanted to die, I lay back down and I was happy to be alive. Hadn't I previously sworn never to give up? Yes, I had, but at that time there had been no way I could have known what was yet to come.

Today, something else was up. Two Russian officers came in. One of them had something wrapped up in a newspaper.

'*Achtung!*' one of them called out, and in broken German he made it known to us that each of us would receive a card from the Red Cross, with which we would be able to notify our relatives. Delighted, amazed and at the same time incredulous, we looked around at one another. The astonishment increased when the other officer handed each of us a card. Both of them had blue caps. Were they with the NKVD [the People's Commissariat for Internal Affairs, the Soviet secret police, formed in the 1930s and dissolved after World War II]? Instead of being excited my reaction was one of apathy. Clueless, I twisted the card in my fingers. The Russian explained how to fill it out and then he left the room, visibly pleased he had done something good for us. The card had been written in Russian and French. It bore the Turkish crescent with a star.

Everyone had a card in their hands, but no one had a pencil. What we were supposed to write with, the Russian had not said. The smallest little pencil stub had long since become a rarity.

Personally, I was very sceptical about this. I thought it absurd to think that these cards would reach our homeland. First of all, what route were they supposed to take, when all connections had been demolished? At best, it was an attempt to persuade the homeland that Russians were not killing all their prisoners, as Goebbels had claimed. But there was another possibility: in the spring of 1943, would German military intelligence acknowledge the number of prisoners which would be shown by the cards if they were allowed through?

So I put the card aside and decided not to fill out anything. Pepsch and the others, however, would not let me alone. They wanted me to fill out the card, regardless of whether it would arrive home or not. They were able to find a small piece of pencil. My dear comrades could not figure out how to fill out the card, in spite of the explanation that had been provided. My knowledge of French was quite poor, but it was sufficient to help fill it out. Even though everyone else had finished, I continued to hesitate, until Pepsch gave me a proper scolding. After some cajoling, I scribbled greetings to my loved ones. The words were a bitter irony: things are going well for me … I am healthy … don't worry about me … with love, Your …

As I read over the card one more time, I noticed that the writing looked muddled. Should this card make it home, then they would understand everything that was going on … yes, everything …

Would one really believe that three, four lines would fully exhaust what a human being would write? In the late evening, when it had already become dark, someone collected the cards. If only I could have believed that this sign of life would make its way home, I would have given a thousand thanks. But I couldn't believe that. For this reason, I was completely indifferent when I handed it in.

The Survivors Reach a Military Hospital

For us prisoners, the changes in our existence remained modest. It began with counting the dead in the morning; after a while the soup would appear, sometimes watery, sometimes with gruel, the next time with cabbage. The rations of bread remained constant, soggy and sour as always; the sugar rations also remained small, albeit regular. Medication was virtually non-existent, except one time when a woman brought a bottle of liquid; it was supposedly a treatment for dysentery that would somehow diminish the bacteria that caused it. Temperatures were taken every two or three days, the *bania* continued to take place once a week. By and large, the routine was settled and regular, and despite everything we had to admit it was progress. Just as before, the major topic of conversation was food. Imagination and boasting produced amazing ideas. Did each of them really have a schnitzel and a goose on their plate every day? The hunger generated these hallucinations that appeared to bring some great delight and to satisfy them.

Fights would repeatedly break out whenever someone was caught being dishonest in the distribution of food or if he was stealing. Nevertheless, due to our feeble condition the skirmishes were always harmless. The hungry attempted to use every means to get two servings of soup instead of one, or to grab one more piece of bread than they were entitled to. In short: whenever food was distributed it was accompanied by a sense of agitation and nervousness.

Later one afternoon we received amazing news: all those who were fever free and capable of walking approximately 800 metres should get ready and wait in front of the barracks; we were to be moved to better quarters.

I thought about it: according to Russian calculations, 800 metres might be more than a kilometre; was I able to endure that? My feet were not only weak, all of my toes had frostbite and that would hinder my ability to walk. How this had happened I didn't know for sure; it was probably due to the room being 'overheated'.

Several of us pulled ourselves up, hoping for any improvement. The plague and our barracks of death were easy to leave behind. The memories of the past few weeks weighed heavily upon our conscience.

It was laughable. The coat draped around me, the camouflage jacket I was wearing, the bread bag with my meagre possessions – a few rags to cover my feet, a piece of fleece that served as a pillow, a rusty can and a wooden spoon – weighed me down so heavily that upon my first attempt to stand I had to sit right back down again.

But on this day the Russians seemed to be in a hurry, so I had to get back on my feet. Along with '*Davai* – onward' and '*Bistra* – quickly' we were driven outside. Look at that, I thought, the snow had vanished! Two wagons were there. Anyone who felt too weak to walk was to be transported in the *panje* wagon. With some momentum from a pair of strong hands, I was roughly loaded onto the wagon. Half-sitting, half-lying, I found my spot for the transport. Those who did not have a spot clung onto the side of the wagon, and off we went with a '*Hü-a-hö* – giddy-up' …

The journey was crazy, we dashed across the open field. It didn't matter at all to our workhorse, and Ivan drove on cheerfully. Those who could not hold on were unable to keep pace, and we lost them, the poor souls. Two more fell down, and no one seemed to care. It would have been the same for me. I was just happy that I had a place to squat in the wagon.

The 800 metres had nearly doubled by the time we reached the end of our trip. The passengers who rode in the wagon, which more closely resembled a box with wobbly wheels, had been tossed to and fro. But even here the old adage applies: a bad ride is better than having to walk a long way. Unloading happened in the easiest conceivable way: our friend Ivan opened the side panel and, one after another, out we rolled. There were no injuries other than a few bruises. We could hardly be called men; at best we were a number. We slowly managed to help each other up and we attempted to gather our gear. In the meantime, my cap had been lost. Where, then, was Pepsch? He was nowhere to be seen. Did he come perhaps by foot?

We stood before a wooden house that from the outside made a good impression. A white-coated Romanian doctor and a Romanian medic were expecting us and directed us to our quarters. Compared to us, it seemed as if priority had always been given to the Romanian prisoners of war. That would be something I could accept, were we to be treated decently. For the most part they had treated us rather poorly, and along with the Russians they brutalised us in order to better their own position. We knew what the Romanians were like, and we resolved to let them neither cheat nor rob us. Concerning the latter, mind you, one had to be very careful or you might end up losing the shirt off your back. We got to know the Romanians, and they had made an art of adroitly stealing from their fellow man.

But to our surprise, things were not half bad. The Romanian doctor made a sincere effort to try to obtain better rations. He regretted that our soup was once again watery. He promised to speak with the Russians, but he had no success for the simple reason that no gruel remained. The doctor even provided opium tablets; however, due to poor nutrition our digestive system was no longer able to process the 'food', and it passed through our system just as it had entered it. Only a proper diet and decent care could help us in this situation.

The rooms were more agreeable, more spacious and equipped with large windows. Although there were no stoves, it was no longer as cold; the sun began to give off its warmth.

As before, our berthing consisted of wooden-framed bunk beds. Unfortunately, we noticed a blemish right off the bat: the entire house was infested with bugs. That could be a big problem when it became warmer! And because the wood was green and the bark had not been stripped, crevices provided bed bugs a great hiding place.

The prisoners suffering from diarrhoea – I among them – came to an isolated room in which a few were already lying. A nasty odour hit us as we entered, because two buckets that stood in the room served as a toilet. Not hygienic, but practical, even necessary for those who were ill, because the latrine was too far for us to make it. We no longer missed having either a table or chair, because we no longer expected such luxuries. Our entire existence took place on the bunk beds.

Due to our doctor's initiative, one day we received *suchari* – dry bread, as a dietary measure. The faces, though, became long when the bread was emptied from the bag onto the floor. There were no longer any slices of bread; just chunks, crumbs and bread dust. Due to a lack of available water, instead of 300 grams of fresh bread, each man received only 180 grams of dry bread.

We needed the entire morning to divide this unappetising amount into thirty-six even portions. It would be difficult to describe its flavour, it was absolutely tasteless, a little sour. Mind you, it had one advantage: it took longer to eat because it was rock hard and it had been a while since we actually had to use our teeth. It also had a more lasting effect: it helped regarding our diarrhoea. Unfortunately, the distribution of dry bread ceased for the simple reason that it was all gone.

Necessity is the mother of invention. I came up with the idea of taking the wet bread that was once again being distributed – I repaid the comrade who had loaned me the knife with a piece of bread – and to dry it in the sun and fresh air.

One morning someone called: 'Do you know what today is? Easter!'

'Easter, why do you say that?'

Not only him, but a Hungarian claimed that, as well. They said they had calculated it precisely. Well, perhaps it really was Easter, we could neither confirm nor dispute it. For me, captivity had already seemed like an eternity. Naturally, it was certainly possible to work out the date. I was alive, that was the most important thing; the day passed without Easter eggs or palm willows [when Christianity was brought to Central Europe, no palms were available, so local plants were used, including willows, which are among the earliest plants to sprout]. Regardless of the situation some people find themselves in, they battle through and endure. Others give up and are gone …

Those of us who remained lived for weeks with barely enough

to sustain us, yet we still breathed. In this, one's constitution and will mattered a lot. That being said, once vital organs like the heart, kidneys and lungs were damaged, under these conditions nothing could help.

About eight days after our arrival in this house, the number of those dying each day began to decrease. We were even louse-free. Above all, we had to thank our Romanian doctor. He made rounds daily, and when he found someone with lice, he sent them along with all their 'bunkmates' to the *bania*. That walk was always harsh, because the distance was very far for us. Transport was no longer provided, the entire way travelled on foot. In the event of a strong wind, some would be knocked down, and it was difficult to help those who had fallen get back up. But the result of being louse-free was worth a great deal.

For the first time we started hearing detailed reports from the front that sounded almost sensational. Rostov, Kharkiv, Kursk were in Russian hands, the entire German southern front was in retreat.

The Russian was disappointed that we did not receive this report with great enthusiasm, and at the end he berated us for being incorrigible fascists. Did he not understand that we had more important concerns? Those who are unable to stand on their own feet have little interest in how the war is going at the front. 'The war will soon be over,' they said, clearly expressing their own desires.

Personally, I was not convinced. Most of us believed that Hitler's chances of winning the war were now very small. But it was dubious what would happen from one day to the next.

What the Russians urgently wished for was the 'Second Front' which the Western Powers had promised and were already preparing for. We heard this from both the commandant and the *politruks* [commissar – an official in charge of political indoctrination]. The phrase *ftoroi front* [second front] echoed again and again.

I can't say exactly what I thought about it, other than it was meaningless to me. I couldn't have cared less about a *ftoroi front* ...

My frozen toes would not allow me any sleep, particularly my right big toe; it was as blue as a plum. Our doctor said to me in French: it needs to be removed. I shook my head in disbelief. But it became increasingly unbearable, and one day I had to call upon the medic. He squinted at me, then at my toe, left the room, and then returned with a pair of common plaster shears in his hand. He sat me down on a bunk, taking my hand to use it to cover my eyes. I screamed – and when I looked, a large piece of my toe was lying on the floor. My entire body was shaking with pain and I felt lightheaded as I softly whimpered to myself. The medic was kind, and even though I did not understand a word he was saying, I knew he was trying to console me. He bandaged the remaining stump and he applied a liquid to alleviate the pain. '*Mulzumesk* – thank you,' I said, and I hobbled towards the door.

When I reached my spot I lay down immediately, ashamedly wiping my watering eyes. This drastic treatment was not without considerable pain. Yet, the constant tingling was now gone. The wound festered, but here there was the possibility of having the dressing changed. With all the frostbite we experienced, my case is hardly worth mentioning.

Beautiful days finally arrived. The sun was like a balm on us invalids. Every day we could sit outside, from early to late, and let it warm us.

8

The Train Ride to the Urals

We quickly slurped our soup and we were just sitting around the house. We then noticed a large group of people walking quickly towards the hospital. We knew they could not be prisoners, because they would have moved in a different way. As they got closer we recognised they were Russian officers and women in uniform. Something was up. We observed them closely. They called immediately for the doctor, who came as soon as he was called. Expressing the utmost haste, they were most animated in their gestures. Romanians, Hungarians and German interpreters were called, and we soon heard the exciting news. A few even thought the war might be over.

'Everyone, inside, grab your gear!'

So, another relocation. What a pity, it wasn't that bad here. In fact, it was hard, but it was clean and reasonable.

The sound of engines roared! Gasoline cans with Stalin markings were suddenly placed outside. 'Whoever can't make it on their own, climb on,' was the command given by a German-speaking Russian Jew. Those of us from the 'shit hole' were aided by a kick in the backside, and those with frostbite and amputations were also loaded onto the vehicle. It seemed to me that things were moving along rapidly. It appeared as though a complete evacuation was in progress. Those remaining were formed into a queue and were to follow later.

The *LKW* drove in an 'unfamiliar' way. We were so packed in, next to and on top of one another, that we didn't have any time to concern ourselves with our destination. With every precaution I attempted to protect my amputated toe from anyone who might step on it, but unfortunately I did not have much success; the road was unpaved, and instead, à la Russian, muddy, rutty and full of potholes.

As I peeked over the side of the truck, I could see we were driving towards the city alongside a rail track. I wondered where it led. The fact that they were taking the time to move us, and weren't simply leaving us to our fate, was at least worth something.

Then came a jolt and the truck stopped. Along with '*bistra*' and '*davai*' we were driven from the wagon. It seemed as if the Russians were always in such a rush! Yet when one considers their countryside, their villages and their cities, one wonders what remained of this urgency when it came to progress. Perhaps it was only when they were urging others to hurry.

We were amazed when we found ourselves at a railway station ramp. On the tracks stood several railcars loaded mostly with war materials.

'*Sadiss*! – sit!' came the command. So we sat down on the ramp and passed the time rolling *machorka* tobacco. My tobacco was mixed with all sorts of things that were in my pocket, and it was somewhat amusing that they crackled when smoked.

A column of about 120 men came from down the road. They were 'heavier' and were stronger than it would have been possible for prisoners to be. They sat down along the ramp. I looked around to see if I could spot Pepsch anywhere. But to no avail. Had he died, or had he been left behind? It was such a pity, there was no one left of those I had met. I wasn't really afraid, but it would have naturally been better to see a familiar face; things would have been easier to endure.

For us, the upcoming transport was a special occasion. There was already a set of trains with the Red Cross emblem, positioned alongside the ramp. Moments later Russian women with pencils and paper busily approached us, and we were divided into groups of thirty for each railcar and carefully registered: first name, last name, date of birth, etc.

I waited with anticipation until it was my turn. Whether I was leaving what appeared to be better circumstances for the unknown, it didn't really matter. The time had finally come.

A small set of steps were lowered, and with the help of Russian medics we were pushed, not always gently, into the cattle cars. I was so astonished with sheer joy that I stopped moving. When I finally got to my assigned place, I found that I had a straw-filled mattress, a blanket and even a pillow. It was actually possible to lie down and stretch out on a mattress! Once everyone was inside, it was cramped, but not half bad. I felt great – after three months of lying on stone, wood, snow and dirt, I actually had a mattress and pillow. I lay myself down and fell asleep.

It was dark when I woke. I pushed the person next to me, wanting to ask where we were. But he was sleeping. Everyone was asleep. It was dead quiet. So I lay back down and I was out in a minute.

The next time I woke it was already light, and thereupon a heated debate occurred over when we might get some food. We were still at the ramp, and there was not a single Ivan to be seen, not even on watch, so we were able to go out and relieve ourselves.

Approximately an hour later, there was movement around the railway station. Then it occurred to the Russians that they should check on us. One brought the news that we would be eating shortly after the locomotive was coupled with the mobile field kitchen. Mind you, that was a rather indefinite time span. But the Russians were moving more quickly than normal, running back and forth, so we expected that something would happen sooner rather than later. Suddenly, there was a strong jolt. The cars were coupled. One of us looked carefully forward and confirmed that the lock was on.

A Russian determined the *starschina* for the car. He appropriately named a Polack [a person of Polish heritage – a derogatory term that was common in World War II] who also served as an interpreter. He was also strong enough, at least in our imagination, to bring us a little soup.

The guard and the newly appointed *starschina* set off together with buckets, otherwise there were only wooden barrels. So the Russians were not entirely without culture. No, no, we were the real pigs: '*Nix kultura*' ['No culture'], we heard them say, reproachfully at every opportunity. I wasn't about to complain, because the soup was coming. In the end, it was nothing more than a transport for sick people, and we dared to hope that there might be larger rations, or perhaps that things might improve.

It took quite a while for the two buckets to reach our car. Ivan carried in one hand a small sack, and in the other a ladle. Our noses told us right away that there was something novel about the soup. Then someone called out from the upper level – since there were two levels – 'pea soup!'

'How do you know?' responded another.

'I see peapods swimming on the surface.'

The portions began to be served. Curiously, Ivan attended to the work himself, which triggered murmuring among us. This intensified as the good fellow only skimmed off the thinner water on top. Ivan was not impressed, and he unwaveringly continued. Despite repeated heckling he did not stir it. I personally received a total of seven peas in my tin, the rest of the soup was grey-lilac water, a little salted, with a glob of grease on it. It didn't taste horrible, but if this was all we were going to get for perhaps the next two weeks, then it was bleak for all of us.

Following the distribution of soup, Ivan lent us a spoon, and sitting on the wagon's edge with his feet dangling, and our hungry eyes growing ever wider, he ravenously consumed the thick portion of the pea brew. He gave part of it to our *starschina*. At least those two stomachs were full. I preferred not to look as it only made me more irritated. With resignation, I lay back down and nibbled on the piece of white dry bread that had been distributed.

Where in the world would one find a soldier devouring this meagre watery soup in front of prisoners? Had the Russians gone to the dogs because of the war, or were they always like this? Perhaps it was only this Ivan who was so gluttonous, or did he simply do this today to torment us? I found it very difficult to find an explanation for what had occurred, and shortly thereafter he was assigned as a medic; there was no doubt he would receive better rations in that position than we would as prisoners, or so I thought.

An illustration of the 'high point' of our so-called servings would be the distribution of hot chai, a Russian tea; a wonderful beverage by our expectations in this dreadful reality, a light-yellow, warm water drink without any distinctive taste. For the first time, a heaped teaspoon of white sugar was provided. It was actually somewhat appetising to lick up this sugar from our unwashed hands, as there was nothing else to pick it up with, not even a scrap of paper, for those who had paper would prefer to smoke it.

A sudden jerk – we were moving. We were actually moving, as could be seen as Ivan tore the ladder away, and soon we were on an open stretch. This journey by train was a complete change for us.

Ivan told us that whenever we stopped at larger train stations, we should close the doors. We soon learned what that meant. As soon as a door was opened in a larger station, gaping crowds would start cursing, ridiculing, and now and then throw stones at us. Occasionally, when the guards weren't looking, Russian civilians would exchange something with us through a transom window or hatch. There were some who swapped their last sweater, shoes, or even pants, for something to eat or smoke. In the moment, we did not even consider the conditions the locals must have had for them to want to acquire our ragged clothes. Every day we would receive some kind of visit from a medical orderly, but there was rarely any medication. When someone died, they would be carried off at the next stop, loaded onto a wagon and carted away. When these wagons did not serve as a hearse, the wood would be taken off and used to fuel the engine. Coal was not available in these regions. Naturally, the dead were stripped of their clothing. In this way, the clothes that had been traded away in barter were replaced.

One day the train came to a stop. There was no more wood to fuel the engine. All the sick who were even partly capable were off-loaded. Resistance was pointless. Heavy logs had to be carried onto the loading dock on the train. It was painfully slow, some even collapsed in the process, until finally this hauling came to an end.

Each day we pleaded to have our dressings changed. The wounds festered acutely, and the infections were so severe that in some cases maggots were visible on the bandages. The stench was also unbearable.

Once again we sat for at least three hours. It must have been a giant train station for some type of industrial plant or military installation. We were still unable to make out the name of the town. As one would expect, we were always placed on a side track as we approached the suburbs of any major city. A T-34 transport accompanied by a number of troops went past. It did not appear luck was with us. The train stopped. We immediately responded by closing our doors. But after some time had passed, a field surgeon appeared and called for all those who were able to off-load. I wrinkled my brow, because it was apparent with the Russian soldiers standing outside that the situation was not favourable. Nevertheless, I bit the bullet because I wanted my bandage changed as well. With foresight, I removed my felt boots and hid them, which was possible because my neighbour loaned me a pair of canvas mittens to put on in place of my boots.

When I got off and the Red Army soldiers saw me looking at them, the shrieking and laughter increased. The dressing-changing station was located six cars from me. Every possible invective and swearword, and then some, were hurled at us, combining Russian and German. '*Deutsches Schwein*' ['German pigs'] and '*Hitler kaput*' ['Hitler is finished'] were clearly inferred.

I must have made a ridiculous and strange impression on the Russians. Because I felt weak and my feet were covered by mittens, I had to stop several times to rest as I made my way along the train cars towards the front. Then I suddenly fell to the ground – it was a kick from behind. As I was trying to get back up, a motley bunch surrounded me. The only thing I was aware of was that I was being spat upon, then I collapsed. A pair of powerful arms pulled me up and took me to the car where dressings were changed. It was the medic from our wagon, a good chap, even though he had gobbled up the soup. He protected me against any further attacks.

The dressing change hurt. But what was that compared to the abuse, invectives and beating I had just experienced? The soldiers were now being restrained by guards who mounted fixed bayonets for protection. I was really glad once I crawled back to my spot, where I could rest after this latest 'excursion'.

I tried racking my brain to understand the behaviour I experienced. Is it not beneath human dignity to treat a defenceless person like that? This had nothing to do with the war; as soon as a soldier becomes a prisoner, he should be treated according to certain standards of humanity. At least that is what the Geneva Conventions state. Or were these conventions agreed upon merely so the people did not have to think much about it?

The previous summer, I personally had had experience dealing with prisoners from New Zealand in my homeland. Against orders, I brought them bread from the post, and bottles of beer and cigarettes in a backpack, as long as I had the financial means to do so. In various ways I sought to better their situation, given the irregular operations of the camp. The food was awful, the work was difficult, and contact with their homeland had not been established, as the New Zealanders were first prisoners in Greece for two months. We had also been misled by deceitful propaganda; but hate, such hatred as was here, had not existed. This was true even with the Russian prisoners and deserters, at least the ones I had encountered, I thought. I did not recall ever hitting a Russian prisoner, or spitting on one, not even when just a moment earlier he was a bitter enemy trying to put me in the grave. The desire to retaliate, or to let off steam, could not be directed against a prisoner. But these people must have been inculcated with a refined hatred and mistrust of everyone, or at least those who were not 100 per cent friend. That had to be the reason. I do not think that mankind is bad, and that includes the Russians.

On the other hand, the mentality was like children who laugh at others when they should have pity.

The train ride had already lasted a while. Our compartment was no longer as tightly packed, and some were already laid out on the wood. The man next to me did not last very long, either. For two days he did not eat his soup or touch his bread, until one morning when he no longer opened his eyes. Was he dead?

In the interim I collected his rations for him, but he remained stiff. So I had to report him, even though his rations had benefited me. Once again, someone showed up to carry him away.

What kind of human beings had we become? Someone next to you died, and you hesitated to report him dead, while you calmly received the dead man's rations. Is this ungodly? I didn't let it bother me. The only thing important to me at the time was that small supply of bread.

'*Smatri, smatri* – look, look! The Volga!' exclaimed our medic, who interrupted the quiet of our rather monotonous ride. We stretched ourselves, lifting our heads from our beds, and saw that we were travelling across an enormous bridge, under which slow-moving, dark-black water flowed. Along the banks, which appeared to be torn by strife, sat barges in a series of rows, where they had been kept during their winter hibernation. The ice and the snow had not yet entirely departed, and even the woods showed patches of snow remaining.

The Russian looked in awe at the large river that belonged to him. It appeared to me that he considered it a shrine. I also looked at the river for a few minutes, wondering … When might I return over one of these bridges? The large river, which at this point was just as wide as the Danube near Vienna, was one I wanted to cross again. I was overcome with homesickness, and I turned away.

Where, actually, were we? Based on the landscape, I assumed it was somewhere near the headwaters of the Volga.

After a few days passed, Ivan beamed with delight as he told us that we would soon arrive at our destination. He was correct.

The train station, where we remained for twenty-four hours, was where we disembarked. At dawn there suddenly arose dreadful shouting. We understood what was wrong immediately, even without the screaming of our attendant telling us we had to remain attentive. '*Sakriwei* – shut the door!' Fist-sized rocks were hurled into our car. We took cover as best we could and swiftly closed the door. Outside we heard Russians yelling at one another, probably because one of our guards had also felt this warm welcome.

After about two hours came the official word to open the doors and off-load. We supported each other in this process. After so much lying down, steadiness did not come easily; indeed, it was the opposite. I could barely move. On the opposite side of the tracks stood a curious crowd that ogled at us, ridiculed us and mocked us. So this is what the 'Fritzi' looked like, these Hitler beasts … actually harmless, laughable in appearance, feeble and gutless, it must not be hard to fight them in war, these gapers would like to believe. Nevertheless, even in my bad situation I would not want to change places with them. How wretchedly they were dressed! The majority of them wore very old, tattered, cotton clothing. In this moment, as we stood opposite one another, they would like to have believed that what they had been preached was true: they were princes fighting against the German riffraff.

Once again, one of them attempted to throw stones at us, but the guard accompanying us intervened.

So our sick bunch began to move in a column along the road, with four to five walking arm in arm, looking downwards, having difficulty placing one foot in front of the other.

Fortunately, this march only took about fifteen minutes. We were assembled next to an athletics field in an enclosed stockyard. We were subdivided into groups of about thirty persons, who would march into the city.

At first we thought this might be our final destination. However, it turned out to be just a trip to the *bania*.

This *bania* was somewhat better equipped than what we had previously experienced. It even had warm water showers. The undressing and dressing ceremony was the same. Each of us was worried whether we would retrieve all the clothes we removed. The room in which we washed was poorly heated. I looked for a little place by the window that would allow the warm rays of the sun to heat my emaciated body. Some of us had to be carried on stretchers to the washing and the delousing stations. For most of us, there was hardly any life remaining. What was the purpose of doing this to us, I asked?

I learned for the first time the terrible consequences of doing something regardless of circumstances, even if based upon scientific findings and evidence. Although delousing was necessary for hygienic purposes, in this case the only basis for it that existed was that they were ordered to do so. Instead of taking those who were barely living to the closest hospital, where they could be carefully nursed back to health, those too sick to endure were dragged to the *bania*. Given the state of some, it was clear they would not survive; with these barbaric conditions, they would lose too much body heat, and they could not endure all the movement and physical adversity. Yes, the *bania* was also intended to protect against disease. But the absurdity of it all was that in trying to preserve life, they actually had the opposite effect.

Along with two others who went through the disinfection chamber, I stood by the exit door, wondering what would happen next. Then a man came – it was not clear whether he was a civilian or a soldier – who instructed us with *davai* and who gave us a big kick in the rear end to set us in motion. Although the first kick did not quite 'throw' me to the ground, with the next one I fell, and then he did the same to the other two. We apparently did not advance quickly enough for him. He cursed and scolded us and thundered, apparently thinking this would make us move more quickly, and that striking us with his foot would help us progress – to the amusement of passers-by. I did not bother to count how many times these kicks caused me to fall to the ground, but without any exaggeration it must have been a minimum of thirty times before I reached the stockyard.

Exhausted, I leaned against a wall and rested. My mind was completely switched off. Although I was still alive, I felt as though I was somewhere between heaven and earth.

Everyone up! Once again we were divided and driven into abandoned houses. This was followed closely by young soldiers with machine guns, somewhere between fourteen and seventeen years old, who came into our rooms and searched us. These poor fools. Searching us for hidden treasures! Flints, rings, safety pins, pocket knives … Of course they didn't find anything. There were still a few crumbs of dry bread in my haversack. We couldn't get over our amazement when the Russki took the mouldy, shrivelled-up crumb and put it into his mouth. Fine young lads – I suppose. They were the *Komsomoltschiki*, Stalin's young guard. Later, they departed in formation, singing marching songs, à la Hitlerjugend [in the manner of the Hitler Youth]. And such, regretfully, was the destiny of the breadcrumbs I had gathered. Nevertheless, I felt somewhat satisfied that I was able to feed a Soviet who felt he was even hungrier than me.

9

Eating Grass on the Riverbank

Towards evening we were all led back onto the main road, and as they say, after only a kilometre the *Maschinen* started coming, i.e., the vehicles. We were no longer so credulous as to believe they would transport us.

The march through the city was about to turn into a nightmare. It so happened that in this small village there were quite a few injured soldiers, and an increasing number of wounded, some supported by crutches, came towards us. Word must have spread quickly that German prisoners of war were in the area. A savage honour guard accompanied us, raining down punches to the face, kicking us, and striking us with their crutches. Our guards did virtually nothing to protect us. Just the opposite, they laughed and even seemed to enjoy it, that these despised 'Fritzi' who had attacked them were now receiving the payback they deserved. Despite being so weak from the off-loading and the delousing bath, I was awakened from my dazed and confused state. In spite of my festering toes, I remained between the ranks, and by meandering I was able to avoid the beatings.

When I was told *'Hinsetzen'* ['Sit down'], I felt as though I was covered in sweat. We sat on the banks of a large river. In the distance another curious crowd gathered. Now and then, one of the wounded would spit at us and strike at us, nearly hitting us. Then the guard was reinforced, and they ordered the crowd to remain a minimum of 50 metres away. That was, at least, a considerable relief, as a few of us had lost some of their teeth.

After some time had passed, a woman in uniform wearing a white scarf wrapped around her head asked if we were hungry. That was truly an unnecessary question. We nodded silently, but our eyes were blazing. In fact, she brought pieces of bread on a tray and gave us some. I also got my scrap and I reverently took a bite.

A large boat appeared and it came down the river, positioning itself a short distance away. I was lucky, because I was among the first to board. There were places for approximately fifteen men, oars were placed in our hands, and with some effort we had to row across the river. It is easy to imagine the tempo at which we advanced. First one would dip the oar, then the other, but the Russian at the helm drove us on without showing any pity. This had virtually nothing to do with sport; we could barely hold the heavy oars in our hands. I prayed we would get through this. We reached the other bank, and for far and wide there were no houses to be seen. We stopped near a meadow in the vicinity of the river, and we settled down on the damp ground. The guards brought some wood and lit a fire. Of course, that meant we were going to bivouac in the open field. It became dark, and as time passed the remainder of our bunch made it over the river.

Distinguishing between warm and cold is something I had long since forgotten; it made no difference to me whether I sat near or some distance from the fire. The experiences of the last days haunted me: one time it was stones, nothing but stones, the next time beatings from every side. They told us we were going to a hospital, but there was nothing to see here, and it would certainly be several more kilometres away. Did anyone even know whether or not there was a hospital? If so, were they even expecting us? I dared not to think about the future, or whether something better lay ahead.

The night passed, a day went by, once again darkness fell, and then it was light, but without any rations appearing. Our troops were so broken that we could not rebel, even if we were not provided the smallest bite to eat.

At first, I just shook my head as I watched a comrade starting to collect sprouting blades of grass; when he had enough, he began consuming them like an avaricious billy goat. Not much later I saw those next to me begin to do the same. A Hungarian – he was, so far as I could observe, a Magyar Jew – instructed me on the best way to graze. He appeared to be a nice person, and his German was very good.

The sun was warmer than usual the next day. We sat with our field caps between our feet, picking out the various herbs, and telling each other about earlier times. Lojosch, the Hungarian, called to my attention two Romanians who were not far from us, hammering at bones with stones until they were broken down into small pieces. They then placed the crumbled bone meal into their mouths. *Prost, mahlzeit* [Cheers, enjoy your meal]! That was our grazing delicacy. Who knows how long those bones had been lying there.

Two full days we sat there, figuring we would remain there a third night. For a healthy person that is not a particular concern, although perhaps one could develop sniffles or a cold. However, for those who were critically ill, when no one knew about them, or how much longer they might live, to leave them in the open air night after night without any kind of nourishment, that had little to do with the humanity that was so widely discussed.

Another night passed, as well as another day, without anything unusual occurring. They just let us sit there, no one seemed to care about us. The guards, who were supposed to keep watch over us, maintained their distance and they did not seem to exert themselves in their duty. One time they approached us, but that was only to begin a search. They probably only did this to relieve their boredom, or did they really think they would find an *uhra* [watch] or a wedding ring? They quickly abandoned that, as the chance of success was zero. There was nothing more we had, except some ragged clothing or torn *valenki* [felt boots]. I had been able to get those boots after a comrade had died during the train transport, and I carried them on the chance that I could exchange them for something.

Yet another night passed. There were not even 200 of us remaining, lying and waiting on this river, and not far from these survivors were the bodies of those who had died during the previous nights. Once again we reached the low point of morale, where no one spoke, and where there was barely any trace of the will to live.

In the evening – a light rain began – the sound of engines approached. We were lying tightly against one another on the ground in order to keep warm.

Davai! Get up, and line up in fours.

With some difficulty we helped one another to our feet. It was already pitch black, and the light rain trickled on our faces and down the nape of our necks. We could not tell what was in front of us. Then I overheard one of the guards say: bread, butter and cubes of sugar!

I thought I had not heard correctly, it must be a bad joke. But as the line came towards us, a woman actually began to place a large piece of bread with something white on top into our hands. Protectively, I laid my other hand on top, so that nothing was lost. I continued moving forwards for what followed. Lojosch whispered to me, 'You, this is actually butter!'

We found a reasonably flat surface and settled down. Enthusiastically, I smelled the fresh bread and crumbled butter. I placed the two cubes of sugar immediately into my mouth. With my fingers I spread the *mjasslo* [Vologada butter, known for its sweet, nutty flavour] over the entire piece of bread, and I ate this first buttered bread slowly with indescribable contentment. It flowed through me blissfully and freely. There was actually someone here who cared about us, who wasn't simply going to leave this wretched group to die on this river. I laid a hand to serve as a head cushion under my cheek and I fell asleep. The raindrops no longer bothered me.

In the morning we were sorted into those who were still capable of marching, those who were able to move, and those who were not. Vehicles were not available: '*Maschina kaput*' ['The machines are broken'], said the Russians. The repair would take four to five days.

I did not want to wait there so long, so I reported to the middle group. The guard who escorted us was very nice. We stopped every 400 to 500 metres, sitting down to gather our strength. I cursed my *valenki* boots, which were dangling on my back – I could not put them on due to my wounded toes – and I considered them as almost useless ballast. Yet, I certainly did not toss them away.

We came across various smaller and larger collective farms. We did not feel any hostility from the people. They only seemed amazed, and for the first time, I saw women taking hold of their apron strings to wipe tears from their eyes. The impression that we must have made upon these people was that we were to be pitied. They were not without compassion, every now and then tossing us potatoes, sugar beets or chunks of bread. But they were not permitted closer. The guard forbade it. Infection was the reason he gave us. Perhaps he was right, as we were all in some manner infected.

One of us was successful in exchanging a shabby pullover and a pair of boots for three eggs and a large piece of bread, without the guard noticing it. The column was already very spread out.

At the next opportunity I tried trading my *valenkis* for something to eat. I was also successful. I received two eggs, a large onion and some bread. This time, however, the guard noticed. But since the trade had been completed, he let it go.

When we rested the next time, I had a banquet fit for a prince. Hardly had I finished drinking the eggs, when suitors came for the eggshells. No, I would eat them myself, by God, no, give them to me. Whereupon they were consumed in front of the others.

Would anyone believe this? No, never, unless he had experienced it and seen it for himself. Only then can one understand how people suffer when they are starving.

By late afternoon, after we had travelled 7 or 8 kilometres, there was a surprise. An *LKW* came towards us, two nurses stepped out, and they distributed bread and cubes of sugar. Then I began to believe that we were near the hospital. We probably stopped about 4 kilometres short, but that was all the strength we had remaining for the day.

For the life of me, I could not manage to climb the small hill that led to the village lying in front of us. The guard saw me. However, no rough words, no kick in the rear – he pushed me from behind, and so I was able to surmount the last few hundred metres. How disparate is mankind. This was a good man. He appeared extremely civilised.

We settled down in the open. The guard offered us encouragement: 'Tomorrow you will certainly be in the hospital.'

We trusted him, so it didn't matter to us very much that we would spend another night without a roof over our heads.

Naturally, breakfast was not served in this outdoor area, but each of us had a little bread left over. In the early morning we continued down along the road, silently hoping in our hearts that we would find our circumstances had improved. We had not even travelled 1 kilometre, when suddenly I blacked out, falling where I was.

10

Recovering from Dystrophy

A powerful rattle and rocking motion brought me back to consciousness. Adjusting my eyes slightly, I looked around and figured out that I was lying in a small truck with other comrades, driving across bumpy ground. I asked one of them who spoke German what had happened to me. He explained that about an hour earlier a few men from our convoy gathered me up and loaded me into a Russian truck, which just happened to be driving by. I vaguely remembered that it might have been the kind guard who had helped me during a critical moment.

We drove through several small villages, until we stopped in front of a large, stone building. Thereupon, a few men with their heads shaven, dressed in hospital coats and wearing slippers on their feet, helped us to get off. They led us to a large wooden table with benches.

'Well, comrade, where are you from? Where were you taken prisoner?' Personally, I was too tired and exhausted to answer.

Still, I found the strength to ask, 'What is this?'

'A military hospital for prisoners of war,' came the answer. 'It's quite good.'

The assurance that I had been brought to a hospital was all I needed to know.

The convalescents passed out red earthenware to the fifteen of us who sat at the table, and poured steaming soup. The *miski* [a bowl, often of wood] was completely filled. Those who no longer possessed a spoon were generously given a *lozhki* [a wooden spoon]. While we were being served, a woman dressed in all white approached us; she was obviously a doctor. However, she did not speak to us. Rather, she gave a few orders that I assumed concerned us.

Immediately afterwards, we were led up a narrow staircase and into a heated room. We had to strip. Our clothes were bundled up separately, and we were provided labels for our names. Naked, we then entered a room where nurses were expecting us for hospital admission. Oddly enough, there was no sense of shame, although it was peculiar that we had to provide our 'nationality' and answer various questions that really had nothing to do with a medical examination.

We were weighed, and the scale showed I was 45.5 kilograms, woefully little for a man who is 1.79 metres tall. Then came the ablution. It differed in that it was more comfortable than the previous procedures. I went through it without saying anything. Fresh dressings were applied to my toes, and I could hardly believe my eyes when I was provided with a snow-white undershirt and a pair of long briefs.

I was finally free of the original clothes I had been wearing. Although there was no reason for it, I lamented those tattered rags, and there was a strange feeling associated with the new uniforms. The only thing still belonging to you was your skin, everything else was gone. That was somehow depressing. Perhaps it is because as capitalists it is difficult to part with a possession, no matter how small.

Viewed rationally, however, it made sense that the Russians would do this in order to avoid introducing filth or illness into this house.

In order to separate the maladies, we were assigned to various rooms of different sizes. Although this was not a normal hospital, but a temporarily equipped battlefield hospital, it still made a favourable impression on us.

I came to the ground floor, which was full of beds and prisoners. Even so, the nurses made a place for me. The beds were particularly close together, and the patients were lying at right angles to one another. I was placed in with them. The straw-filled mattresses were cosy, covered with linen sheets, as were the pillows. It was just a little cool, since we were given only one blanket that had to be shared between two persons.

The passing of the monotonous and peaceful days cheered us up. At an appointed time each morning the nurses came, took our temperatures and recorded them. Then the medicine was distributed and each man received 200 grams of bread for breakfast. A little later soup was served, which was tasty, but it could have been thicker, as we continued to be terribly hungry. We needed soup in which you could stand a spoon up.

Before lunch, rounds were conducted by a female doctor, three nurses and a prisoner of war who served as interpreter. In the first examination a detailed medical history was taken, beginning with childhood up to the present. Hearts, lungs and kidneys were checked, oedema was noted, a proper diet was ordered; in short, they actually followed hospital procedure. Every third day the bandages were changed.

Since I continued to suffer from dystrophy and my stools were very thin, I was transferred. In the new room even more men were lying side by side, which made it warmer.

At lunchtime we again received another 200 grams of bread and soup, in the afternoon medicine was prescribed and in the evenings it was again bread and soup. Bread three times a day! We had not seen such splendour since our captivity began. For this reason, rumours began to circulate that we would also get sugar and butter, but that was not the case yet.

Two days later we received a midday snack of baked fried eggs, a large mouthful in size, which only served to tease our stomachs. But the Russians claimed that one should not overfeed someone with dystrophy, and for this reason we were only served small bites several times a day. Perhaps they were right, if only we would all recover.

Rounds were repeated every two to three days, and I must say, always with the same attention to detail. Yet, I could not help but have the impression that a lot was being written down that had nothing to do with prescribing what we needed most: an ample diet. There were several among us who held the absurd notion, which cost some their lives, that by pouring another cup of warm water into their soup it somehow increased what they needed. For a little while they naturally had the feeling that their stomach was full. But not long thereafter it began to growl, and it had the harmful effect of over-taxing the heart and kidneys because they were unable to process the water, and this only made the oedema worse.

                                    Stalingrad Survivor

The Russians could never understand why we did not wait to pick up the bread until we received the soup. An explanation was pointless. When someone is hungry, this is not easily managed, even if it is only holding back for a short period of time. I only tried to do this once, and it seemed to me an eternity. It is also not advisable to leave the bread on your plate or to set it aside to make room for the soup. Either way, you risked it being stolen. Hunger makes a thief of any man, and among us there were many. A few times some of them were caught, and they were harshly chastened with clubs. But I did not think that even this summary judgement was sufficient to deter someone from doing the same thing if given the opportunity to do so.

In the meantime, the meals were enriched with the well-known *kasha*. It was either sorghum, barley, grits, potatoes or cabbage in the form of a slurry. Sometimes there was roasted miniature fish, and as a snack, sour milk; but as before, always in tiny portions. One time I was able to get a little more, and soon thereafter I experienced the following: a never-ending diarrhoea accompanied by cramps.

After four weeks I picked myself up and I attempted an excursion to the floor above us. There were supposed to be quite a few Austrians there. What encouraged me even more was that there was supposed to be a mirror hanging about halfway. It was certainly not because I was conceited, but after such a long time, and particularly because of my condition, I was very interested in my outward appearance.

So I began to climb up the stairs, using the banisters as a support. Indeed, a large mirror was located there, in which I could view my entire body. How I looked! I saw in the reflection a thin, gaunt face, head completely shaven, and with ears protruding that somehow no longer belonged … You look splendid, older; not even an old fogey made such a miserable impression or had such unsteady legs as you. Shaking my head, I continued on my way to the upper floor.

In the corridor a radio was blasting. Aha, once again 'for everyone, direct from Moscow'.

The rooms were enormous and full of patients, but they were lying on bunk beds instead of regular beds. There was even a dining hall.

I took a brief look inside and spotted three giant pictures: Stalin, Molotov [Minister of Foreign Affairs] and the third was likely Voroshilov [one of the original five marshals, the highest rank in the Soviet military, and one of only two who survived Stalin's purges]. Next to them was a large bandage dressing room and a sign which I believe read, 'operating room'.

The nurses were rushing around busily. They weren't wearing actual nurses' uniforms, but a white coat with a kind of small cap made out of cotton. The infirm were being carried in and out of the bandage room. This hustle and bustle gave me a certain sense of security and peace of mind.

This first excursion had so exhausted me that I could not continue further to find my fellow compatriots, so I began to return. It was then that I saw for the first time the aborted foetuses. They were extremely mangled and unsanitary, lying in a heap near the single hole located in the corner of the room. The people who left the foetuses in these heaps must have been from homes where they were too lazy to trouble themselves with cleanliness.

The next day was the big *ramasuri* [Romanian for a medley of things]: bed linen changes, *bania*, mattresses stuffed with straw. Clean-shaven, haircut. Lathered up as normal, and this time without being tortured. Part of the straw mattress was removed in the yard and refilled with fresh straw. That was a good idea, one slept much better. Clean bedsheets were handed out, the pillows received new covers, and the blankets were beaten to remove the dust. The linens were counted by the room elder and handed over, and in exchange he received the same number of fresh sheets in return. This careful checking had its reasons: nurses or prisoners readily set aside a piece of linen; in one case to take home, in the other to exchange for a small sack of sugar or something like that. A few even traded them for a small sack of bread or *machorka*.

None of this took place at the tempo the Russians desired, because we were still very weak for this work. It took the entire day.

My Hungarian friend, Lojosch, was already stronger, and he worked his way into becoming a soup provider. So when there was soup remaining, he was given an extra serving. The senior in the room also enjoyed this privilege. Envy was naturally great among the rest of us. But it is always that way: a director, a superior, usually has it better, even in communist Russia. Those who work should also eat. I have no problem with that. But what of those who are unable to work, but would gladly do so if they could?

But in this place it would be better not to be too eager to work. One day approximately a hundred men who were 'strong enough' were selected – I was not even close – old uniforms and wooden shoes were provided, and they were sent off. In the evenings they would return, after having loaded heavy, wet wood.

Actually, this is just the way it was; once someone was nursed back to health they were employed as part of a workforce. Their reward was more to eat – but at our expense, because the *kasha* would then be thinned for the rest of us.

The daily rations were precisely prescribed, they had to be complied with, and they could not be exceeded. Therefore, if one was to receive additional rations, it could only be accomplished through trickery. Each time the work details were sent out was a day that resulted in watered-down portions for the remainder. Many of those who went out ended up bedridden later or their illness returned, coming down with colds or even pneumonia.

It seemed to me that although the doctors were against this, there was a higher authority who had ordered it. After all, it was war, and men were in short supply in the villages, so prisoners of war were used even though they were not fit.

In the meantime, summer had arrived here in the north. During the day we were led into a large garden. My first sunbathing did not go well for me, I became extremely ill and I ended up crawling on all fours into the shade. My skin appeared hideous, sagging and flaking off, a consequence of avitaminosis. Almost all of us suffered from this.

The sight of the private, walking barefoot in his shirt and underpants, is something we became accustomed to. Nevertheless, I was pleased to receive a hospital coat from a nurse. It was a little more comfortable to wear. And I protected this coat like a holy relic, as I noticed a couple of 'friends' were looking at it.

Sunshine and fresh air are a wonderful medicine for both body and spirit. My interest in different things increased. I also had a desire to learn to speak Russian, even though it was very difficult. I traded a piece of bread in exchange for a pencil stub. I obtained some paper from the female doctor, and so we began, Lojosch and me, to learn the Cyrillic alphabet.

It went very slowly, because we had hardly any suitable resource. We received a copy of *Izvestia* [the Soviet newspaper] from the *politruk*, who was added to supervise us. It served as our text. We timidly made our first attempt at reading. With some persistence and making it a priority, we got past the first step. We did not give up, and when we sat outside in the fresh air we quizzed one another. The importance of learning this language lies in the fact that even a limited knowledge brought significant benefits.

The Russian believes that most, if not everyone, must learn to understand their language. When that was not the case, one was met with contempt and disdain. After a few weeks of avid learning we sensed we had met with some success. We grew in favour with the domestic staff, and we were no longer seen as the usual fascist swine.

The relationship between the doctors, nurses and prisoners was very distant, and sometimes hostile. But some demonstrated compassion and were extremely civil; I might almost say a few even mothered us, and those were female Jewish doctors. The nurses also varied considerably. There were those who would prefer to spit in our glasses as they were distributing the medicine, others would look away, some displayed a contemptuous smile, and there were those who stood above the rest. They were the real Samaritans, providing kind words to console those who were dying, and alleviating their suffering with painkillers.

The hospital staff consisted to a large extent of those who had been evacuated from the European portion of Russian. It is therefore understandable that so many displayed hostility towards the 'Fritzi' who had driven them out of their homeland and dwellings; they had lost possessions, and their family had been scattered to the winds. As the German withdrawal progressed, they had no way of knowing what they might find when they returned.

The latest addition was to distribute chess sets to the rooms. So I finally began to learn this stimulating game, which I always had an inclination to do, but I had never had the opportunity to practise it at home. Here, there was enough time available, and I was far from being eligible for work. In our room were two excellent Hungarian chess players.

Even the commandant of the hospital heard about them. One day he unexpectedly entered, he watched the two play, and then he challenged the winner to a match. They played over four hours nonstop. The Hungarian won more games than the commandant. This repeated itself from time to time, even in the evenings.

11

First Encounter with the NKVD

One time, however, the door opened and a young officer appeared, looking at us. The commander, who was a lot older, stood up, a little embarrassed. They exchanged a few words and both left the room. The commander never returned to play chess. Who was this young officer with the well-tailored shirt, the blue peaked cap and the red stripe? The interpreter claimed he was with the NKVD. I already knew this four-letter acronym from the time our troops were advancing. NKVD troops were opposite us in the trenches, and they were people who very rarely surrendered; they fought to the end. We compared them with the SS [the Schutzstaffel – the paramilitary wing of the Nazi Party]. But could there really be something like this in Russia, which always described itself as democratic?

That we would come across such people in a hospital was not surprising. First, they were looking to avert any subversion within their own ranks, which could easily arise if one were to believe our narratives. Second, it was possible to get all kinds of useful information out of prisoners. Now and then a few of us were questioned extensively in an informal conversation.

In addition, the guards who were posted in the four towers around the building were wearing the blue caps of the NKVD. We were well guarded, because these towers were connected via telephone. It was unclear to us why these guards sounded the whistle at regular intervals during the night. Were they used to keep each other awake? They stood watch for four hours.

One time something rather comical took place. A few of us noticed the guard was sleeping during broad daylight. Mischievous as we were, we opened the window that was next to the guard, one of us opened the door, and then slammed it forcefully shut. The poor man fell in horror, and because he was still confused from sleeping, he almost fell out of the guardhouse. There was resounding laughter from our side. He immediately recognised the prank, scolding and threatening us. Then we closed the window.

NKVD guards also accompanied the work details. They were responsible for a specific amount of work. When things progressed too slowly, they helped things along with the butts of their rifles.

Once, two privates attempted to escape, in spite of the obvious futility. What was the result? After being chased by dogs for three days they surrendered. One lay dead from being shot during the escape, the other was disfigured and bruised after being beaten; and with a shot that had grazed his upper arm, he was led back into the hospital. This event led to stricter regulations; the guards were very harsh towards us because they had failed to notice the escape and they had to search day and night for the refugees.

This matter had another consequence: A work detail of roughly ten ill prisoners were given hoes and shovels, and they had to dig a 4- to 5-metre strip from the fence in such a way as to remove all grass and to till the soil until it was all level. This area was identified as a restricted zone, and marked with small sticks. The purpose was clear: the footprints of anyone trying to cross it would be noticed immediately.

Following this, those carrying soup were also prohibited from leaving the area, and the kitchen was outside the area. That slowed down the distribution of meals considerably. But this led to another change, because the Russians themselves were then given the arduous task of lugging the stockpots. Hence, after a few days this restriction was removed and we returned to the old way of doing things.

The survivor of the two who had tried to escape was placed in a detention cell, and having atoned, was sent back to his hospital bed because a high fever had set in. The doctors attempted to rehabilitate him, but to their consternation they had just discovered that he had sustained a broken lower jaw from the beating. A prisoner who was a dentist attempted to fix it with primitive instruments. He again tried to mend it, and though it was a little crooked, it held.

A change was made. We ate in the dining hall instead of the rooms. For the time being they stopped serving us soup for breakfast, and instead we received four or five 'boiled jacket potatoes'. In addition, there was dried fish. Naturally, we ate them with their skins. It was also tasty, but as before it was not enough. In the morning, we received 30 grams of butter. Inscribed on the peculiar packets was 'Mayer & Co., Chicago'. We received 40 grams of sugar daily. Printed on the packets of sugar was 'Sugar from California'.

We were not angry about this. If the Americans had not shipped it, we would have received even less to eat. We realised, mind you, that the Russians also received this *Ami-butter* [American butter]. If you asked them how it tasted, then the answer they gave was, 'Our butter is much better'. Perhaps they were right about this, but we had still not received any Russian butter that would enable us to judge.

The verdict of the Russians was the same in each and every circumstance: ours is always better. How well they had been taught. They only acknowledged their own; it was quite impossible for anything bourgeois to be good. When it was discussed, we often tried to persuade them that the conditions in Central Europe were actually better than here. Any such attempt was pointless. When they could not think of anything to say, they would reply, 'In Moscow we have at least everything you have.' From then on we remained silent, and let them believe what they wanted.

When a person sees this behaviour, it only confirms how effective propaganda is at producing the desired outcome; it shapes people and becomes normal. In our land we also had experience in this regard. The difference between east and west lay mainly in the fact that in Central Europe the indoctrination took longer and it had to be more intense before the idea took effect and a person was willing to sacrifice himself for the cause. In comparison, he was more critical. People in the east, however, were far more naive towards propaganda. The masses believe what they are told, especially when it is skilfully done. It did not take an artist to pretend to make promises to the Russian people. The living standard was so poor that even the smallest benefit, whether it was vodka, foodstuffs or clothing, triggered an enthusiastic defence of their system. They had convinced themselves that they were a great and powerful people. That this was a great war to defend the Fatherland had been drilled into their heads. We also had to acknowledge the responsibility: that we had brought this war into their lands as far as the gates of Moscow, to the banks of the Volga, and as far as the Caucasus mountains, such that they regarded this as a heroic war, especially after the initial crushing defeat.

Although homesickness weighed heavily on me and I longed for the day I could return from Russia, I still wanted to learn more about this land, its people, and most of all, its system. In this regard, I had seen and experienced little. Until now I had only been fighting for what was left of my weak life. In all probability, like the others in this hospital before me, my health would only be partway restored, and I would be sent to some other location. It could be that I would learn nothing of Russian enterprises. The region in which we found ourselves did not appear to be our final destination. We were in a notably wooded area somewhere in the Asian section of the Urals.

This information came from a reliable source. I personally heard it from a Russian cleaning lady, who grumbled about the '*same husche oblast mira*' – 'the worst oblast in the world' [an oblast is an administrative territorial region or province within Russia and the former Soviet Union]. I imagined that sending us to the Crimea to recuperate was not something the Russians would choose – and to the best of my knowledge it was still occupied by the enemy.

The climate here was very harsh and inhospitable. It took a long time for spring to arrive. It only lasted a very short time, like all transitions between winter and summer.

The summer was very hot, during the day heavy thunderstorms descended upon us, and the nights were warm. It never got really dark. Even at midnight, one could almost read a newspaper outdoors.

The view from my window did not offer much. I could only see a few fields where potatoes and beets had been planted. We also received our first vitamin supplements, and cabbage with onions and carrots were distributed. The young onions were a very special treat. Along with a piece of bread and salt, they were a delicacy. At home, such morsels would have surely stuck in my throat.

A particular problem in this hospital, probably everywhere, was the short supply of paper of any kind. Paper was an extremely scarce commodity. Given the vast supply of wood, this was hard to believe. But as long as the trees were standing, there was no paper. Therefore, it was a problem either of production or of distribution. One thing was certain: the doctors did not have any paper with which to write out their orders or the medical histories. But the Russians knew how to work around this. They would take paper that had already been used and write diagonally across it. Or they would take any newspaper they could find and write on that. Toilet paper was something they knew nothing about.

The following was also amusing: the nurses had the task of attaching additional sheets of the paper to the previous medical histories. At a minimum, they used a needle and thread – staples and a stapler were unknown here … 'We have these in Moscow,' I thought to myself. They went to the prisoners to borrow needles. But there was no thread or twine, so they helped themselves to the gauze bandages and they removed the threads.

Neither was there ink. So they went to the prisoners, from whom they sometimes found a pencil stub with an indelible tip. They would then place the felt-tip in the water until it was completely dissolved.

There is always something that can be learned, when one improvises.

12

A Stalingraders' Reunion

It was a sunny morning. We were not allowed to stay in the garden. It did not take long before we knew why. Silhouettes began to appear through the large gate. From a distance we could already tell they were people like ourselves. Emaciated and feeble, they entered in columns of four. There were over a hundred, each seeking a place in the shade among the few trees.

'Where have you come from?' we shouted through the window. 'Stalingrad,' was their answer. We didn't ask anything further, because we knew these survivors had endured a difficult journey.

They were fed, stripped of their clothes, washed and distributed among the rooms. They had much to tell us. They had also been in transit camps, the worst of which was supposed to be the Frolov Death Colony. The pitiful remnant of the army had witnessed terrible things. They had also lost their colonel and cannoneer in less than humane conditions. Only a very select few were sent to special camps near Moscow, such as Paulus [Field Marshal Friedrich Paulus, Sixth Army], Seidlitz [General Walther von Seydlitz-Kurzbach, LI Army Corps], Korfes [Major General Otto Korfes, Divisional Commander, 295th Infantry Division] and various other divisional commanders. One of the soldiers told me about the formation of the Nationalkomitees Freies Deutschland [National Committee for a Free Germany] and the Bund Deutscher Offiziere [BDO] in der Sowjetunion [the League of German Officers in the Soviet Union – shortly after being formed, the BDO was combined with Free Germany – operating out of the Soviet Union. The purpose of both was to deliver anti-Nazi propaganda aimed at the German armed forces].

'Have you still not received any of their newspapers?' I had no idea that such a thing existed, but it was possible that we were simply too far from the Moscow headquarters, and that this news and their newspapers would reach us later. I further heard that these few emaciated men had just come from a military hospital in Saratov [a port on the Volga River about 390 kilometres from Stalingrad]. Their treatment by the Russians had been good; only the Romanians, who held positions in the hospital and camp, shamelessly deprived the German-speaking prisoners of their provisions. It seemed to be the same everywhere. Hitler's Balkan allies did not behave themselves well. One had the impression that these people, in particular, had a lot to learn. Several persons confirmed that in Camp Frolov there were over 5,000 men, of whom no more than 400 remained by the time they arrived via military rail transport at the hospital. Perhaps the numbers were somewhat exaggerated. But when I consider my own transit camp experience, in comparison those casualty figures were in roughly the same proportions.

Here in this hospital the Russians aimed to help us using all means at their disposal. However, what we had been through had afflicted many of us so severely that even well-intentioned drips of glucose and emergency injections could no longer help [hypoglycaemia can be caused by long-term starvation].

Not long after, a TB [Tuberculosis] isolation ward was prepared in the event of an active case of TB. An X-ray room was also made available. Most of the TB cases were Italian. For them the climate was understandably the most disagreeable. Nevertheless, they were the first who found themselves singing. They sang in order to cheer each other up and to entertain one another. We enjoyed their melodious folksongs.

The Germans did not sing. The lyrics of their marching songs were for the most part forbidden, and other songs did not come to mind; the root cause was their mental state.

The *politruk*, a small, inconspicuous man, called me over one day and said that in the autumn a celebration would be held in the dining hall to honour the October Revolution. He thought it would be good for the Austrians to also put their best foot forward. Song lyrics would need to be translated and approved. I promised we would do something. But it was a mystery to me who would translate

'Das Fiakerlied' ['The Coachman's Song', a song composed by Gustav Pick in 1885] or 'Mei Muatterl war a Weanarin' ['My Mother was Viennese', a song composed in 1908 by Ludwig Gruber] into Russian.

In September the *politruk* called us into the dining room. It was not a demand. The commissar, I believe with the rank of major, told us of the Russian advance on all fronts. We believed him, and no one bothered to deny it. Thereupon, he spoke of the Soviet–English–American friendship. We also believed this, but we were not fully convinced. One person from our circle asked the unassuming question as to whether he could imagine two totally different world views in the Soviet Union, once the war had been brought to a triumphant conclusion. To our amazement the commissar gave '*Moschna* – it is possible' as an answer. We seriously doubted, however, the possible coexistence, because when two world powers with so divergent world views occupied the heartland of Europe, it would naturally result in a thousand economic and military difficulties.

With the word *moschna* came a certain renunciation of the ideals of the worldwide proletariat revolution. We also noticed the Internationale [the anthem of the Socialist International Movement, adopted at the Second International in Paris in 1889] no longer rang out each morning, but was replaced by a characteristic Russian hymn. Rumours even began to circulate that the commissar would soon be abolished and that the NKVD would be transformed. Nevertheless, we regarded these measures as a disguise to placate the Allies. I did not think the Russians would deviate from their interpretation of the ideas of Engels, Marx and Lenin.

When a commissar spoke or discussed a matter, one felt immediately that his thoughts were built upon a certain view. He was educated, but partisan; he was intelligent, but indoctrinated. He gave passionate speeches, but always with a certain leaning. But above all, the speeches featured an absolutely uncompromising bent towards political or similarly related matters, or those that directly concerned their land.

One day we received directly from the commissar a few copies of various editions of the newspaper *Freies Deutschland*. The front page described an assault, and each hoped to read something from home or the front, or simply something we could read in the German language. The most important thing, however, was that the newspaper was a valuable bargaining chip that could be exchanged, as it could be used as cigarette rolling paper.

Famous names had authored the articles: in part, well-known emigrants, but mostly former German commanding officers. Reading these articles, one was, at first, speechless. How is it that these gentlemen changed their beliefs so suddenly? Did they write to extract personal benefits, to alleviate their situation? Anything was possible. One cannot see into the soul of a person, not even a general. We understood that in the mind of some Stalingraders, a world had come crashing down. But how does one morally justify preaching one thing one day, and the opposite the next?

We primitive-thinking soldiers in Russian captivity didn't believe such a rapid change in opinion. It was our view that it would have been better for these gentlemen to remain silent. In our eyes, they were nothing more than willing pawns of Russian propaganda. There is little honour in being a turncoat when the cause is already lost, simply to receive better treatment than the others. Another, even more offensive case was if a wartime German father figure swapped and gave speeches full of praise for Russia – simply to gorge himself and fill his potbelly, and to receive an invitation for a trip down the Volga River.

We all had to play-act here to a certain degree. We had to guard ourselves against speaking anything negative, and to agree here and there if we wanted to have peace. But we did not have to sell ourselves out.

Nevertheless, the newspaper was suitable as cigarette paper. We hoped we would receive these consignments on a regular basis.

13

Reflection on the Russian Mentality

The celebration of the October Revolution would also come and go. The lyrics were approved, performed and listened to in silence. Any type of outbreak of emotion was out of the question, because a few days before there had been a huge crackdown to prevent any disturbance. Anything that even resembled a 'weapon' – handmade and sharpened knives – were once again forfeited.

The celebration also had amusing parts. The emcee made jokes and tried hard to entertain us. He succeeded and we laughed our heads off. The Russians appeared angry, because they could not understand us, and they believed the jokes were about them. The commissar suddenly jumped to his feet and furiously yelled, '*Schto on goverit*? – What did he say?'

The interpreter, a Banater Jew [the Banat was a region of the former Hungarian and Romanian kingdom along the Danube River], was incapable of translating the *Bobby-Witzel* ['Bobby Jokes' were a chain of jokes about a fictional, out-of-touch Viennese aristocrat named Count Bobby, who had little money, and who continued to think of himself in terms of the Habsburg Imperial Court]. We smirked – the celebration was abruptly ended.

That's how it was when the Russian didn't understand something. He always felt as if it affected him. It never crossed our mind to ridicule him in public. But they didn't trust us. How in the world could someone be so suspicious? The only thing that could explain this was an inferiority complex.

The autumn was short, and the transition between seasons passed quickly. The snow came overnight. The sight of this frightened me a little, because with it would come the cold, and it would become even more bitter here in the north.

Every other day the sled team went out into the woods to cut metre-long logs and bring them back for heating and the kitchen. According to the comrades, this work was not that difficult; just the opposite, it was a stroll that would strengthen and refresh those involved. We only asked ourselves why the Russians had not already made provisions during the summer. They were always doing just enough to get by; in the figurative sense, they were just living from hand to mouth.

It was now December 1943.

There was a big push for those who had recovered to leave the hospital. They received a clean bill of health. Where were they going? No one gave us any information, although nurses accompanied the transport. They remained silent. In truth, those of us who were left behind didn't really want to know. We would find out soon enough.

I also slowly started to become a human being again. When I looked at my body, I saw quite clearly that it was beginning to once again take shape, the skin became smoother and healthier. Muscles, mind you, were slow in developing, and what there were of them remained flabby.

I owed much of this to my female doctor. She took good care of me. I was even promoted to dishwasher. I only did this type of work every once in a while, because cleaning ladies were there to do this. However, they preferred this type of work only because it would enable them to take a little *kasha* or soup from us.

One had to wonder why these women always tried to steal some of our rations. They did not feel ashamed when they did it. When we also had peas and cows' eyes, even the female doctors did this. It even happened that buckets of mush were taken. Since they hid the food under their skirts to get past the guards, it was probably because the children of our caregivers were going hungry.

To everyone's delight, we once again received roasted fish and mashed potatoes. Suddenly, they said the fish was all gone. A murmuring began that slowly grew into a tumult. The nurses attempted to calm things down, but it was in vain. The noise became ever louder. The chief physician was also standing in the room. 'What is wrong?' he thundered. Everyone began to speak at once. The interpreter did not want to admit what was being said. To be sure, he tried to hide himself along with the nurses. Fortunately, some of the comrades spoke Russian and they shed light on the situation. A tray then appeared with fried fish hidden under a cloth. The chief physician was furious and he left the room. There was no doubt the sermon would be delivered during the next *sobranje* [gathering]. After that, the senior female physician accompanied us during every serving, and instead of a nurse, a prisoner distributed the meal.

We soon learned that the menu was being altered. Instead of millet we would be served peas. However, since these contained more calories, we would receive smaller portions. Apart from the soup, the meal contained twenty-five to thirty peas, but instead of being green they were a tawny colour and full of wormholes. In addition, we sometimes received offal: for example, cooked testicles or cows' eyes. Sometimes I would dream about the peas, but it was just an illusion. One time I wanted to eat through an entire mountain of peas.

There was also *mustard-senf* [*senf* is a common form of mustard in Germany and Austria, and can be either spicy or sweet]. We enjoyed it in moderation, but the Romanians greedily stuck the entire lump in their mouth. The effect this extremely sharp condiment had was enormous. Bright tears streamed down their lobster-red cheeks, they began to sweat, and they acted like they were going to burst. Naturally, their weak bodies did not tolerate the sharp mustard. But it served them right, the greedy devils.

Christmas was just around the corner. We pleaded with the commissar to allow us to get some Christmas trees. He said yes. The next forest duty returned with a few trees. In every room we enthusiastically put up Christmas decorations. One would not have believed it was possible to create beautiful decorations from wood, cotton wool and paper. We obtained the dyestuff from different medications. Yellow and green from malaria tablets, red from streptomycin and purple from manganese came from dissolving them in water. Charcoal was used for labelling. From paraffin wax, which was supposed to be used for packaging, we made candles. Finally, the time came. We decorated the tree.

Suddenly, we received bad news: we were allowed neither lights nor to sing songs; a command from on high.

At first, we were very depressed. We lay down. Sometime around ten in the evening – everything was dark and peaceful – I stood up and looked through the keyhole to see if there was any light. The coast was clear. We quickly lit the lights, and very softly we hummed 'Silent Night, Holy Night'. That made us happy. We thought about home and fell asleep with that in mind.

The next day the commissar, the *politruk*, the chief physician and a few NKVD officers came with their children. They went from room to room, looking at the Christmas trees that the *njemzi* [elsewhere spelled *nemtsy*, this literally means 'mutes'; it was a nickname given to Germans and other foreigners who did not speak Russian] had put up. The children were obviously delighted. The dignitaries said nothing, but they satisfied their curiosity.

The new Russia knew nothing of the European way of Christmas. They only celebrated the *Novigod* – the New Year. They also put up a tree for *Silvester*, but it did not have the same meaning. The older ones looked forward to this because they received vodka, regardless of service or achievement, rank or age. On New Year's Day there was scarcely a Russian to be seen, and those who remained wore their caps low on the nape of their neck. It was also *brasnik* – a holiday. And holidays meant vodka.

From time to time, one felt sorry for these people and their poverty; they had not seen anything else, and they were content with whatever was set before them and had been offered. What would it be like if they had seen Germany?

With all their traditions surrounding the celebration, they felt themselves superior. Setting up a manger or displaying angels seemed absurd to them, and in relation to this they held themselves to be far more advanced than the other nations.

I learned about the Russian concept of 'progress' more clearly on the occasion of Women's Day, which took place each year in March. On this day, on which no one worked, the commissar lectured us with a verbose commentary that nowhere in the world does a woman enjoy equality of rights in comparison with Russia. Here, a woman could study to become a doctor, engineer, in short, every profession was open to her. She could vote, everything which our countries did not have, he said. There was no reply. In my observations, the effect of this practice meant more than that: not only were women allowed to do the same work as men, they were given the most difficult manual labour and used as a workhorse until they were worked to death.

The '*komi*', the nickname we gave the commissar, was in charge of our spiritual and political care. That is to say, purely the party line; he entertained ideological questions no more than once a month, and attendance at lectures and the discussions was voluntary. At our request, he obtained instruments for us, a guitar and a violin. Unfortunately, this became a bone of contention between the individual rooms. In the end, the violin was awarded to a Romanian Gypsy, who played quite well, with the understanding that he would also entertain us.

The Gypsy naturally played in his own way; one time he would fiddle a superb variation in oriental style, and then he would play a sensuous melody, singing in the Puszta tradition [the Puszta is a grassland extending from Hungary to the Burgenland in Austria]. His appearance was cheerful. His shirt hung out over his pants in the Romanian custom, with a rope tied around it; he used all sorts of facial expressions. Each time he stopped he received abundant applause, and then he would play anew.

Another musical talent was also here, a Westphalian. But he refused to play because he was too weak to hold the violin and guide the bow. With considerable persuasion we were able to get him to do it.

Mozart's *Eine kleine Nachtmusik* echoed. With it, I buried my head in the pillow; I was gripped by homesickness.

The Westphalian was first chair violinist with a German orchestra, and truly a first-class artist. What he was able to get out of the shabby instrument – the bow had only a little hair, there was no rosin available – was wonderful. He played with his eyes closed, and one felt as though he were not even with us. Without respite, he alternated from lively to soft music. We were all grateful to him, and we begged him to come to our room. Soon, the doctors and the nurses heard of his art, so he played in the dining room in the evening for everyone who was in the hospital. The enthusiasm was unanimous. Doing this he created friends, and the nurses secretly slipped him some extra food.

One evening – we were once again sitting around together and our Westphalian friend was entertaining us – the door opened, and two sisters entered. There was nothing exceptional in that. Then one said in a rather imperative tone: 'Heinz, play something from *Carmen!*'

She was the sister we did not like very much; she let her hatred be felt with every opportunity. We had always ignored her behaviour, and we simply nicknamed her 'Shotgun Woman'.

Heinz fulfilled her wish, and fiddled powerfully 'Auf in den Kampf, Torero' ['March of the Toreadors', from Carmen Suite No. 2, by Georges Bizet] ... Then he suddenly switched to the children's song, 'Ein Männlein Steht im Walde' ['A Little Man Stands in the Forest', a song based on the German nursery rhyme by August Heinrich Hoffmann von Fallersleben, 1843], adapting the melody to his own imagination, only to return to the 'March of the Toreadors'. He played this original composition for a while, and it was authentic Bizet. The nurses looked on with respect, and appeared solemn and appreciative. We turned away, and a few of us even ran to the door because they could not hide their laughter. Heinz, however, without batting an eye, laid his instrument aside and bowed elegantly. The sisters thanked him with '*Otschin karascho*' ['Fabulous, well done!'] and disappeared. That's how it is when men who behave as though they are educated, as they were, begin to mock another.

Among the sick prisoners was a dentist. The Russians asked him whether he was willing to work in his profession, probably because they did not have anyone with that 'specialty' in the vicinity. The dentist – who the Russians began to address as doctor – requested tools like a drill and probe, as well as the bare essential medications. In a corner of the first-aid station he set up something like a modest surgery station. He stood there in long, white pants, wearing slippers, a white lab coat and a white cap – like a chef. Officers, soldiers and even civilians, those with special permission, came to him to be treated. I had the great honour of operating a foot-powered drive whenever the drill was needed. Otto was always urging me to tread more quickly, because he could not both drill and power the machine at the same time. However, I could not always accommodate his wishes because the tempo was more than I could handle. Incidentally, I also assisted him in arranging the instruments, stirring the dental cement, etc.

Initially, the extractions were without any anaesthetics. Novocain did not come until later. Even then, the Novocain was apparently not very effective because our patients had pain from the injection. Occasionally, the procedure was drastic. It often had to be done with leverage, and without the proper instruments.

One day the Russians asked the dentist if he could make 'new teeth', in other words, whether he had the technical ability to attempt this. He said yes, and he listed which materials were essential. They provided a vulcaniser from ages ago, rubber and other material were brought from a hospital in the vicinity of Bolniza [Bolnisi is a city in the Republic of Georgia that was originally settled by Germans]. The work could have been started, except we lacked gypsum. They offered plaster of Paris, but that didn't work. Finally, he received at least some white gypsum that was suitable. Then it didn't take long before the first dental prosthesis was removed from the improvised vulcaniser. It actually held.

As the Russians observed that things were going well, he had to accept appointments from nearly half the hospital staff. The work was paid in kind: onions, dried fish, *machorka*, pickled cucumbers, tomatoes, eggs, two to three pieces for each denture, or one piece of white bread.

But the Russians were more vain than we thought; after a while they wanted gold teeth. That, however, was outside the range of possibilities for Otto. He had neither gold nor the appropriate facilities to deal with this. But the Russians didn't back down easily. At a minimum they wanted a metal cap, the shiny kind they frequently saw among the Romanians. That, however, was not easy to do.

One day a young, pretty, dark Georgian came bashfully to the *subnoi vratsch* [tooth doctor]. 'What do you want?' asked Otto, not understanding when he looked in her mouth and saw a set of white, healthy teeth. She responded rather brusquely that he should remove a healthy incisor and replace it with a metal cap. In vain he tried to convince her that such a beautiful tooth should not be removed. She continued to insist, but to no avail. But Otto remained firm, adding that technically he was not in a position to comply with her wish. Outraged, she left and then after a while she returned with the senior female physician. After much back and forth, she finally gave up the struggle when the doctor sided with Otto's point of view.

Kommissia budjet – an investigative commission was coming! Rumours spread that high-ranking officers from Moscow would visit the hospital. Some even spoke of an international commission. Early on, a *bania* was arranged, everything was scrubbed, washed, dusted, beaten and cleaned. The entire staff was in a state of flux. The shine was restored to everything. For us, such a commission was not so disagreeable, as we expected something decent to eat and, above all, larger portions.

The time came. At the crack of dawn the senior officers arrived, unfortunately no foreigners were among them, and they inspected the building from top to bottom. On that day the food was good and portions were somewhat larger.

In our room they asked whether we were satisfied with the treatment, whether we thought that Germans treated the Russian prisoners of war as well, that the war for Germany was finally lost, or if we would ever again raise arms against Russia, and some other things.

We answered the questions as best we could. Whether they were actually satisfied with them, I don't know. Unfortunately, the question concerning whether we would once again fight against Russia was directed at me. I asked the officer, how was it that he could ask such a question since we had been prisoners such a long time, and that we would not be able to hold a weapon until after the war was over. He added that he was referring to once I was released back into my homeland. To that I said: never again, why would I!

'Fascist,' he snarled at me. 'You lie, you would fight against us again if you had the opportunity.'

I was silent, because I saw he was angry. How else was I supposed to answer him? One way or the other, however one answered him, it would not be right. If someone was silent, then they assumed we believed ourselves to belong to a 'higher race', and that we would not lower ourselves to speak to them. If one were to answer with how he really felt, he ran the risk of getting punched in the face. In saying something positive, one was then called a fascist and a liar.

The best tactic was to try and not be noticed, and never to ask a question. I was happy when these gentlemen once again left our room.

I was approaching ten months in the hospital, and I was beginning to feel like a little Hercules. My arms, my legs, my entire body began to fill out and take shape. I found myself needing to go outside, to get out of this building, into the fresh air. So I volunteered to join the wood transport team into the forest.

The guard accompanying us was well known from the hospital. He was a dear, chubby uncle, who always wore his *furaschka* [military cap] tilted on his head, and not without good reason. One could not help wondering how he always managed to have vodka when there was such a shortage of alcohol. Was he among those who knew the secret of distilling alcohol? He called everyone Sascha [a diminutive of Aleksándr], and we said the same to him. The ten of us received only old, but clean, pants, felt boots and a coat.

Sascha trotted along next to us, whistling something. I was

breathing the cold air with deep gasps. In the meantime, I considered the condition of my body from head to foot, fully dressed and physically stronger, and I was overcome with a strange feeling that I had rediscovered my existence. I felt human once again, and I was exhilarated as I happily strode along.

We pulled our little sled behind us along the country road that was relatively busy with cars and sled traffic. One sled stopped, and the occupant, a bearded Russian, spoke a few words into Sascha's ear that I was not able to make out. Sascha nodded sympathetically and we continued further. About 2 kilometres later we saw something dark lying on the road, which had just forked towards the left into the woods. Sascha took me and another along, and he told the others to wait.

We moved quickly towards the dark spot. Someone was lying in the snow – a woman. Sascha bent down, stood up again, and with resignation said: '*Skora kaputt* – she's going to die soon.'

I kneeled down and felt for a pulse. In fact, I felt a very faint and irregular beat.

'Let's go,' said Sascha. In disbelief I stared and I asked him if we could simply leave this woman to her fate and let her die. '*Nitschevo* – it doesn't matter,' Sascha said and just shook his head.

We returned to our group, veered off into the woods, loaded heavily snow-covered metre-long logs onto the sled, and returned to the main road about an hour and a half later. Instinctively, we directed our eyes towards the place where we had found the woman, assuming someone had either helped her or taken her away. Should one be amazed or think it was possible? The woman was lying in the same spot, despite the ongoing traffic and all sorts of carts. Apparently, it did not occur to anyone to take the dying woman into the next village. She was probably already dead. Sascha didn't consider that either, but instead he stuck a *papirossi* into his mouth and asked us to pull the sled towards home.

How much was a life worth here?

The 'outing' refreshed me, and every once in a while I went to the woods. This type of work was not too taxing, and it strengthened the body. The muscles were again reforming, although they remained soft. Every time I returned I was very tired, but gradually I noticed I was becoming stronger.

In the meantime, I switched quarters. I was moved from the room for the seriously ill to where one would convalesce. Instead of being placed in beds, we had wooden bunks with straw-filled mattresses, pillows and covers. It was also quiet here, about twenty lying in a row. Just one thing became increasingly bothersome. When we turned off the light, the bedbugs became very noticeable. The nurses, and even more so the doctors, cursed when they saw bloodstains on the wall, stemming from our squishing them. It is not very attractive to have whitewashed walls splattered with the pests. However, there was no other way to cope with them. During the day they would hide in the cracks and in the nights they would become active.

As the nuisance became unbearable we suggested to the commander that we be allowed to take apart the planks and plane them smooth, because the nests were mostly in the cracks. Then we would pour boiling water on them. The stench from this procedure was overwhelming. It seemed to work for a short time, but we could not get all of them. The Russians knew well that unless treated with sulphur they would return, but that was nowhere to be found. It was our opinion, of course, that the bunks should be gathered and collectively burned.

There were also spot checks for lice, and despite the emphasis on cleanliness they continued to be found. They were introduced along with the new arrivals.

One day a sizeable number of serious cases arrived, completely emaciated, filthy and tattered – always the same picture. This time I was among those who helped bring them in, dress them and carry them to their rooms. A few with high temperatures were admitted to the TB ward.

Suddenly, shocking news spread through the hospital: the high temperatures were not caused by a lung disorder, but from typhus fever.

The Russians, who themselves were deathly afraid of the fever, quickly took precautions. All those running a fever were taken to separate rooms and isolated, and only those medics who had previously been infected with typhus were allowed to tend to the sick. I also helped out for a short period of time.

For the first time I realised what I must have experienced a year earlier when I came down with the disease. These poor men, many of whom had already lost consciousness, moaned and hallucinated day and night. The Russians did everything possible to help. The worst cases were given injections with 90 per cent alcohol. In this way, the patient became completely intoxicated. However, that was a therapy only used when it was a matter of life and death. It had some success, because only two succumbed to the fever while all the others survived.

At this time I also experienced my first dissection. We carried those who had died from the fever to a shed in the yard. A Romanian *feldsher* [doctor's assistant] did the preparations. He cleaned the body and he cut open the chest of the deceased with a sharp pair of scissors, and then the senior physician performed the dissection, using the opportunity to provide visual instruction to the young female doctors.

In the course of this I learned that each time a patient died in the hospital, an autopsy was performed to determine the cause of death. The examination was recorded and the conclusions were written down in the medical history.

While I stood there and watched this scientific enterprise, I said a quick prayer to Heaven that I would not one day be the one they spoke of as they dismembered my body.

The burial that followed was more than sobering, I might almost say gruesome. A half-starved *panje* horse along with a wagon was brought through the gate, giving one the impression it was always about to lose a wheel. In the wagon was a 2-metre-long wooden box, 1 metre high and 1 metre wide, along with a lid. Once the body was released for burial, the *feldsher* would then take the organs from the dissection and stuff them in the rib cage, and then he would sew it shut. Then the corpse, just as it was, naked and stiff, was loaded in the box. It was customary to wait until more bodies were collected, and then the draughthorse, driven by a Russian civilian, would depart along the bumpy road away from the hospital. Sometimes it even happened that limbs would be sticking out of the box to the point that the lid would not close. Somewhere out there in the countryside they would find their final resting place. Only after a while did the hospital administrators allow us to make a simple wooden cross, branded with the name and birthdate of the deceased. Although we were never allowed to go to the grave site, we learned later that the crosses were actually placed there.

14

Ready for the Labour Camp

It became obvious that the doctors and nurses had finally accepted us. In addition, several new American medications began to arrive. Vitamin tablets of all sorts were administered. A nurse revealed to me that the commissar had made it quite clear in a meeting that the mortality rate had to be reduced considerably. The directive had come from high up, she said.

That was totally new. Until then, one had the feeling that the staff were not especially concerned when a 'Fritz' closed his eyes for the last time. Even more surprising to us was that a surgeon was assigned and that he would be conducting operations. I personally had the opportunity to help with appendectomies and haemorrhoidectomies. The impression I had as a layman was that they took the work seriously and they were conscientious.

The prisoners recognised the situation immediately and lined up by the dozen to have their appendices removed in order to postpone their transfer to the labour camp.

There was quite a commotion when an Italian developed a high temperature after an operation, indicating the existence of an infection. The attending physician and nurses worked around the clock to watch over him. Despite doing everything in their power to help him, he died. The doctor appeared to take it personally, as if it was due to a medical error, but it is unlikely he was at fault.

All of these things led us to believe that a lot had changed since we arrived at the hospital. Even more striking was the relationship between the prisoners and the nurses. From week to week things became noticeably better, even downright friendly. It got to the point that the Russians even sent patrols at night to see if perhaps the nurses might be 'entertaining' the prisoners.

These nurses, who had already been with us an entire year, found that we were not so wicked, violent and cruel as we were made out to be; that not every one of us would shoot someone in the back of the head, or pluck out the eyes of small children. The longer we remained here, the less they saw us as soldiers and the more we were seen as human beings. The one-sided picture painted of *Nemez* [Germans] that they had from newspapers, radio and political instruction slowly began to fade. In addition, they could never understand that the Austrian mindset was distinct, not necessarily better, but definitely different to the German. It always resulted in an incredulous shrugging of the shoulders and the response: 'But it is the same tongue.'

As I said, much had changed. I, myself, came to have a good understanding of Russian, and every now and then I would serve as a translator, often having splendid conversations with the Russians. They also became more open. Even the big, tall NKVD officer came once in a while to chat. He promised to bring us a soccer ball, which he did, even playing with us! One time, however, he was pulled away by the officer on duty, because he, being a little tipsy, was taking the conversation too far.

Those who had convalesced, and for what it was worth, those who were even partway recovered, joined in kicking the ball. Even the guards in their huts amused themselves, laying their rifle to the side and watching the action. In truth, it must have been a priceless sight, seeing this barefoot soccer team in their long briefs.

We were made up of a veritable collection of nations. First up was Italy versus Austria. It was an exciting contest, causing some light banter between the spectators and the players. The space was small and the surface somewhat hard. The constant striking was very painful on our feet. Although we were clearly the better team, the Russians favoured the Italians. Of course, they had to do that, because Italy had surrendered and they had become allies.

We played the Romanians as much as we could, as well as a Hungarian team. The Germans, who at the time remained in the hospital, still did not have the strength to play. As soon as they recovered, they were sent immediately to the labour camp. I wondered myself, after such a long period of starvation and bodily deprivation, how I could muster enough strength to run, take a header and shoot.

Subconsciously, I began to fear that the day I would be taken to the labour camp was not very far away. I was now strong enough to go.

Once again, we were visited by a commission for physical examinations. Just the thought of it awoke uncomfortable feelings. We had absolutely no idea where it would be or what it would be like. We simply learned from the nurses that it was better here. When they said this, we knew it must be true.

For the first time I stepped before a foreign doctor. After a thorough examination they wrote that I was fit for work. I happily looked forward to the end of the war. Until then, I just had to endure it.

Much to my surprise, the next day my name was not on the list to move out. That meant I was able to remain. At first I couldn't believe it, thinking it was an oversight. But the chief physician assured me that I was staying, and that in the future I would assume responsibility for supervising the seriously ill. My job was to keep things clean and orderly, and ensure that the sick would be properly fed. They had to receive their soup in bed and they required considerable care. The Russians wanted the prisoners to be able to increasingly look after ourselves.

This task was not always easy to do. From experience, the fellow prisoners saw such a *starschina* as using his position mostly as a way to increase his own portion at the expense of the others. They were right to do so, because that is what normally occurred. Such duty was often given to a very dubious character.

In this regard, I attempted as much as possible to be objective and to present all requests, complaints and matters of concern to the Russians, and in most cases I was successful in addressing the situation. The leftovers that remained after the portions were served were divided according to a precise process, and second helpings were distributed evenly to each of the sick.

It was not to be forgotten that in every room five to six nationalities were represented, and doing right by each of them required real artistry. As a German-speaker I was particularly seen as an

Ausländer [foreigner], and I was subject to strong criticism. The common language in this small Babel was principally Russian. This 'Russian' could only be understood by the prisoners themselves, because it sounded almost like Esperanto [a language constructed in the 1870s by Polish ophthalmologist L.L. Zamenhof, which some Central European nations taught in their schools in the 1920s and 1930s]. I often had a good laugh when petty squabbles broke out among the different nations. They made themselves understood in broken Russian, but they cursed and swore in their own language. It was good that they did so. That way, the epithets were not understood, so the insults did not hurt.

The number of TB cases in my section increased. They could no longer be housed in one place; instead, they required several rooms. The worst dysentery cases were placed separately, and these were further divided into those suffering oedema. The sight of these disfigured bodies and faces was always heartbreaking. There was nothing that could be done to help them. Even inserting catheters didn't help. They only lived as long as their heart held out. It was dreadful with these patients; they could see their impending death. They screamed. They didn't want to die. They only wanted to go home. One began to sing and to laugh – he apparently lost his mind. Half an hour later he was dead.

Even though no German soldiers remained on Russian soil, the war went on. Hitler and his generals refused to give up the fight. Then one day the news came of the beginning of the Second Front. Americans, British and Canadian troops landed in Normandy.

The Russians in the hospital were beside themselves. The war would end soon, we thought to ourselves. 'We will soon be in Berlin,' they said. We believed that was possible, but the matter that concerned us was whether somebody, if not Adolf, would prevent the Russians from invading Central Europe and establishing themselves with a massive presence. Perhaps Hitler would even make a separate peace with the Americans. Such was the daily gossip that proceeded from this news.

But does the little man ever know what the powerful man has in store for him? Were the leaders in the homeland aware of this? The most fantastic rumours began to circulate about a failed assassination attempt on Hitler's life, a conspiracy involving mass arrests of high-ranking officers in the Wehrmacht. *Freies Deutschland* confirmed the details in its next edition.

This brought to mind a part of one of the Führer's speeches, which gave me a sense of angst now that I understood the meaning. 'If I should someday be forced to exit this world theatre, I will slam the door so hard that half the world will be smashed to pieces,' or something like that, so I read. Now it seemed to be so. It appeared to me that Hitler was really going to bring this about, destroying everything around him.

I continued to make progress on once again 'becoming a man'. The *Parikmacher* [the German term for a Russian barber – literally, a wigmaker] granted my request to not take as much off the top, so that after three months my hair was long enough to comb. As the situation of others improved, they were also allowed certain privileges. However, these pleasures did not last very long. The commissar discovered that the nurses, and even some female doctors, had become attracted to the prisoners. Was the hair directly to blame? Regardless, once again Samson had his hair shorn.

This simple-mindedness seemed rather amusing to us. Nevertheless, there were nurses who were devoted to us, even without our headdress; some would come and stay with us surreptitiously. It was unusual.

In the next *sobranje* I heard they quarrelled badly. Even the senior female physician was given a tongue-lashing. The relationship with the prisoners had to become distant once again. We were and we remained the enemy. At least, that was how we were viewed.

The effect this would have on me was clear. No female doctor was going to be able to save me from the next commission. I prepared myself mentally and physically to go to the labour camp. No matter how indispensable I made myself here, it wouldn't matter. When one fell out of favour here in Russia, one fell a very long way.

One day the time came. I once again put on my old clothes, the ones I had handed in when I entered the hospital a year before, as well as a nice pair of *valenki* boots and two pairs of Wehrmacht socks. At the height of summer, it was rather grotesque.

About sixty men stood ready to march outside the hospital. For marching rations we received bread and fish. As we moved away, the ladies waved, having carefully tended to us for a year. It was strange for me. After the first kilometre I felt eager for the new situation.

I saw the road where I had once collapsed and been removed as a half-skeletonised body. This day, I stepped firmly forwards, healthy and with an erect posture. It's not that I was truly happy; I was rightly concerned about the future. This uncertain, indefinite situation continually gnawed at me and made me feel uneasy. One dared not think about home, or what might happen to us once we got to where we were going.

We passed by peaceful, serene villages, both small and large, and then we were soon marching in the woods and past vast fields. For the most part the land was relatively flat, but sometimes it was also a little hilly. The locals barely even noticed us. Apparently, they had become accustomed to such movements.

It was actually the first time that I was able to appreciate the landscape up close. Before that, I had been too absorbed with myself. The region did not look that different to what I had seen during the previous march. Endless forests alternating with partially cultivated farmland and open fields.

In silence, I compared this with my homeland. No, this was no place for an Austrian. Even if parts of this land had some natural beauty, I took no pleasure in this countryside.

How one sees a land also depends upon the people in it. Even flat land can be charming, when lined with beautiful villages, hamlets and lovely towns which speak to the people who make the best out of it. But everything here was gloomy and bleak, it all appeared so pitiful, so primitive, so neglected, like nothing I had ever experienced.

How undemanding these people must have been. I felt that someone living in our country who chose to live on an abandoned farm had higher expectations than the people here. Stalin could have offered me the wealthiest collective farm, and my answer would always have been no. The only thing I wanted was to go home, even if it meant I was the poorest devil there.

But look, I had to stay here, I said to myself. The war would soon be over, but now I had to go there, to work for two years, thereby atoning for having taken part in this war; then, they would, I hoped, send me home. The commissar had assured us of this often, that they were not interested in keeping us. As soon as the war was over they would send us home. I hoped he was right.

These thoughts occupied my mind throughout the entire day of marching. We spent the night in an abandoned house. For the first time in quite a while I lay on the floor. But it didn't bother me any more. I slept well.

We spent the next day there, because other groups were joining us and this was where we were gathered together. The next morning a considerable number, somewhere around 300 men, left where we had been staying for the nearest train station and further transport. Before leaving, we were given bread and fish.

Where we were going was anyone's guess. The hospital guards continued to accompany us. I assumed that meant it couldn't be much further. We travelled through the night and throughout the next day.

We stopped at a large city. We asked for water because we were totally parched. This was understandable, because salted fish causes tremendous thirst. The guards procured an empty barrel close by, and they had some of us take it to a *kipitok*, a reservoir that contained potable water, to get some.

Lojosch, who was released along with me from the hospital, brought to my attention a buffet at the railway station. They were selling hot, brownish water as *tschei* [chai]. I knew about this drink. One could hardly call it tea. I wondered why someone would pay rubles for it. Naturally, one had to remember a war was going on, and that no one was paid anything in money, just like in Germany.

'Where are the sausage buns, sandwiches, or frankfurters?' I mockingly asked Lojosch.

He tapped my forehead and said, 'You must be daft …'

We drank like fish. The hot water that our comrades brought us tasted superb. The food was easier to digest now that we had enough to drink.

We spent another night on the bunks in the train. They were very hard because we didn't have any straw.

The next morning we were totally surprised when we looked through the sliding door. Woods, nothing but woods, but instead of a green forest all the trees were completely dead, burned down, barren and lifeless. One of us said there must have been a huge fire. I answered no, because the landscape appeared too desolate to me. Nothing but arid wood, singed and charred. The barren stumps appeared like windswept ghosts in the gloomy morning sky. There were no green spots, no undergrowth; instead, the grass was yellow and withered.

Our train drove on and on. It hardly ever came to a stop. Every now and then we would encounter oncoming trains loaded with timber. Throughout the entire day all the woods we passed looked like that. Then, finally, we saw a light coming towards us. *Oy vey* – guard towers – a camp. As we passed, we didn't see any prisoners, only the red pennant with the hammer and sickle blowing in the wind. Once again, we were enveloped by the woods.

We saw camps similar to this nearly every 8 to 12 kilometres, some near and some further away from the tracks. At times, we would see people standing before the barracks, but we could not make out whether they were prisoners or some other people.

Towards evening the train came to a stop along an open section of track. The guards distributed fish and bread. Our meals were not very balanced. Not that we complained: we were happy just to get something to eat. Then the train continued into this desolate, primeval forest. Were we already at the taiga [a northern forest characterised by conifers]? We could only guess, because no one knew where we were. Without a doubt, it was either in the north or in the east. 'How much longer?' we asked the guard.

'*Skora* – soon,' was all he replied.

Another night passed, then the train came to a stop. Were we at the end of our trip? At dawn, we saw that the locomotive was gone. Not far away was a sentry box, a little further distant a few barracks, and behind them the camp with the watchtowers looming.

In the background was nothing but woods. Surrounding the camp were large open spaces littered with tree stumps. It was picturesque. I imagined how I would be as a lumberjack. I thought I would probably make a complete fool of myself. But when it came to getting a daily supply of bread, I would learn how to do that. I was no specialist, so there was nothing left for me to do but set about making myself useful. Then again, why was I worrying about this? I had no idea what kind of work I would be assigned.

'Everybody off, fall in in columns of four!' We moved at a quick, steady pace towards the barracks. We stopped before the gate! It took a while for someone to enter a *zona* ['zone' or camp – the Russian word for a Siberian prison camp], but even longer before one would be able to leave.

15

In the Taiga

A few Russkis with caps low upon their forehead appeared, lists in their hands. Names were called out. Those whose names were read off stepped through the gate into the camp. Strangely, my name was not one of them. Approximately forty men, I among them, remained. That meant 'Take a seat and wait.' An hour later two soldiers came, a machine gun across their backs, and with '*davai*', things proceeded. So I thought this camp might not have been for us; perhaps it was already full.

We began to move along a small path away from the rail line. Some distance from us, we saw chimneys protruding. Our course, however, did not head in that direction. We passed a huge timber yard. It might have been a paper mill.

The path suddenly came to an end, and we continued along an even narrower logging trail, and because the ground in the taiga is so soft, wet and impenetrable, the logging trail was the only way through it. On this path was a narrow-gauge set of wooden tracks for a handcar, which was a suitable method to transport long, bundled logs through this area.

Following the example of both our guards we tried to balance along these wooden tracks, because it was easier than the uneven, irregular beaten path that served as the entrance way. We followed in pairs of two, progressing side by side, our shoulders touching.

These tracks led us deep into the taiga, and several junctions headed off in various directions. The further we penetrated, the more sense this method made. This was because beneath the moist, mossy surface was often a pond. One time we came to a glade, created by the clearing of trees. The ground was a little drier here. For a long way it was nothing but tree stumps and the roots of trees which had been uprooted by a storm. On the left-hand side stood these desolate, dead woods, untouched by the axe, dull and grey. Only the ground had vegetation, some green undergrowth, pasture, and young birch trees. There were no flowers, no birds, no living things; here, the silence of the grave prevailed.

After another hour, we were led through the forest on both sides of this strange path. The trees were quite thick, extending along the logging road. Above us was a somewhat overcast sky and before us was a long stretch that we had to pass through.

Then we came to another clearing. Through it ran a makeshift rail line that was placed perpendicular to the path. The broad-gauged tracks were not embedded on a road, but simply next to each other facing outwards. We took a short break here. The surroundings made a lasting impression on my mind. Could it be that people worked and lived here their entire life? In that moment, this was incomprehensible to me.

We continued on this wooden section of track. After a large bend it became lighter on both sides. As far as the eye could see there was nothing but tree stumps. The sun was already beginning to set. Then it occurred to me that something stood out about this landscape. Now we saw it quite clearly: it was a gate. A watchtower in the middle of these moors? As we came closer we noticed that it was unoccupied and it was very run-down. Whatever could it have been used for?

The landscape alternated between standing and fallen timber. Then we saw roofs and towers; right in the middle of this godforsaken area a camp appeared. The tree stumps had been uprooted and a few hectares of the land cleared, principally for growing potatoes and beets.

The logging road led right up to the prohibited area of the camp, opposite which stood some wooden houses. In front of them, to my amazement, children were playing. What were children doing in this land of exiles?

The Russians had truly chosen a good place for our continued captivity. No one would run away from here, unless he was completely insane. One could not deviate from the path, and the forest offered nothing but charred tree bark. We were all very despondent.

We were already expected at the gate, the names were read off, and we entered immediately. It was called *proverka-platz* ['verification place' – i.e., roll call or parade ground], and we fell in and waited.

So this was the work camp, of which we had only heard rumours while in the hospital. The prison camp commandant, a Romanian Jew, informed us how the barracks were organised. Nine large barracks of approximately the same size housed the prisoners and were divided by nationality. There were Italians, Romanians, Hungarians, Germans, Austrians and a small barracks for Jews. For the time being, Germans and Austrians were not separated, because there were still not enough Austrians. One barrack served as the *ambulanzia*, which meant an infirmary in Wehrmacht German. One barrack was dedicated to serving as a 'club'. The explanation for this was anyone's guess. A small cabin was clearly for the Russian camp commander. Next to the parade grounds one would find the kitchen, the *bania*, and the supply depot. Near the command post and administration buildings stood a little fire department house. Next to this was a tall fire observation tower. Primitive latrines were located on the edges of the prohibited area. The rectangular perimeter fence surrounding the camp – an ordinary fence – was equipped with the all-too-familiar watchtowers. The *karzer* [detention cell], the air-raid shelter, in which punishment was served, was outside the camp. Perhaps this was so the rest of us could not document what happened to the 'criminal'. The bakery and the equipment storehouse were located in the already mentioned housing units across from the camp entrance.

Finally, the commandant pointed to a large, elongated blockhouse at the back of the camp, where the collective farm was located. It was already twilight, but the warehouse team was still at work.

'They have very long work hours,' I commented to my neighbour.

'Don't complain, we are in workers' paradise, there is no need to worry. Everything is well organised,' he responded sarcastically.

One could only hope, I thought, saying nothing.

From there we were taken to the clinic. In the vestibule of the barracks, we undressed. We were going to be 'commissioned'. What was that supposed to mean? The camp commandant explained briefly: 'There are four categories of men here: 100 per cent, 75 per cent, 50 per cent and 25 per cent.'

'When is someone 100 per cent and when is someone 50 per cent?' one of us asked.

'You will all see what this means later.'

We stood there naked and were called in one at a time. In the examination room sat a Russian doctor, the Russian commandant and the Romanian storehouse manager, who served as translator, and a scribe.

The doctor examined me, pulled the front and back of my skin and said: 'One hundred per cent,' and then I could go. So it was with most of us. We assumed this meant we were responsible for reaching 100 per cent of the quota expected from the work, or who the devil knew what?

As it became dark, the work detail entered from the woods. I was aghast at the mere sight of them. Oh, Lord, how these men looked. Emaciated, starved, filthy, tattered clothing, sleepy eyes and injured feet. Many of them could move with only the greatest difficulty. However, we did not have much time to inquire, because our working group was being assembled for the next day.

The group leader assigned to us was an East Prussian. He seemed to be a good man.

'What is there to eat, what does our work consist of?' were our first questions.

He assured us we would not be used to cut down trees, but instead we would construct a new camp. At any rate, that was supposed to be better. We would be given soup three times a day, and whoever fulfilled their quota would receive 800 grams of bread in the morning 200 grams of *kasha* in the evening.

I wondered what my work would look like as a carpenter?

Finally, we were brought to our dwellings. It was as dark and gloomy as a cellar. And the space? On the bunks, which were constructed one on top of the other, men were already lying side by side. The senior man said to me that at this time there were no empty places remaining. It would be like this for a few days. So we lay ourselves on the ground for the time being.

Late at night we newcomers were led to the kitchen and served a little soup.

The first night there lasted an eternity for me. For the life of me, I was unable to get any sleep. It was hot, the air was bad, and it was overflowing with people. The majority of them had to go out and relieve themselves a number of times, even though they were dead tired from the difficult work. One would stumble over another, and the next would kick someone else with their foot. And so it continued.

As ordered, I arose early in the morning, patting the dust off my clothes. Washing appeared to be a luxury here.

Some soup was made for us. It issued from three counters. With 600 grams of bread for the entire day, we headed to work. Our team leader assured us that we would certainly achieve our quota, so that we could expect to receive a full set of rations the following day.

The soup tasted like …? It was difficult determine. It was like warm water with a little salt and green root vegetable leaves.

On the parade ground the nationalities were formed into groups. The Russian commandant had two Russkis determine the count. The numbering never agreed the first time. During this *proverka* no one within the area was allowed to move. One soldier went from barrack to barrack to count those remaining behind, and those who had office duty. At least twenty minutes passed before everything was checked and the numbers agreed. On the left wing stood the infirm. This was checked against the work list to see if the doctor had really authorised sick call. Then the Russian officer gave the signal to move off.

It was about seven o'clock. As ordered, we began to sing as we marched. Marching songs jumbled together as they resounded from every language. The Italians sang 'Avanti Populo', the Germans 'Die blauen Dragoner', the Austrians 'Das Südtiroler Lied', the Hungarians 'Ledöle, Ledöle', and so on. As we passed the gate, the number of people in each brigade were counted once again. Outside the camp we were given saws and axes. An Italian, a Russian and our group took off in a different direction from the rest. It was approximately 6 kilometres to our workplace. [The lumberjack brigade reportedly had even further to go.] No thanks, one was already tired before he even began to work.

The building site represented nothing other than a clearing, which meant it was located wherever they pleased. The tree trunks were still there. In the middle of this clearing was a piece of land which had been cleared. But the contours of this expected camp were not yet recognisable.

The convoy brought us to a spot where the foundation for a new log cabin could be seen, and we were handed over to a Russian civilian. The team leader said to us that we had to learn to get along well with him. He was the supervisor, himself an exile, just like almost all the Russians who were sent here to do forced labour. *Saklutschoni* was the name they gave to these banished exiles.

He looked at us calmly and asked if any of us were 'specialists'. Only a few of us understood anything about this craft. I already had some concerns about achieving my quota, unless I could find a type of work that relied more on hard work than it did technical expertise.

Our team leader understood my concerns and assured me, along with another, that we would gather fallen timber from the woods. The logs could be no smaller than 15 centimetres in diameter, and no larger than 25 centimetres in diameter. The two of us carried timbers 4 metres long in pairs, those that were lighter we carried individually. Moving along this uneven and impassable terrain was exceedingly difficult, and not infrequently, we ended up falling on our knees.

So we hauled these logs the entire morning, like the coolies [a derogatory term for unskilled labourers, especially from Asia]. At noon we had a short break. We received soup. Supported by a massive root, a giant iron pot stood over the embers of a recently extinguished fire. Each one of us received 600 grams of hot *kapusta* soup [a Polish dish of sauerkraut or cabbage, usually containing bacon, mushrooms and onions]. It was only cabbage and water.

When we returned to work, I asked the team leader how many of this type of log we needed to haul here in order to fulfil our quota. He couldn't tell us exactly. The amount of wood and the thickness of the logs had to be calculated according to tables. So it had to be somewhere between fifty and seventy-five logs, he said. That meant a lot more, since we had only moved about thirty logs thus far, and that was without any breaks. With these kinds of rations, in three weeks I would be lucky to be able to carry five more pieces. After that, I no longer carried any wood at shoulder height.

About 4.30, a siren sounded from afar. Our *desjatnik*, the foreman, gave us the signal to stop working. Then he and the brigade leader looked over what was accomplished together. First, he measured how many logs had been moved to the construction site. Then he measured the length of the logs, and how many had been cut into squares. Then he measured how many we had stacked. He didn't count two of them because they were rotten. I did not know I was supposed to take that into account.

'Did I meet the quota?' I asked anxiously.

'That cannot be known for sure; it depends upon the mood of the Ukrainian.'

On the way home our leader revealed that the *saklutschoni* were also hungry themselves, meaning that if we gave our supervisor some of our rations, he was more inclined to calculate the quota in our favour, even if we sometimes did not completely fulfil it.

We immediately comprehended the necessity of paying homage with a token of our good will. From then on, one of us donated his portion of bread to the Ukrainian each day. Nevertheless, sometimes he wrote that we did not meet our quota, because we did not give him enough – which we did not have to give – or he wanted to extort more from us. Many only met 75 per cent or even less of the quota, so they stopped receiving *kasha* and their bread ration was greatly reduced. Here it was revealed how finely and precisely everything in Russia was thought out, calculated and organised.

According to the wishes of the Russians, our work output should have been increased further, an impossibility given our rations. Even when the quality of our bread, which was as wet as a sponge, was improved. Just the opposite: the output could not be maintained, but instead fell from one week to the next as our bodies became weaker and our physical stamina diminished.

The hauling of these tree trunks was hard work. After transporting

4-metre-long logs all the way by ourselves, we were reinforced with other prisoners, but then we had to haul 6- to 8-metre-long logs. These were lying at a considerable distance from the work site. The load was distributed unevenly during transport on an individual, mainly due to the uneven ground. Sometimes we thought the wood would crush one of us to death.

One other time I was assigned to tree-felling. But this skill was something I could not master. The foreman complained about me. What was I supposed to do? The next day I received 200 grams less bread.

The barracks on which our brigade was working slowly began to take shape. The barracks the rest of the teams were working on also began to rise. Our construction was supposed to be a 'garrison', a house for the guards.

'For whom is the entire camp being built?' we once asked.

A shrugging of the shoulders. 'For people such as me', the *saklutschoni* said, 'or for prisoners of war. No one knows for sure.'

Every now and then an engineer would appear with his assistant. He was a large, powerful Russian, and from what one could see, he gave a good impression. He was no slave-driver. We often saw him sitting on a tree stump gazing off into the woods. He was also a *saklutschoni*, one of the exiles.

Everything was so unclear to me, I could not see exactly what was happening here. Who were these people? For what reason were they sent here? How long did they have to remain here?

16

Hard Labour

Some distance from the camp was a wide, cut path with a narrow-gauge railway that was supposed to be used to transport the wood. One afternoon I was randomly assigned to the person in charge of gathering a few boards for the flooring.

Then I noticed that there were Russians under heavy guard working on this railway. They begged for bread and German cookware, and offered *machorka* in exchange. I witnessed such an exchange take place between a Russian and a German prisoner of war. In the haste of the exchange, however, the Russian ran away without handing over the bag of *machorka*. The cheated prisoner complained loudly, and the remaining prisoners added their voices to the fuss. The guard observed this, running after the thief and screamed: '*Stoj, stoj!*' ['Halt, halt!'] The exile, probably out of fear of a hail of bullets, stood still. The cookware was wrested from him, and he received a few kicks as punishment.

In fact, I found myself in a sort of penal colony, for serious cases indeed, primarily political prisoners, but also some criminal ones. My knowledge of Russian, which was improving from day to day, would certainly provide me with more information.

Our brigade was split up. The supervisor measured the site for additional barracks. At specific intervals he marked the spots where we were to dig holes. With spades and pickaxes we went to work. The holes were to be 1 metre in diameter and 1.4 metres deep. Tree trunks of 40–50 centimetres in diameter and 2 metres long were to be cut, set in place, and then the hole filled in.

The tempo required to meet the quota was made much more difficult by the partially bluish clay soil. The quota for two men consisted of cutting down three trees, digging out a hole in the ground, putting the cut logs into the hole, filling it up, and then respectively, stomping on the dirt to pack it down. If the quota was met, we received 800 grams of bread, soup, and as usual, *kasha*.

Of course, work done in such haste could only be described as clumsy. And where possible, there was cheating. The most important result of the day's work consisted of hearing in the evening, '*Norma jest*' ['The daily quota was met']. Quite frequently, when the supervisor didn't notice, we dug the hole a little less deep and cut the logs a little shorter. Using this trickery made it easier for us to make our quota.

At the time, all men were used to drive the piles into the ground because frost was imminent, and then the ground would be as hard as rock. With the primitive tools we would no longer be able to work on the frozen ground.

Once again I was sent to the rail line, where I was supposed to be able to find a heavy-gauge steel wire. We found it, all right, but instead of being coiled up, it consisted of a tangled mess that we had to remove from the undergrowth. Only with considerable effort were we able to bring this material to the work site. The garrison barracks, which was already 2 metres high, needed scaffolding. We lacked the proper nails that would have been useful in building the framework. 'Oh, of course,' said the supervisor, 'you have a wire.'

Out of this we were supposed to be able to cut off 10–15-centimetre nails. How? An axe was used, cutting upwards into the wire that was clamped onto a stake, and with another pickaxe we would beat on it until it broke off. We also had a quota for this: 700 pieces per day. Naturally, these nails had neither tips nor heads, but in the softwood they were fairly easy to knock in.

We did not have boards for the scaffolding, so we placed large round branches next to one another. It was not easy to maintain our balance, clinging like monkeys to keep from falling. It was ironic to be thinking about safety devices that we would naturally have had at home.

Although I was never really a 'specialist', I always found enough work for me to earn my daily allotment of bread. A new duty awaited me: gathering moss. Armed with a spade and a Russian tarpaulin, I went into the forest and looked for moss. Digging it into large blocks,

I placed them together onto the tarp, and then I dragged the load to the work site. Would you believe it? There was a chart displaying a quota for this type of work. It amounted to a cubic metre per day. The work was not too strenuous, but one had to keep at it the entire day in order to manage it.

The moss served as an insulation layer between the beams. That's why the bedbugs felt so at home, they had their own reserve to support them.

Another time we had to dig a ditch for the construction of a latrine, 8 metres long and 2 metres wide. Here we were not able to make our quota. Some of the comrades didn't want to; their strength had diminished too far, so they chose to make do with 600 grams [as opposed to 800 grams of bread and 200 grams of *kasha* porridge]. That day we also took clay bricks with us back home, because a comrade with an amputated foot wanted to bake the clay into bowls. He was a skilled potter, and in exchange for some of our rations, he gladly gave us one.

The outline of one of the barracks in the new camp was now discernible. The site supervisor tried to increase the tempo, and in exchange for more work, he offered *machorka*, as well as the possibility of a small piece of cooked lung or some other similar innards that otherwise might be thrown away.

We would gladly have done more work for something more to eat, but the watery soup we were given did not contribute to our strength. I realised that my own strength had begun to wane. It became most noticeable at the end of the day as we were marching home. Specifically, we always came to a small hill that each day became more difficult to cross.

In addition, the accommodation had taken a toll on us. It was impossible for anyone to rest; instead of lying on a bunk, we found ourselves on the floor. The consolation that we had fewer bugs wasn't worth much; instead, we had rats with their long tails scurrying across our faces.

After a few days there was finally more space, and we were given bunks to sleep on.

It grew increasingly cold, and days became shorter. It must

have been sometime in October. After we set the pediment for the garrison barracks, it took many unsuccessful attempts before we were able to finish the roof truss. I went with the 'specialists' and worked along as a carpenter. The most difficult part was to bring the long girder onto the roof. One time the entire scaffolding, which was so primitively nailed together, collapsed, and along with the beam we came plunging down. But we were lucky, receiving nothing more than a few scrapes. For the time being, the loft consisted of loosely stacked round logs. It was like walking a virtual tight rope.

During the entire construction I saw no other tools than axes, saws, drills and, for the laying of beams, a jack. There were no pliers, no hammers, no crowbars – nothing else. Everyone could learn to be a carpenter!

Then we moved to the interior. The weaker pilings were reduced to a pulp and they served as support for the floor. Strictly adhering to the quota, two men had to cut forty logs and two men had to place twenty of them in a day. The supervisor no longer trusted us completely, and he checked the depth of the holes and the length of the pilings. Then the floor would be laid and next it was the panelling for the walls. A grid made out of wooden slats was attached to the wall, and then loam was applied over everything.

In the meantime, there were the '50-percenters' – that is, the brigade of people who only achieved half their quota – who worked to erect the fence for the zone. The gate with the small guardhouses outside had already been completed.

We were supposed to lay the floor. A smile came to me as I realised neither I nor the others knew anything about laying a floor: two bakers, a musician, a postal worker and a precision mechanic.

A stack of beams was brought to us. The supervisor drew out a long plank and showed us how to plane it. We actually received a plane, across the middle of which ran a strip of wood. In a straddled position, my comrade and I sat across from each other, and between the two of us it was comical as we planed back and forth. What we planed did not look pretty. But it didn't matter to us because we were sweating profusely.

Suddenly a man stood next to us. Even though he wore Russian clothes, he gave us the immediate impression that he was no Russian. He laughed and he spoke very good German to us. We put the plane aside in order to talk with him a little. He first looked around a few times, as if he felt he was being watched. Then he said we should continue planing, and that he preferred to sit with us.

His pronunciation betrayed a Swabian accent. I asked about his origins. He was a German from the Caucasus; his parents were Swabian. He, personally, had never seen Germany, but he spoke enthusiastically about it, saying he knew many German songs. His wife and his children had been scattered to the winds. He knew nothing about their whereabouts and they knew nothing about his. Until the war came, things had gone well for him. After Hitler's invasion they were scattered across the entire Soviet Union, because the Russians considered all Germans spies and defeatists, irrespective of which Soviet republic they came from, even though they had long been Russian citizens.

'What are you doing here?' I asked.

'I have been a woodcutter the past three years, working under the most severe conditions. Many of us who were transported here in 1941 have perished. We have suffered unbearable hunger. Ever since prisoners of war arrived in this region, I have been removed from the camp for exiles and placed along with the prisoners of war. At first I was working in inventory, but now I am a *normirovtschik.*' That was the man who calculated the daily amount of work in terms of percentages.

'What is that?' I asked perplexedly.

'I provide the daily percentages of work necessary to achieve the goals set by the brigade commander. Another bookkeeper then enters the corresponding portions of bread that are to be supplied.'

'Thank you, thanks,' I wanted to end the conversation. He then attempted to excuse himself, because he was also being monitored. I reassured him and then I asked him one more thing about the rationing system. Instead, he quickly stood up, placed his finger over his mouth, and said, 'I have already told you both too much, please say nothing!'

We understood and assured him that he had nothing to worry about.

I would gladly have learned more, and I hoped to later.

We continued planing our boards. But our thoughts remained on those who were among the exiles. How impoverished these people were; just because Hitler invaded, what had they done to deserve this? What crime did they commit? None. These people weren't criminals. The only reason they were banished here was because their mother-tongue was German, or because their ancestors decided to set up a colony in this land and do valuable work. It was appalling to see what was going on here. Did the world even know? Little, very little!

One can imagine the level of enthusiasm we had in laying this floor. We were able somehow to attach the boards and cover up the uneven areas as best we could. The main thing was the report said that our daily plan was accomplished. The how was of minor importance, including for those who made the report.

Once again I was assigned another type of work. The work team leader made it known to me that for a period of time I was allowed to work on the shingle machine. Two barracks already had a gabled roof, with thin planks serving as the support for the shingles. With curiosity I went the next day to my new work station.

The shingle 'machine' is an incredible apparatus, and one cannot imagine how it works. The Russian explained to us how to operate it. Two men were employed to feed long, thick logs into a few reels that sawed the logs into the length of a shingle. From this came little rectangular blocks of wood. This block of wood was then wedged into some sort of vice. Over the wood was a crossbeam that was free on one end and attached with a hinge on the other. A knife was clamped underneath. Four men raised the crossbeam on the free end up and down and produced shingle after shingle, when, of course, it was working! One felt as though you were at the helm of a ship. So they would cut the entire day, feeling like they were galley slaves of the twentieth century.

The quota per day per man was 1,000 shingles, so a total of 4,000 together. Naturally, we never reached that number because half the day was spent in setting up or in repairing the knife. When the cut was too coarse, the knife had to be removed and sharpened with a stone. And when it appeared to come out correctly, we then found the piece of wood was no longer of use. Maggot-infested wood was of no use for shingles, and neither was a heavily knotted piece.

If our Tyrolean farmers, who probably were not among our wealthiest, had the same difficulty in generating shingles for their houses and Alpine huts, I would feel very sorry for them.

The supervisor realised that under such conditions we could not achieve our quota. Despite this, he wrote 'met', and we thanked him. In doing so we brought him one of our servings of soup from the kettle. We received warm soup each afternoon, whereas the *saklutschoni* received nothing from the time he left his dwelling in the morning until he was served his warm soup together with the *kasha* upon returning in the evening.

I also never once saw the two guards who accompanied us get something to eat, from the time they led us to work until they escorted us home, including while they waited for us at the work site. Around one o'clock, when the prisoners were fed, they always walked around the soup kettle, waiting to see if something might be left over. The Russian guards were embarrassed when someone saw the cook, who was Hungarian, giving them a mess tin full of soup. It also happened that they looked dejected when there was nothing remaining. Sometimes the cook had to stress that he was not obliged to give them anything.

I heard from the other side that our guards had likewise been sentenced, and that they were banished to this godforsaken area just as we were.

In one respect, working on the machine and spending the entire day in constant motion was not all bad. It had become severely cold, and the snow was deep. When the storm blew the snow crystals into our face, we would pull the crossbeam to and fro all the more.

As before, the outfitting supplies became absolutely dire. Day after day we were promised we would receive trousers and jackets, felt boots and even fur coats for the winter. Apparently, it was not yet full-blown winter, even though the temperature was -10 to -15°C and the majority of us possessed neither gloves nor any protective covering for our hands.

The supervisor removed me suddenly from working on the

machine and instead assigned me to kitchen construction. Some of our brigade had been working there for quite a while, and the roof needed to be covered before midwinter arrived. The boss said to me I was already a specialist in collecting moss, and that I should endeavour to go and fetch some because the supply had run out and the building could not be completed without it.

At first I thought he was messing with me and I looked at him incredulously. There was no way someone could collect moss when there was half a metre of snow and the ground was frozen and as hard as a rock.

The Russian looked at the expression on my face, and then pointed his finger to his forehead to exemplify how stupid I was. Without further ado, he placed a shovel, an iron spade and a tarpaulin canvas in my hands and said, unmistakably: '*Istschi* – search for it!'

So, shivering, I and another man went off looking for moss. To do this one needs a nose like a hound, being able to sniff where one might find moss under the snow. We shovelled away the snow in various places, encountering only rocks and dirt. All things come to those who wait. All of a sudden we found a spot where we unearthed a wide strip of moss. We first placed some wooden boards on the ground around the large area of moss, and then, in fits and starts, we began to separate the frozen solid sheets of moss and dig them up off the forest floor.

When we brought the first large load to the construction site, the *desjatnik* detained me. The team leader explained to me why. I was

to be in charge of cooking the moss. At first, I could not imagine what he was talking about. Then it made sense to me: in its present condition the frozen moss could not be placed between the beams. It first had to be thawed.

A fire had been kindled behind an uprooted tree trunk in order to warm up the ground below. Accordingly, I took a spade, stuck it into the ground, and dug a rather wide and deep hole. Opposite the root, I set up a wooden frame on the other side of the hole, so that I could lay a mesh across the hole. Part of it was supported by the root and the other part by the wooden frame, creating a grille that was approximately 1 metre across. The frozen sections of moss were lain across the grille, and then I lit a new fire in the hole below. The flames in this cooker should be neither too big or too small, they had to be just enough to warm the moss in order to thaw it, without burning it or setting it on fire.

This work, even though it gave off a lot of smoke that caused the eyes to sting, had its advantages: it was pretty warm and the physical demands were not even worth mentioning. Mind you, you had to pay attention, or you risked burning both the moss and the cooker, and in addition to the loss of the moss, even more bitter was that it snowed more and more.

I remained as the moss roaster for a considerable time, and naturally because of that, others became envious.

In the meantime, the other roofs for the other barracks were completed. On top, slabs of wood served as an underlay and on them the shingles were fixed. In order to finish both living barracks, all the men of the brigade were used, half of whom pounded in the wire nails, and the other half made the shingles. The wind nearly blew us down off the roof, while we also had to deal with the heavy snowfall. With stiff fingers this was not easy, and these often got badly struck with the hammer, instead of the wire nail we were supposed to hammer in.

But still, we had no room to complain over the work, because the remaining brigades envied that we were working on construction. The 'forest brigades', that is, the woodcutters, supposedly had it much worse than we did. They always came back to the camp later from work than we did, and I believed that I was no longer in a physical condition to be able to fell and cut 3 cubic metres of wood.

One evening, a lasting commotion arose. The Russian camp commandant came personally and called before him all those who were not fulfilling their quotas. He listed the excuses, such as being too weak, malnutrition, and inadequate apparel, but he said they were not acceptable. He placed particular emphasis on the cold, arguing that the real winter still had not even begun.

I was too tired to be able to follow this debate, and I fell asleep early. Anyone who did not meet their quota was placed in the *karzer*.

A few evenings later and the tumult began again; it was so loud that even the most tired men could not sleep. The people who had not cut enough wood would be deprived of some of their bread and soup. Two team leaders were dismissed from their position, because they were held responsible for their team failing to achieve their quotas.

17
Murderous Forest Work

The *starschina* in the barracks suddenly came to me and asked whether I was in a condition to lead a brigade of woodcutters, because my understanding of Russian was pretty good.

The camp commandant hoped that I would have more success, and he gave me the essential instructions.

As the team leader I did not need to work. I was responsible for the bread that had been prepared for the team, as well as the soup to be served twice. If the brigade fulfilled the quota as a whole, the team leader would also receive *kasha* along with the bread, but if they underperformed, a reduction in portions would result. The duties consisted of providing the team with the rations each was due, according to the calculated percentage; making sure that their apparel was mended in the *masterkaja* [master workshops]; that the felt boots, which had in the meantime arrived, were worn into the disinfection chamber and dried; and that the gloves and boots were either mended or replaced. On *bania* day, the team leader would shave and have his hair cut along with the others, and all would be deloused. At the time, freshly washed clothes did not exist.

The team leader was further responsible for ensuring his twenty men were all ready to begin work. In the evening he had to accompany those who were sick to the doctor, and during the march to and from the work site he had to keep track of his people. He couldn't lose any workers and the column had to remain intact. Outside, he helped the foreman to ensure all his men were in their place. At lunchtime he led those men under his charge to where the soup was distributed. However, when the soup pot was too far away from the work site, and too much time would be lost, he had to take a bucket by himself into the woods, collect the soup where it was cooked and, through the deep snow and fallen and overturned trees, he would bring the bucket to each individual labourer. In the evening, along with the *desjatnik*, he had to review the work that had been completed that day.

So the next day I no longer marched to the construction site, but instead I set off with my people to the tool receiving area for a new assignment. It took for ever to get there, nearly an hour. On the one hand I was sorry that I was no longer assigned to construction. We got along working with each other rather well there, and I could not know what awaited me here. The brigade that was assigned to me was completely foreign, and I hardly knew any of them. Moreover, I had practically no knowledge of this type of work, I knew nothing of the work practices, and there was no help to speak of.

All these lumberjacks and members of the path-clearing brigade were subordinate to a Romanian prisoner of war, a 'master of the forest', who in turn split his duties with a *saklutschoni*, who was also a master of the forest.

As we arrived at a large fire, around which sat a few men cloaked in fur coats, one of them jumped up and inquired about the team leader. He was a Romanian. He glanced me over and said he hoped that the people under my command would work better. The *nemtsy* were certainly capable, but they did not want to work. I did not respond, thinking only about my role. Mind you, I contemplated what he said. What did this Gypsy expect from men who in any case were exhausted by this type of work, and devoured by the cold and snow? But, after all, he had to say something to hold his ground. He was chosen by the Russians, and if the plan was not accomplished he would lose his position.

My few boys went immediately to their workplaces, each of them had plenty of wood in their assigned section. I went from man to man, spoke to each one, and watched them work, primarily to learn for myself.

What did one man have to complete here? He sawed around the largest trees. This was hardly imaginable to someone who has not seen it, and it was done with only the typical Russian one-man saw. It consisted of a single narrow blade, which was serrated between four to six times, and these were separated by a wide, curved tooth. The sawblade was held by a wooden frame, and like our cabinetmaker's saw, it was taut on the surface. These saws were extremely delicate, especially if caught when the tree began to fall over, as well as sometimes when it was bitter cold. A good conventional crosscut saw, which was sharpened and had only a few soldered joints, worked very well, provided that the man who operated it was in good shape.

When felling the tree the man remained in a crouched position, because he was only allowed to cut the trunk 10 centimetres above the roots. Likewise, the axe had to be sharp, and several swings could be saved by notching and scoring the tree. In this way, the trees fell easily, and the wood being dry and the limbs being seared off, it was rare that the treetop canopy remained. If the tree was cut poorly, or there was a strong wind blowing, the felling was more difficult. Then the team leader had to help, so I made myself readily available. It also happened that despite the tree being cut all the way through, it remained standing. In this case, one used a push rod. If it still didn't fall, a second rod would be laid under the first, and this would be lifted up; with this leverage, the tree would fall.

The winter made jumping out of the way of a falling tree very difficult. The men were slow to get out of the danger zone, especially when the tree snapped. Enough time was already wasted clearing away the snow from around the tree. But this was only done so there was sufficient freedom of movement for the saws on all sides. However, it was not only the snow; there were also the twigs that needed to be hacked off.

If you were sure enough trees had been felled so that the quota of 3 cubic metres was achieved, then the limbing of branches would begin. Hardwood is typically knot-free in the first 5 to 8 metres from the ground. When falling to the ground, a considerable number of the branches were detached, and the treetop usually splintered because the forest had been burned out and the wood was dry. Unfortunately, the thick branches near the trunk did not break clean off, but only partially, so the trunks had to first be trimmed. This took time, but the *desjatnik* didn't like that. With green wood the limbing is much harder, because the branches are not chopped off in one or two strokes, as they were here.

Large birch trees that were scattered here and there were especially dangerous to fell, because the branches at the crown of the tree were completely rotten, and with the smallest jolt they fell off vertically towards us. The most gnarled branches were from pinewood. There was also another type of tree we were not familiar with. The tree was completely bare, and having no bark it glittered an almost silvery-white through the gloomy woods. We christened these trees by naming them *pappeln* [poplars].

Then, the long trunk was sawn into 1½-metre logs. It depended upon the skill of the loggers to bring the tree down in a way it would be well situated so that the saw would not get pinched while cutting. If one was careless, the result would be a broken sawblade. Each time that happened, a great amount of time was lost. There was also an *instrumentalnik* [equipment maintenance crew] in the woods, who provided replacements for the broken sawblades.

The deep snow made not only felling the trees more difficult, but even more so cutting them into logs and stacking them. The prisoners of war or other coerced labourers were left alone in cutting and stacking the wood. Working in groups of two as a way of distributing the work was unknown here, and it was quite simply impossible because the people were completely foreign to one another; there was no trust among the workers, camaraderie was lacking, and in these demoralising circumstances each attempted to deceive the other. Besides, the relative strength of each was so different that working together was not advantageous.

When enough trees had been felled per man, and enough logs had been cut, then began – usually in the late afternoon – the stacking of the wood. The stacking area was assigned by the team leader. It was located on a path that had been cleared by the 50-percenters, who then had to take the wood by horse-drawn sled to a small rail line.

The stacking area was worked by the loggers, who used the axe to clear off the snow. Two or three short sticks were used as the base and rammed in place with a wedge, so that the stack did not fall or roll over.

Lugging the wood to the stacking place was the most difficult part of the work. Heavy logs helped to meet the quota, but they required tremendous energy to transport them. Only by exerting oneself fully could the prisoners drag or carry the wood to the stacking area. In this completely uncultivated forest, the surface was very uneven. Only now and then could one find level ground. Then, one would bury the axe into the end of the log and drag it. In this way, a trail could be created for the remaining logs. Of course, this was the ideal. Most of the time, there were countless obstacles lying in the way. One was then either forced to carry the log on his shoulder, or stand it up and overturn it forwards, pick it up again, and move it forwards in this way.

Before planing the wood it had to be checked over again to see if it had any knots. Rotten wood had to be tossed to the side of the stack. Everything was closely monitored to make sure nothing hollow was sneaked through. Any gaps in the stack were deducted from the work total. Minor cheating, such as placing really short logs in the front of the stack, were often uncovered. After the stack was inspected and the logs counted, the *desjatnik* would mark it black with charcoal, but he often did not take the time to mark all of the stacks. Whenever possible, the prisoners would take advantage of this by throwing snow on the unmarked stacks to cover them, and then they would claim the next day that it was freshly cut wood.

Even after all this, the work day was not yet over. The work site had to be cleaned up, which meant that all the brushwood and pieces smaller than 10 centimetres in diameter, as well as the treetops and the branches – or any other wood that was lying around the place – had to be collected and loaded onto a pile and burned. That often led to quarrels as to who had to pick up this or that treetop that fell some distance away and clear them from the site.

Most of the time we lit a fire at the beginning of our work and we threw the branches into it. At the same time, we could warm ourselves somewhat. In addition, there was little time to waste, because in order to meet our quota we had to work the entire day. Naturally, it goes without saying that there were people who went around with their axe, going from one cigarette break to the next.

As night began to fall – the days were already becoming shorter with winter approaching – the day's output was written down. The team leader wrote the results of each one on a small board. There was nothing like a notepad or anything similar to that. Using a shard of glass, the old entry was scraped off when it was no longer needed, and the board was reused. Not until we reached camp was the output recorded in ink in a ledger.

The work in this wretched, dead forest crushed us mentally and physically. The sun was seldom visible in the heavily overcast sky. So far as one could see, all that was visible was the parched, blackened trees; if one looked up into the sky, all appeared gloomy and dark; and the ground was covered by deep snow. No animal, no bird could be heard; just the drubbing of axes, the crashing of falling trees; what stood out was the continuous cursing of the exiled Russians who loaded the chopped wood onto sleds, and with small, emaciated *panje* horses, they transported the loads across the arduous open country. It was an everlasting curse for the horse, to carry the load on the way.

The one alluring feature of this landscape were the many fire pits that blazed up to the sky; they lent to the woods an unearthly character.

Now I understood why the forest brigade always returned so late to the camp. Assembling the entire brigade on the main path took a long time, because in the dark the guards miscounted a number of times. We could not continue until the number was correct.

On that day my brigade met the required quota. A few had worked above it and three below it, because they had to manage clean-up operations in an unfavourable place. The camp commandant only accused us of trying to rebel when the group as a whole were under the quota. So that night we were left alone and no one was placed in the *karzer*.

I was utterly exhausted, because I helped saw, limb and stack the entire day, even though my physical condition had already gone to the dogs.

For the next few days my people remained in good stead. By expending all our strength we were able to make 100 per cent of our daily quota. But I immediately recognised the downside to this approach. We could not keep this pace up for long. The men were incapable of continuously completing such difficult labour given these rations. Glorious Russia! Only every tenth day was a day off work, and when the monthly plan was in danger of not being achieved, even this free day was cancelled. So it happened that we worked an entire month without one day's rest.

In fact, even if a free day was earned, it was not really a day off. On those days we were still used for all sorts of administrative duties.

On one free day, in groups of two we had to schlep 80-kilogram sacks of millet from the train station to the camp. We would place poles on both our right and left shoulders, and the sack would be placed crossways over them, between the person in front and the person behind. The guy behind me could not resist puncturing a hole into the sack in order to steal some of the millet. A Russian caught him doing it, requested some of it, and then the sack fell to the ground and burst. Now we had a real mess. Needless to say, as we were refilling the sack we stuffed our pockets full of the grain.

On another free day we had to pick up salt. We came to the rail line, and the salt had been poured into a large pile on the snow. Using shovels, we filled bags with the salt and carried them home.

We often travelled this stretch of road, mostly to carry planks. They were used on the muddy, soggy paths inside the camp.

This was how the morning routinely passed on our so-called 'free days'. In the afternoon, we would all lie weary and worn out on our bunks. One would sleep, being spared the bedbugs as long as it was light. That was our Sunday.

The senior man in the barracks received 100 to 150 grams of kerosene oil daily. Our 'kerosene lamp' was a tin can with a hole through which an improvised wick of coat fabric was placed. Naturally, this did not supply sufficient light for a barracks in which 100 men lived. Furthermore, the amount of kerosene was too little, and often there was none, meaning we had to move around in the dark. After work we would grope our way to bed in the dark, pick up our food in the dark, get up a number of times in the dark, and have to rise in the early morning in the dark – the existence of a mole.

Sometimes we would make do with wood chips, but the risk of fire stopped us from doing this. If we set fire to the cabins, the Russians would divide us among the others, and our lodgings would become even more crowded.

Each barracks had a wash area attached. It consisted of two wooden troughs, the upper one to serve as a small cistern, the lower one for drainage. A peg was used instead of a tap, and water would pass through when the peg was pushed upwards. Four such 'faucets' served 100 men for washing. A water tank was filled during the day by the senior man and those who remained behind because they were sick; this was how the reservoir was refilled.

The senior man, along with those who remained behind, also had the task of cleaning the barracks. The Russians showed us how to wash the floor quickly with the simplest method. The floor of our barracks was just as uneven as the ones I had laid earlier. A piece of rubber from the broken-off sole of a shoe or from a pneumatic tyre was clamped and then screwed between two boards, and the rubber was left to stick out about 2 centimetres. A branch was then attached to it. One would pour water over the floor and then scrub with the *'Gummischruber'* [squeegee] the water-infused area in front of him. By and large, most of the dirt was removed. Some rags were then used to rub it dry.

The small iron stove that stood in the middle was steadily fuelled to dry the floor quickly. The team leader was responsible for ensuring there was enough wood for heat, and in the evening the brigade would bring back small pieces of wood into the camp. Sometimes our return trip would go past the small train line, and a few of us could often get small cuts of wood that the exiled women had stacked there as fuel for the locomotive.

The thermometer dropped from day to day. I could not imagine that one could work when it was virtually 35°C below zero. The camp commandant even announced that we would work to 40° below zero; in storms to -35°C. I saw the *saklutschoni* working in every weather condition.

We finally received fur coats, better felt boots, cotton-wool pants and jackets, but there continued to be a shortage of gloves. There were some available, but they didn't hold up for twelve hours. Many things were destroyed in the woods. What's more, flying sparks would start one cotton-wool jacket on fire, and then another, and in no time they would burn.

October Revolution Day, which was celebrated on 6 November as a result of the Julian calendar [the official date was 7 November according to the Gregorian calendar] passed us by without any kind of ceremony, apart from the usual search. We actually had two days of rest. Roll call took place early and late; however, we were counted in the barracks and so we didn't need to go outside in the cold.

It became increasingly common that someone would suddenly collapse when they began working. They would be picked up and carried to the *ambulanzia* [infirmary]. The commandant saw this, but he showed no emotion. One morning – two comrades fell at the same time, a Romanian and an Italian – however, he gave the command to let them lie were they were. The rest of us marched off in song through the deep snow and darkness towards the gate.

Then another fell, but no one dared to lift him. The commandant appeared to view the collapsing men suspiciously, and perhaps with some of them he was right, i.e., that they were simply feigning illness.

18

The *Schlappkommando* and the *Oberrekordisten*

In the evening the team leader and the senior man were called to the camp commander. He talked with us at great length, saying that the fainting at roll call had to stop. He claimed that those who were collapsing were workplace saboteurs and fascists. He impressed upon us that we were no longer to pick them up or carry them away. When they became cold, they would get up by themselves.

It was clear he had not thoroughly considered why the comrades were collapsing. Whether they fell down deliberately or were really collapsing, the fact was that they were too weak to work and they could not continue to make it all the way to the work site.

One evening the monthly health inspection commission arrived to complete its examination of the all the prisoners.

The camp doctor, a *saklutschoni* – they were always called *SK* for short – was not without sympathy. He had the final say on the diagnosis. In addition to him, the Russian camp commander, the *technoruk* [the person responsible for organising the forest work] was there, as well as a Russian officer and a soldier who had the personnel list. He belonged to the so-called *ftoroi-dschast*, those in charge of personnel, who worked closely with the NKVD.

The first ones picked were the forest workers.

The *kommissia* [commission] entered our dark barracks with an actual oil chimney lamp.

The prisoners had to undress and were called in by section. So the enfeebled Adam stepped forward before the critical commission and the haggling began, as if it were a cow or horse market. The doctor checked the thickness of the skin on the chest and the buttocks. Then the commandant asked how many percent each could still produce:

one hundred, fifty or even if the percentage was less. Whereas the doctor was trying to evaluate as objectively as possible, the commandant was trying to squeeze out as high a percentage as possible in order to not place the prescribed monthly plan at risk. The doctor appeared to have a difficult dilemma: If he wrote too low a percentage, it would be insinuated that he was aiding the saboteurs. If he wrote the percentage too high, the men would become sick, and if they died, he would be held responsible for the losses and the reduced capacity to work.

If the skin was nothing but wrinkles at the buttocks and stretched out against the ribcage, those concerned would be written down as 25 per cent; that meant *Schlappkommando* [literally, 'slack' or 'weak' command; i.e., light-duty brigade]. It was not uncommon for the commandant to hold the brigade leader responsible. That was more than absurd. Even the strongest man would be driven into the ground by these conditions. What could these unreasonable assertions and accusations mean? They could only serve the purpose of the ultimate slave-driver.

This 'cattle market' terrified all those who had the fortune to work in either the kitchen or the bakery as a bread slicer. If they recovered at all while they were working there, they would now be written down as 100 per cent.

The consumption of men was enormous. Whereas these troops were replenished during the summer by approximately twenty-five new *etappen* [resupply] brigades, the number of those brigades at 100 per cent shrank to seven.

The work within the zone could not be achieved without the lower percenters. Carrying water and sacks also required stronger workers.

To fulfil the monthly plan, a recording day was included when the cook, the baker, the scribe – virtually everyone – had to work.

The *Schlappen* – Category IV with the 25-percenters – were combined into their own barracks – at that time, four of them. They were no longer separated by nationality, and considerable dissension prevailed. They quarrelled, stole and fought with one another, and they could not understand each other. These poor men, they were completely finished and they appeared as though they were in their first few months of captivity. Nevertheless, they were supposed to receive better rations, presumably so they could return to work – nothing else could explain it. But there were no more foodstuffs available from which they could be assigned additional portions. There were also supposed to be camps for the *Schlappen*, where agricultural work was extracted from the inmates.

Although I personally did not have to work for an entire month, but instead occasionally with helping out as the team leader, I nevertheless did not become any stronger. I was written down as a 75-percenter. However, as the team leader there was no change in my responsibilities.

As I looked at the different categories of work for the men, I wondered if this type of system was being used anywhere else on earth. Here, mankind was a working machine. He worked as long as he could until he could work no more; he could only last so long. Shortly before he broke down he was left in peace. Either he would die from some type of illness, like dysentery, pneumonia or oedema, or he would recover and slowly climb back to life. He would then be added back to the number of those working, and the dangerous game would begin anew.

The 50-percenters didn't have it good, either. That had to leave for work at the same time as the others, and they had just as far to walk. Although they did not need to fell any trees, they did have to build trails. They had to clear the many access roads and make the paths usable. Removing bushes was no small matter for these emaciated figures. But the Russian was humane. The path builders were allowed to return to the barracks at three o'clock, provided they had fulfilled their reduced work quota. Despite their infirmity, they also brought wood for heating the barracks. Unfortunately, sometimes they had to carry that wood by hand to the Russian garrison, so they were deprived of the fruits of their labour. Of course, one could not expect the Russian guards to carry their own wood when they had prisoners to do it for them.

The 75- and 100-percenters served together in the same brigade, with the only difference being that Category II [75-percenters] had a correspondingly reduced work quota. Otherwise, the work was the same.

As the work team leader, I acquired practical skills relatively quickly. Along with the forest master, the team leader had to find a good spot for cutting down the trees. The more effort the team leader took to find the right place, the more likely it would be that his people met with success in their work. In woods where the largest trees were no more than 10 to 20 centimetres in diameter, one could saw and cut around the tree until their hands and arms couldn't take it any more. In the best case, he could cut 1½ metres, or only about half the quota. The result was less to eat and, eventually, the *karzer*. In this case, it was not a lack of willingness to work that was the problem. Only now and then was a worker petulant, and that was because he was already at the point where he couldn't care less. As a general rule, everyone was willing to work because they were hungry, and that was an effective motivator.

The Russians tried to increase the amount of work with *machorka* rations. Anyone who was able to cut an additional cubic metre would receive 10 to 15 grams of tobacco leaves. The desire to smoke really did push some to cut 4 cubic metres on average, in deep snow and when it was nearly 30° below zero.

The Russians referred to anyone who cut more than 4 cubic metres as a proud *rekordist* [record holder]; one man even cut 5 metres, so he was awarded the title *Oberrekordist* [chief record holder]. The record holder received a double portion of soup and tobacco, and the chief record holder three times the norm. Bread rations were not increased. Unfortunately, they used the same trick they had when we were in the hospital. The porridge and soup were simply diluted with water. In the end, everyone was disadvantaged. They received no more calories than we did. So the extra work they did for an additional serving was not a fair trade. In reality, it only served to weaken their bodies in comparison to what they were fed. Despite having done the record work, the cost–benefit ratio was negative.

In my team I had one worker who, because he was known to be a good worker, was allowed to serve in the kitchen while he recovered. When he was in good condition he cut between 5 and 6 metres daily. I was amazed every time I came to his work site at how quickly he could fell and cut the trees. I could not have stopped him from doing it, but I feared one day he would overdo it. What then? No one would care about him, no one would appreciate he was a record holder. At the time, he was praised for being a 'hero of Socialist labour'. Robert did not talk a lot, but one evening by the fire he confided in me: 'Don't mention this to anyone. I want to do this amount of work because it weakens me quickly, so that I can be sent back to the kitchen. This is how I have been able to survive the last three years since I was captured. In this way, I am able to get almost enough to eat. I have long been alternating between record work and kitchen duty.'

I tried to talk him out of doing this and I made it clear to him that this exploitation would take its toll on his body and would eventually destroy him. To develop this train of thought, to deliberately and completely exhaust oneself, was only possible given certain circumstances, such as they were here. One could never know, however, how going from one extreme to the other would affect the body, and it was impossible for anyone to know how long this captivity would continue. In these terrible woods, I often began to doubt myself, now more than earlier. Would I ever find a way back home, or would I perish among dead trees in this bleak forest?

I could hear the siren wailing from afar. It was one o'clock. I quickly took my pail and ladle and went to find the forest kitchen. I arrived a little late, as I was the last one to reach the cook. The guards were prowling around us. The soup they were serving in the woods had recently improved somewhat. It had been made thicker with the addition of bran, millet and chopped beets. It tasted excellent. I received exactly seventeen portions for my seventeen people, and two extra servings for the record holders were counted out and placed in my pail, as well.

The journey back to the work site of my people was not so easy, because the path was full of a host of obstacles. I had to be careful not to spill one drop. That would have meant each one received less. I carefully trudged through the snow from one comrade to another and poured a ladleful into each mess tin. Many took no time to spoon down the soup in quiet, fearing to lose too much time that could keep them from finishing their quota.

'I can't do any more, I can't do any more,' I heard one of them stammer, 'even if you beat me, I cannot do any more.'

This man was shaking all over. He was sweating and he had a fever. His eyes were somewhat shiny. His axe and saw were lying in the snow – he had only felled a single tree, and from it he had cut two logs. Were a Russian to see this, he would assail him and call him a saboteur. There was no consideration given here. Sickness or feebleness was interpreted as unwillingness to work. In addition, I could not help him as the team leader, other than to take him to the doctor when we returned, who might place him in sickbay for a day.

I led him to the fire, I tossed on a few branches, and I said to him he should try to warm himself until I returned.

I continued to distribute the soup that had in the meantime become cold. At Robert's workplace it was quiet. How so? I heard neither chopping nor sawing. Where had he gone?

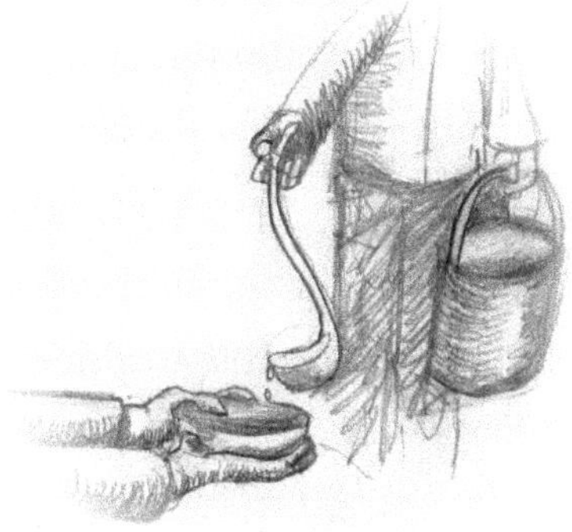

'Robert, Robert!' There was no answer. There were freshly felled trees, some of which had already been cut into logs. 'Robert!' I called again, but without receiving an answer. I set down my pail. Three servings of soup remained: two for Robert, one for me. I crawled and climbed over felled trees. 'Robert, Robert!' – there was no answer.

There, what did I see lying on the ground? Despite the deep snow, I burrowed quickly towards it.

'Robert, what happened to you, did a tree hit you? Why are you lying in the snow?'

There was no response, only mumbling and the rolling of his eyes. I quickly tried to lift him up, but I had great difficulty doing so because he was like a heavy brick in the snow, and he wouldn't wake up. Giving everything I had, I pulled him up and I lay him on a large tree.

I rubbed his face and hands. He was ice cold. His pulse was slow and irregular. How could I help him? I attempted to resuscitate him, as I would if he were drunk. It helped, his eyes became calmer and he started taking deep breaths. He slowly came round.

This was quite some day! Everyone could curse about anything he wished. I took the rest of the soup and I walked as quickly as I could to the nearest fire. There, my biggest problem child was sleeping. I yelled at him to warm the soup, and told him I would be right back.

To make matters worse, heavy snow began to fall. I returned to Robert. He was lying completely still on the tree. In vain I tried to speak to him. I drew his arm over my shoulder and dragged him to the fire. I was exhausted when I arrived, and I proceeded to give him some warm soup. The first spoonful trickled down the side of his mouth. Then he reacted and swallowed. You poor devil, what have they done to you? A record holder? A physical wreck! I continued throwing wood on the fire until the flames reached into the sky, so he was able to warm himself somewhat and thaw out.

I said to the other sick worker that, in the meantime, he should watch Robert closely until I was able to find the forest master and the medic, who was also serving with us. But it was always like this. When you went looking for one of them, it was certain you could not find them.

In the evening, as it was becoming pitch black, the medic took Robert away. He was able to move, but just barely. In his work obsession he had completely broken down and he nearly froze to death.

A few days later I heard that the fingers in his right hand and both feet had suffered severe frostbite. As he was being evacuated I saw him again. He was loaded directly onto a sled. With tears in his eyes he looked at me and said, 'You should have let me lie there, so I would finally have had peace!'

What did the Russian guards do as he was being pulled out through the gate? They laughed and spat contemptuously to the side. That was the final thanks the record holder received. Those who were unable to work, sick or helpless were a trivial concern to the Russians.

My small group of troops had already sunk to twelve. Soon this brigade would be dissolved, and then I would have to take an axe on my own shoulder so that I could cut my own cubic metre.

One day, a few men asserted it was 24 December, reminding us it was Christmas Eve. There was not a hint of the Christmas spirit among us. That day we all wanted to return a little earlier. Even though we could not celebrate, we still wanted a little time to think about home.

As we were marching back an order came down: we had to take along wood for the garrison. Today of all days? My people refused to load up any wood. I didn't say anything, but I feared something would drop.

Just as we got to the garrison, they told us: 'Go back!'

We had to return the entire way back into the woods, but no one dared to contradict the order; otherwise, the Russians would have kicked us or worse. So we loaded a bunch of sticks on our shoulders and headed back home. That was our Christmas celebration. It was certainly later than ten o'clock in the evening when we returned to the gate and reported back.

We lay there dead tired on our bunks, no songs rang out, no candle was lit – nothing. The only thing that burned in our hearts – homesickness. Once again, I cursed the land and the people who did all this to us. My dear Soviet Socialists, what was taking place in these woods was definitely not what you advertised it to be. At best, it was in the secret text of your constitution.

19
Scurvy

Here among the extensive network of forest prison camps, it was said that there were hundreds of thousands, if not millions, of slave labourers. Anyone who did anything against the system or in any way violated the laws was deported. The Russians boasted that they did not have a death penalty. Under normal circumstances this was true. But for many, death brought deliverance.

The most recent sacrifices to this peculiar labour market were the prisoners of war. The new arrivals would ask what they would be doing, where they would stay – at the same time, countless numbers of them would perish, no matter what part of the Soviet Union they found themselves in. Would Russia never be held accountable for this? Or did it think itself so powerful that what the rest of the world thought did not matter?

Before we arrived, only the *SK* were said to have been here. But during the war they were assembled into a penal battalion and sent to the front. The only exception were those deported for political crimes.

One had to be strong, very strong, in order not to lose heart.

We were glad when the cold was so bitter that we did not have to go outside. We spent three days in the barracks when the temperature fell to -45°C . The small windows were iced over on the inside because they were not well sealed and it was damp. Naturally, even during the day it was dark.

We used this forced slack period to put our own things in order. We also used it to carry out the long-planned assault against the bedbugs, pouring boiling water into the cracks in the boards and crossbeams. However, the following night was even worse because the remaining creatures became downright rabid.

Then, out of the blue, my right leg began to show considerable redness and swelling. I suspected it was an abscess and would go away on its own.

To our disappointment the severe cold abated and we had to go back to work. As we marched to the site I began to limp badly. On the return march the pain began to intensify and I could barely keep up. So I had to go to see the doctor.

'*Schto, Brigadier balnoi*? –What's wrong?' he asked. 'Are you sick?' He examined my leg, and without further ado he took a scalpel; before I could cry out, puss and blood squirted from the open cut. The doctor wrote that I was sick – scurvy – and admonished me to be careful of the danger of acute inflammation. He spread a black ointment on my leg and then bandaged it. As I was leaving he said that I should spend most of my time lying down and keeping my leg elevated.

I reported the matter to the senior man in the barracks. It was probable the recovery would take a while. It meant they had to look around for another team leader.

Was it not a gift from Heaven that I developed a case of scurvy shortly before my team was to be broken up? In addition, I had the advantage that I continued to receive full rations in sickbay. Since I had fulfilled my quota the day before, I received the usual 800 grams of bread, soup and *kasha*.

Day after day I lay on the bunk. I gladly kept my leg elevated because it hurt in any other position. It didn't spare me, however, from going each day to the clinic in order to remain on the sick roll for the next day. The queue continued to increase daily, as the number of those who were ill skyrocketed to almost catastrophic levels.

The main illnesses in the camp were physical exhaustion, scurvy and frostbite. Sickness was familiarly known as *slaby* – weak – everyone knew that, and whether Hungarian, German, Romanian or Italian, everyone wanted the doctor to diagnose them as *slaby*, so that they didn't have to work.

The cases of frostbite began to pile up because the gloves were tattered, or simply because the clothing was inadequate. Scurvy, on the other hand, was mainly due to our poor diet. Among the sick were also frequent cases of pneumonia and pleurisy. They would lie in sickbay, and were well taken care of by our doctor; two German doctors were permitted to help. They all did their best to limit the loss of life. Each fatality resulted in the worst reproach from the commander. The two German doctors, who had been captured in the vicinity of Voroschilovgrad [Luhansk, in the Donbas region of Ukraine], were fine young men. One was a surgeon and had recently been named the *bania-natschalnik*. His job was 'the battle of the lice'. The other oversaw the latrine, which meant he had to continually supervise the emptying of the latrine. They didn't worry about the other things. They did not have to go into the woods, except on recording day. With the permission of the head doctor, they were also allowed to make rounds and prescribe who was sick. That was something they did not enjoy, because from their standpoint 99 per cent would have qualified.

The camp commandant then issued an order that 25-percenters had to go out and get fir trees. Where, in this wasteland, were we supposed to get these when you could not find green branches for miles around?

The orders were passed down to the senior man in the barracks, who put together a team who were actually able to drag back some firs. Not that far from camp was a stream in the woods that was barely noticeable. In one spot it flowed around a small island, which had been spared the forest fire. On it stood green fir trees. At the time this stretch of water was frozen, and it was easy to get there.

The needles were plucked from the limbs and delivered to the cook. They were cooked in a large pot. The greenish-yellow liquid was distributed along with the evening soup. It was a horrible swill that most of us wanted to pour out the first time we tasted it. The commandant labelled such acts as sabotage and he posted a guard to ensure each of us drank the entire cup. The Russians claimed that this was the only possibility for us to take vitamin C.

Then, we received something else: vitamin B. The Russians called it *droschi*. This liquid was what you get when you allow yeast to ferment in water. It had to be repeatedly stirred and then left to sit for some time. This drink didn't taste that bad, but it was also simply water. Likewise, according to regulations the brown bread for the prisoners was 60 per cent water. This caused a fair amount of heartburn. Consuming water was supposed to make us well?

The Siberian winter returned with a vengeance. The thermometer showed -45°C. Until further notice, the door remained closed. We were living like cavemen. No one stepped outside, not even to look, unless he had to. It defied description. The latrines were barely usable. Piles of dung were frozen there, as hard as mountains. For urination a barrel was provided in the entrance hall.

They stopped receiving food at the kitchen window, and instead it was carried to the barracks in barrels. It was distributed by the senior man. It was strictly controlled, each receiving one full ladle so that nothing was left. A 'palace revolution' [*coup d'état*] was in order if there was any cheating. Hungry eyes are quick-tempered.

We always viewed our senior man with a degree of suspicion, because he always filled his mess tin, whether it was soup or *kasha*, up to the rim. He didn't work, either performing indoor duties or out in the field. He only helped when it had something to do with the barracks. It was rumoured that he was an antifascist and had previously been part of the commune in Berlin. He was supposed to be connected, somehow, with the NKVD. One would also find the writings of Lenin, Marx and other pamphlets on intellectualism and materialism by his bed.

One day, around the time we would otherwise have gone to work, a *sobranje* was held to prepare us to take advantage of this downtime for political instruction.

The brigade commander and the prisoner of war camp commandant, accompanied by NKVD officers and our senior man, marched into the barracks, equipped with an oil lamp. They spread a cloth sideways across the one table.

The commander spoke. Everyone had to listen. Although I was able to speak everyday Russian, I could only understand portions of what was said. It had something to do with events along the Polish and Romanian fronts. The Russian troops were even supposed to have already entered Hungary. He also mentioned the advance of the Allies in Italy and in the west. The longest part of the speech, however, had to do with the work done by the prisoners of war in the Soviet Union, and especially with us.

The long and the short of it: a good antifascist was one who demonstrated it by completing a high percentage of work. He promised that we would receive better rations in the spring. Meat, fat, fish and more tobacco. The basic requirement, however, was not that we fulfilled the monthly plan, but that we exceeded the required quota.

The Romanian prisoner-of-war camp commandant provided a 'Yiddish-German' translation that we found rather amusing. Several of us were already snoring deeply. That's why I was convinced over 90 per cent of us had no idea what it was about. The German antifascist also thought it necessary that he display his wisdom, so he babbled on about how to increase production. His speech was similar to someone shouting 'give us more to eat!' in broken German.

With shouts of well-being for the great Soviet Union and the Red Army, the meeting was ended. The antifascist screamed at the top of his lungs: '*Smyrna!* – Stand fast!' Half-sleeping figures jumped quickly to their feet from their bunks and the honour guard saluted the commander as he was leaving. '*Dasvidaniya* – until we meet again,' he called, '*dasvidaniya.*'

Another month passed, I continued to remain in my bunk and despite poor rations, despite the lack of any mental activity, and despite my abscessed lower leg, I felt quite well. In the meantime, most of the Romanians had left the camp. Not all of them were taken as they were supposed to be combined into a Romanian legion; to do so they could only take the ones who were dependable.

We were not angry that the majority of these *Rucksäcke* [backpacks] were taken away. They were nasty lads. For example, they were capable of ripping soup and bread out of your hands, but they were too cowardly to do it alone. They would organise small packs for such muggings. They continued to practise this until the Russians caught them in the act and put them into a detention cell.

This gap was replenished with new 'troops'. Along with these newcomers were a considerable number of Austrians. For this reason, the commandant assigned us our own barracks. So we settled together, most being from Burgenland, Lower Austria and Vienna [eastern Austria].

One day, I was changing the bandage on my foot, and a Russian officer came through the door. He was not familiar to me, but I sensed he was a curious George. I knew them, these NKVD officers, without even having to look at their lapels.

He looked around, and I was astonished that he called me by name. He had various questions, but I made it clear that I was not interested in politics.

'But you were interested about this on the front, as an officer, and now you are trying to pass yourself off as a simple soldier.'

How was I supposed to respond to that? In reality, I was not even a non-commissioned officer. '*Njet, njet* [No, no], a man with your intelligence is no everyday German soldier. Perhaps you did something very bad and so you are trying to live here under a false name.' At that I became somewhat indignant, so I said to him that assuming the Red Army were to soon enter Austria, then he could inquire then and there who I was. '*Moschna*' ['Possibly'], he said with a smile, and then he changed subjects. He wanted me to work for him, writing for a wall newspaper as an antifascist, saying I could choose the topics. With a straight face I said yes. I would draft something. Satisfied with my answer, he politely excused himself.

A few days later someone brought me a large piece of white paper and pencil. At the top I sketched an Austrian landscape; underneath I wrote an essay about the beauty of our homeland, that the war would likely be over soon and that we would be allowed to return home.

The NKVD officer reviewed it and did not raise any objections. I was actually a little surprised. I had written nothing about socialism and its glorious effects in the USSR. Did he not understand what I had written?

I was never keen to be a soldier or an advocate of national socialist ideology. In any case, I was against the war because I enjoyed nature and I loved that I was free. I always despised terror and the system. How could I now join this communist order and work for this man? Perhaps he did not deliberately impose on me what I should say in my next wall newspaper essay. My mind was made up: no, I wouldn't do this, especially when I had to go back out in the woods. Against my better judgement I wasn't going to write any more.

When the NKVD officer returned and brought me documents for another topic – a comparison between Russia under the tsars and today – I played dumb and said I didn't understand. My dismissive stance apparently didn't surprise him, and he said only, 'You continue to be a fascist' … What my stance had to do with fascism, I had no idea, but this much I knew: anyone who did not agree with Lenin and Stalin, and who therefore was not a communist, was an enemy of communism, and by implication, a fascist. I had the feeling that he regretted asking me. He could not understand that men existed who did not think like him. Then he said, 'One day it will all become clear to you, that true democracy and perfect socialism is personified in the Soviet Union …'

Perhaps I had made a terrible mistake. But what did I have to lose? I was already living in exile, and it couldn't get much worse. At any rate, this was the worst case. The most they would do to me was throw me in the detention cell and leave me there. However, they would not do that because everyone alive was a number, and they needed all of us to work.

It was still cold in March, but the sun would break through the clouds so we could occasionally go out into the fresh air in front of the barracks. My foot was still not completely healed, but it was much improved and no new scabs were forming.

20

The Fate of the Exiles

I was already well known to the 'doctor' in the clinic. Each time he saw me he said, '*No, Faschist, kak dja la*? – How's it going, fascist?' and then he would laugh. He was a lovely person. At the time, I was visiting him again. I arrived later than him because I had spent the day shovelling snow. He examined me impishly and said, 'I heard the Austrians can sing well. I could accompany you with my guitar if you stop by in the evening.'

I was glad that he invited us despite the prohibition of any gatherings between the *SK* and prisoners of war. We were simply supposed to knock three times.

His accommodation was a small room in the corner of the barracks. We stepped in through a separate entrance. The whitewashed room was just big enough for a single bed and to hold a basic table and chair.

The four of us took a place on the bed. The doctor broke the ice of a somewhat awkward situation by grabbing his guitar and playing a soft chord. He started by humming some songs without

words. From that, he transitioned to a song resembling a ballad, in which the melody repeated itself. The songs evoked feelings of melancholy.

The songs that we brought must have sounded to him very different. *Gstanzln* ['rude' songs, generally satires mocking authorities like the state, emperor, landowners, the Church or the peculiarities of women], folk songs, *Heurigenlieder* ['new wine' songs, typical of Vienna], a real musical potpourri. Our way of singing pleased him and cheered him up. He did not find it difficult simply to pick up the guitar and accompany us. He had a good ear for music and the combination was impressive.

I then had the opportunity to pose a question: 'Tell me, doctor, how long have you actually been here?'

In silence he held up four fingers in front of his eyes.

'And how much longer?'

He shrugged his shoulders and held up his fingers again: eleven.

'That is dreadful! You are supposed to live in this awful place another eleven years?'

'Yes, and afterwards I will not be sent home, because I am a political prisoner.'

I did not want to probe any further, because it was obviously distressing to him. Then he began to tell us what happened:

'You would like to know what crime I committed. Now, my crime consisted of me telling another person one day during a discussion that I thought Germany would win the war. That was at the time that Germany had overrun Poland, France and the Balkans. I also said I thought German weapons were better and that German industry gave it greater potential in war than our own. Overnight I was taken from my home and imprisoned. From there I went before a summary court, where I was found guilty and sentenced to fifteen years' hard labour. Since that time I have not heard anything from my family, even though this was before Germany invaded our country. I worked in the woods just like you. It was a terrible time, and countless *SK* starved to death. Once the first prisoners of war started arriving here, I was once again used as a doctor. Now things are much better for me. But I am not really a doctor here, but rather a slave-driver … I am limited to how many I can prescribe as sick. There is no difference between an *SK* camp and here. The loss of human life is unparalleled.'

He appeared lost in thought as he stared out of the almost opaque window, he shook his head, and then he again played some chords on his guitar. What could he have possibly been thinking? What kind of mental anguish was he going through? Or had he simply given up?

What disturbed me most was that there was not a person that could or would help him. Aside from the exiles and the prisoners of war, not another human being would set foot on this reservation.

He was banished, condemned to be an outcast. The fact was, he was a good and competent doctor, as German doctors who were prisoners of war could attest. Despite all this, he had to have some faint hope in his heart, otherwise his despair would have led him to hang himself on the nearest tree. Was his hope in another time …?

His story made us silent. Then he said nobly: 'You, you are prisoners of war; one day you will return to your home … But me?'

Then he consoled himself. 'I am not alone. Millions have been imprisoned in this way.' He did not say the word imprisoned out loud, but instead he illustrated this by spreading out the fingers of his hands and placing one set of fingers on top of the other in front of his face, as if looking through them as one would from behind bars. He took great care not to say certain words out loud. Then he laughed and said:

'Do you have any idea what NKVD stands for?'

I thought: 'People's Commissariat for Internal Affairs.'

'*Njet, njet*. It is an acronym for *Nej Kakda Vernush Mamoi*! – Never again will you return home!'

This interpretation did not sound very encouraging. I asked myself whether the Russians would even allow us to leave, since we now had a view of their system for exiles, and given the fact they treated us worse than a dog. This was a question that tormented me now and then. Of course, that was a subject I did not want to think about any further.

After a few more songs we shook hands and left, because we did not want to get caught by the night patrols. Our doctor laid a finger on his lips and admonished us to say nothing. It could cost him his job. He would much prefer to be doing this than to be sent back to an *SK* camp where many criminals were living.

I was surprised that he was so open with us, since even among the prisoners of war there were pigs who would inform against someone if it meant they could get another piece of bread. However, with us the doctor had nothing to fear; none of us would tolerate any leaks. 'Silence is golden!' was a fundamental principle in this primeval forest.

But the doctor was not the only *saklutschoni* in this camp. In the administration offices there was an older gentleman who served as a messenger. The only thing we knew about him was that he was a counter-revolutionary at the time of the revolution. He was one of the few who survived the big forest fire that had raged here. No one went near him. He said nothing and smiled little. That was it.

Another, a man in his forties, already grey, served in the rations storehouse. I became aware of him when I was limping on the way to the *bania* while whistling a Viennese tune.

'Comrade, are you from Vienna?' he said to me in German. Rather delighted, I just stood there and asked him how he surmised that.

'Really, did you think I have never been to Vienna? Do you know the Weissen Hahn in Josefstadt [a district in the centre of Vienna] or the Café Siller on the waterfront? You know, there were times I flew from Riga to Stockholm, Berlin, Amsterdam, Paris, etc. ...' He listed all the great cities of Europe that he had visited.

I whispered into his ear, 'And why are you here?'

'I was a wholesale merchant in Riga. During the occupation of the Baltic states our families were torn away from each other one night, and I left carrying only two suitcases of belongings in my hands. Today, I naturally only have what I am wearing. I was sentenced to ten years' hard labour for being a member of the bourgeoisie. I am a Jew, I speak five languages, I am a business school graduate, and now I weigh out bran and millet as part of the daily rations. Of all the acquaintances I made in the first few days of my captivity, almost all are now dead. We felled thousands of trees, slaving away and starving to death. There are hardly any left now. I am a Jew. Maybe you are fascist, maybe not. One day you will go home, but I have lost my homeland for ever.'

With those words he left, touching his index finger to his lips.

Another Balt sat in the storeroom. He was always very concerned with doing his job in the prescribed manner. He was a splendid person. One day when I was the only one with him I asked, 'Why?'

He shook his head and said: 'Don't ask … By the way, are you a communist?'

'No.'

'No, and neither am I, you see?'

Any further questions were pointless. He stuffed his homemade pipe with *machorka* and he appeared lost in thought as he looked out of the window. He had also been sentenced to fifteen years.

In this vast territory of exiles there was allegedly a small city that had been quickly built and inhabited by freed or pardoned *SK*. Out of forced labour a penal colony had developed. They were given a piece of land or a place to work, and they were also allowed to take a wife and raise a family. However, they were not permitted to leave the area.

We were told that a Soviet culture brigade would come to us from there. It was supposed to be a special surprise. They would sing, dance and act. It was meant to increase our work output and morale.

This long-anticipated brigade finally came, escorted by Russian police guards with fixed bayonets. They carried their own instruments and meagre baggage. They were accommodated in the lobby of the club barracks; they spent the night not on bunks or beds, but on the floor and on tables, husband and wife together, something that must not have been disagreeable to them. You would only meet this culture command in this way, since it was otherwise kept in a separate labour camp. They called one of them the 'Seven-Metre-Lady', allegedly because she cut 7 [cubic] metres of wood in a single day. She was a cabaret singer by profession.

In the evening, we assembled in the 'club'. It was a barracks just like all the others, only it stood empty; on one end a makeshift stage was built. Bedsheets from sickbay served as the curtains. For lighting they brought all the available oil lamps from the commandant. For the distinguished guests, officers, etc., benches were carried in. The forest workers, for whom the event was intended, were way too tired and after reporting to the 'club', they left. Sleep was far more important to them.

A few work team leaders, the senior men in the barracks, office duty workers, as well as a scattering of those who were convalescing, and several members of the *Schlappkommando* could be found there. An authentic jazz band played. They weren't bad at all. Male and female artists sang solos or duets of a variety of songs, most of which were melodies from Kalman [Imre Kálmán, a Hungarian composer who was influential in Viennese operettas]. They performed Cossack dances and other national dances in colourful costumes.

They also performed a stage play, the contents of which I couldn't quite follow. It had to do with scenes from the present war, and especially the evil deeds done by the *nemtsy* and 'Fritzi'. Poetry, both solemn and light-hearted in style, was recited, and the Seven-Metre-Lady sang Russian hit songs.

Our dear doctor also stood in a corner and listened enthusiastically. He knew virtually all the performers from having cut wood with them, and as exiles they shared with him the same destiny. As professional artists they had the advantage of being able to relax from time to time, and to provide entertainment as they moved from camp to camp.

They were fed from our kitchen. They received the same portions as those who were sick. White *kapusta* and some potatoes and fat were in the soup; in addition, they had roasted grain patties. I was familiar with these patties because the medic from Revier, a Styrian [Styria is an Austrian state in south-east Austria which extended into Slovenia during the Austrian Empire], gave me them sometimes when the critically ill were unable to eat.

I enjoyed the music and the dances, even though I was not familiar with them. It would be fine with me if the culture brigade came more often. I then heard from the senior man that in the future there would be a monthly performance for the best workers, and the artists would be invited for those events.

The cook, a German, described for us how such a reward would happen. He had even received instructions to set aside a little flour and millet each day.

There was something else that we did not expect. The 'prize winner' would be served from what was being set aside. There was nothing we could do about this. If a team leader brought forward a complaint, he would be sharply reprimanded, and he would be blamed for his people being dissatisfied. If he refused to remain silent despite this reprimand, he would be labelled impudent and he would be deposed as team leader. With this in mind, most would back down.

The worst of the winter storms came to an end. I managed to make it through these terrible times without having to march on my hurt leg. From all our barracks there was only one brigade that continued to work, of 100 men a total of eighteen. Everyone else was either sick or on light duty. Nevertheless, the commander continued to press us to fulfil the monthly plan, which was an impossibility.

It was understandable, given that not once did anyone receive a sufficient quantity of dark grain. It would be quite some time before we received enough food to work. It would even have been in the Russians' best interest. There was no sense in giving people barely enough to survive, simply to end up sending them to an *O.K. Lager* [Austrian concentration camp], where it would actually be easier for them to survive on the same amount.

Suddenly the news broke: Vienna had fallen.

In the evening, all those living in the camp were gathered on the parade ground, where the commander delivered a solemn speech on the news. Italians, Romanians, Hungarians and Jews clapped with enthusiasm. Perhaps it was because the commanding officer was illustrating it. Among us, only the antifascists were clapping, two or three people. The rest of us just stood there calmly and listened to all of it. On the one hand it was encouraging that the war was coming to an end; the news that Vienna had fallen and Soviet troops were before Berlin. On the other hand, the news filled us with regret. These same Russians, whose character we had come to learn here in every nuance, were now in the centre of Vienna and would rule the city. We did not want to think about it, although we could only imagine how they were behaving.

21

The War is Over

In a shrill voice, the commander asked why the Germans and the Austrians weren't clapping. Our interpreter shrugged his shoulders and said that he didn't know.

'Ask them!' the very incensed Russian said in a harsh tone.

But there was nothing he could get us to say. Who was going to compel us to applaud? Enraged, the old man left the area. He wasn't going to harm us, because he needed our manpower to fulfil the monthly quota.

One evening, a *sobranje* was suddenly scheduled in the 'club', for all Austrians. Attendance was mandatory! The first time. Illoschenko [the commander] began with a harangue. It turned out, however, to be rather relaxed. He excused our behaviour, even that we were incorrigible fascists, but he said that one day we would come to see the light, and what was more … He proceeded to give a detailed report of the glorious advance of the Red Army along the Danube, from Budapest to Vienna. A Burgenländer [from Austria] translated the commander's speech, during which the majority of those in the audience slept. We had actually expected the worst insults, especially since the Russian did not usually restrain himself from using vulgarities, but after an hour the assembly simply dispersed.

Day by day the sun began to radiate stronger and warmer rays, melting the snow. My foot had also got noticeably better over the past month, as I began receiving vitamin C tablets from the Americans. As luck would have it, I was once again named a team leader because newer troop arrivals were sent to surrounding camps.

We were already expecting the war to end any day. One morning, it was a rainy day, the Romanian commandant raced through the camp shouting, 'The war is over! The war is over! Germany has surrendered!'

Then the barracks really came alive. The lamest crawled from their bunks and eagerly debated the long-awaited news. Dances of joy were performed by those who thought our release was near.

The commander strutted through the barracks and officially announced the Red Army and the Allies had triumphantly ended the war. The *upravlenje*, the headquarters for the camps, even gave us the day off!

Some began making the most amazing plans. There was no shortage of pessimists, but on this day they were the minority. Nevertheless, they remained very pessimistic about the future.

'What do you all think? That because the SU [Soviet Union] has won the war, we will be fully supplied by them? That we prisoners of war can do what we really want to do for the first time? Our homeland is certain to be in chaos, like never before. No one is going to grieve for us there. We will remain here to serve in this isolated wilderness for many more years. Who knows how many of us will survive?'

Others were afraid that we would become like the *saklutschoni*. Then, no one would know of our existence here. When they forced us to settle here, what could we do?

It is not good for someone to be so pessimistic, in my opinion. The war was over, and now was not the time to lose hope. True, it remained to be seen whether or not we would be allowed to write home. Maybe we would even receive mail from home now that there was no longer any front lying between us. But how was a letter to find its way here? For practical purposes it was inconceivable. I was convinced that none of my relatives knew about my fate. Since submitting the one card that I was allowed to mail, a full two years had passed. No answer. In the west, I believed, my friends certainly had the chance to communicate. Where was the much-vaunted International Red Cross that was so much discussed by the people during peacetime? Russia was a member of the Geneva Conventions! Did war toss all the agreements and laws of civilisation overboard?

[In fact, the author was mistaken. Russia was not a signatory of the Third Geneva Convention (1929), which covered prisoners of war, because it did not agree to all the terms, including the inspection of prison camps during war. Other stipulations of the treaty included a prohibition against dangerous work for prisoners, sending and receiving postcards to and from family members, and that the release of prisoners should be part of the armistice agreement.]

22

Hard Labour Continues

The Russians were completely indifferent to the concerns we brought up. When we started becoming a nuisance to them, they merely replied that it was our fault that we were here.

As we soon learned, instead of [the end of the war] making things easier, severe disciplinary measures were taken. Administrative changes were also carried out. The prisoners were combined into a single work battalion. A prisoner of war was named the battalion commander, and a company and platoon leader were assigned. Sometimes these positions were held by guards. Insignia were introduced: from the platoon leader on up they took the form of letters. As customary, each prisoner had the letters WP in the Cyrillic alphabet sewn onto their sleeves: Prisoner of War. The designation 'brigade' disappeared.

Roll call became more militaristic than ever. The platoon leader accompanied the company commander, and they accompanied the battalion commander. With this, determining the number of those absent went much more quickly. The company commanders had the most to do; they were responsible for the entire office staff. The order in the barracks, the serving of meals, roll call duty, all of these things belonged to them.

The underlying cause for all these measures lay in the increasing number of those refusing to work. The company commanders, who most often were the barracks' *starschina*, were held responsible for all those going to work. After the march to work began, the platoons provided their report to the company commander. The commander checked the count, both the sick list as well as the count of those marching off to work. Woe to those commanders when the counts did not match. If they were in any way lower [than they should have been], then the company commander had to take charge of finding the missing man. There were always a few nooks where prisoners would hide, in the *bania*, under the bunks, behind the latrine, near the fire house, etc.

A few days later, one man again went missing, a Romanian. He was nowhere to be found. The Romanian company commander searched desperately throughout the entire camp. There, in the corner of the camp, they found a small, inconspicuous wooden shack that was occasionally used for carpentry work. At that time its principal purpose was the camp morgue. When someone died, he was brought there during the day, because burials were only conducted at night. And that only occurred when there were enough people to bury. Gorgescu, the company commander, began walking towards the shack for the dead. Perhaps his runaway was inside? As he peeped through the keyhole he saw three bodies lying peacefully next to one another. As he opened the door, the one lying in the middle rose up; terrified that he would be beaten, he begged for mercy. Flogging, even in the camp, was customary for the Romanians.

The other two remained at peace. They never had to work again. The camp commandant, whom the runaway was brought to, must have been laughing to himself. This man was literally lying between two corpses simply to hide himself. In reality it was a tragic truth, that one of the company would prefer to live among the dead.

From then on, each *otkaschtschik*, meaning someone who refused to work, was regarded as a saboteur, locked up and placed on half-rations. The cases also multiplied where people would injure themselves in order to not be able to work. One gashed his lower leg with an axe, another used it to strike his toes through his boots, and a third cut off three of his fingers. In each case of self-mutilation the individual was charged, without any review as to whether it might have been an accident. The *karzer* was the punishment.

The pressure became more severe. There was a proclamation: anyone in the future who self-mutilated would come before a summary court martial and he should expect a sentence of no less than ten years. Those concerned would be expelled from the prisoner-of-war camp and deported to an *SK* camp.

This was how the end of the war was supposed to look? Deported to an *SK* camp? Yes, that is precisely what we feared the most. The mere idea of being alone to live among banished Russians was incomprehensible. Or was this simply a precursor to making all of us exiles?

This decree on self-inflicted wounds was written in all languages and posted in the barracks.

The result of this was that just two days later one of the men hanged himself during the night with his braces. He was found lying halfway off the bunk beneath, his comrade above him. This German had never feigned weakness, but at that moment he must have been overcome with immense despair, deciding that he no longer wanted to live in this camp.

My foot began to fester anew in another spot. The kind doctor placed me on the sick list again. As a result, the commander placed me in charge of the *Schlappen*, who were supposed to be moved to a newly prepared accommodation. He gave several directives all at once: the barracks were supposed to be treated with sulphur [for its anti-bacterial properties] and freshly cleaned. The bunks were to be partially torn out, transported by wagon and used to construct bunk beds with more space between them. 'Specialists' were used to do this. I supervised, as best I could, the course of work. A house painter offered to create a mural once the whitewashing was completed. Medicine was used to create dyes.

When the art was more or less finished the commander came to have a look. He was pleased, and he even promised bedsheets, pillows and freshly filled straw mattresses. That would certainly feel good to the sick. The main thing, I thought, was that we were well fed. Unfortunately, I couldn't really say that. Then the commander announced we would have healthy meals.

Just as he was getting ready to leave the barracks, he pointed angrily with his finger at the painting. He was very agitated, and expressed his displeasure in a rather unexpected degree. I didn't quite understand why he was so angry. I only heard him repeat the word: bourgeois … bourgeois …! Then I realised what was wrong; the good painter had created his caricature with a big belly.

'We don't have big bellies,' screamed the commander, 'only

capitalist countries have this, where the bourgeois is at home. This is a product of your minds!'

I tried to reassure him that the painting would be changed. Nevertheless, he was still full of rage, and with an expression of the utmost contempt he spat on the floor. As is quite common with Russians, he cursed at us without giving us a chance to respond and he left the barracks.

Things happened slowly for life in the camp, but there was a noticeable transformation. On one hand with regard to discipline; on the other with regard to our rations. The quantity was not changed, but the quality improved. The standard portion was 30 to 40 grams (1 ounce to 1½ ounces) of pork fat placed 'on the hands' – '*naruke*'. The soup became tastier. Most of the time it was fish soup that was so well cooked that the fish bones, head, tail and innards could be eaten. Sometimes salted raw fish was distributed *naruke*. We even experienced dried, salted camel meat. Instead of bran there was millet or gruel.

More attention was paid to cleanliness and routine in the barracks. Eventually, every man was able to lie on his own mattress. By the express order of the commander, no one was permitted to lie on the floor, although many preferred to do so because they were less affected by the bugs. The barracks were no longer over capacity. Anyone written as *schlapp* was immediately expelled. Each man possessed one or two satchels, a pillow and a pillowcase. There were no bedsheets.

The company commander had to ensure carefully that each man washed and was stripped of his clothes when he 'went to bed'. The floor, which had been repaired, was carefully cleaned and required to be kept in order.

The barracks also began to be fumigated with sulphur. Sealing up the room was very challenging, because hardly any glass actually fitted the small windows. The workforce was billeted in another barracks, and three small heaps of brimstone were placed on the floor and surrounded by earthwork. It was a wonder that the sulphur did not ignite the wood. The only thing remaining were black circles. But that didn't bother us here.

The prisoners also contributed to decorating the camp. Each, according to their nation, painted an image of their homeland on the rear wall. For the Austrians we saw a rolling hilly landscape, for the Hungarians it was the Puszta with its tall wells, and for the Italians it was the sea and a small harbour town. What the Romanian picture was supposed to symbolise was difficult to discern. It displayed a strong peasant dressed in national costume next to a house, and somewhat disjointedly, a pair of hens. Something else looked like a bouquet of flowers, but it could also have been some bushes.

What was the reason for this? Why were they trying to make things more homely and feed us better? Some of us believed, and hoped, that we would soon be repatriated to our homeland, but before doing so they wanted to put us in a condition that was fit for human beings. Others, however, were convinced this was only occurring in order to increase our capacity to work so they could exploit us longer. It proved to be that the prisoners of war were more willing, and by far better, workers than the *saklutschoni* and other coerced labourers.

One evening I was sitting with the comrades in the O.K.-barracks [Austrian barracks]. We were talking about our different experiences as prisoners of war. It came to light that one of the comrades had been in the same hospital where I had been. He experienced the closing of this hospital. What he told us was very interesting.

'Weeks ago, before it was closed there were rumours that the military hospital would be abandoned. It was almost exclusively the critically ill who remained. Literally, overnight, it was determined to shut it down. The few medics and all those who were at least able to stand on their own feet were used to gather together the blankets and linen. The rest of the inventory, wooden bunks, etc., were thrown out of the window and into the yard. Iron beds and tables were carried down so that the rooms were completely cleared out.

'It rained continually when we evacuated. A number of *panje* horses pulled up in front of the hospital, loaded with hay or straw. Steed, man and wagon were dripping with water. Those too sick to walk, TB cases, those with gastric disorders and others were dressed in some way or another, whether the clothes fitted or not. They made a pathetic impression. Like a coat hook, everything was hung on them.

'The critically ill were placed on stretchers and laid on the wet hay. You can imagine how those with fevers felt. But orders are orders, and it was impossible to delay the transport until more favourable weather arrived. Any success the hospital had had in caring for the sick was wiped out in a single blow. The absurdity of it all was irrefutable. Only days before, we had been given every possible injection and treatment to preserve life, and now every sanitary measure was thrown overboard.

'Those capable of marching went along the long road to the train station by foot, and those going there on the vehicles were laid on the wet grass during the distribution of rations.

'In the vicinity of the train station we were housed in a large hall and we had to wait three days before we were loaded. There was one female doctor and a nurse there, but they didn't do much to look after anyone. The rations for the entire transport were passed out to a few German medics, three days' total, who administered them at their discretion. Our numbers declined because the evacuation had accelerated the deaths of many, if not caused them. During the transport a few more died. The majority were then placed in a hospital for prisoners of war, and I was only there a short time. Then I was sent along with other comrades capable of working to a labour camp, and that is how I ended up here.'

I was glad that I had not participated in this evacuation. I had not missed anything.

Another told about his experiences in the Plesetskaja Labour Camp in Onega [a town in the north-west of Russia, near Arkangel] on the northern railway. Similar to us, they also had camp after camp, overcrowded with *SK* and prisoners of war. The working conditions and rations were likewise miserable. A third was in the Bessanovskiy Labour Camp in Kuybyshev [Samara, at the confluence of the Volga and Samara rivers in the south-west of Russia]. There, also, Russians worked as slaves. A few in our company had also been brought here from central Siberia.

The forced labour system was, as we discovered, a type of slavery present everywhere. It constituted a well-organised network, requiring a colossal effort of administrative authorities and an army of guards to ensure the coerced system operated properly.

The system had to be directed so that it was rational for the state. The men had to produce far more than was required to simply exist. That was the basic requirement for slavery to be profitable. The idea of slavery was not new, but at this time in the Soviet Union it was mostly designed to develop the state culturally and, in addition, to make it more 'socialistic' and 'progressive'.

Coerced labour, as an educational measure, had already been supported by the author Maxim Gorki, and Stalin had borrowed the idea from tsarist times. It was probably only further expanded and streamlined. [Maxim Gorky (1868–1936) was an apologist for the 'gulag'. According to historian Paul Johnson, author of *Modern Times* (Harper & Row, 1983), the Cheka, which reported directly to Lenin, began operating concentration and labour camps by the end of 1917. This was 'the nucleus of what was to become the gigantic "Gulag Archipelago"' (Johnson, *Modern Times*, p. 69).]

We asked ourselves repeatedly how, one day, the Soviet Union was going to justify this to the outside world. Even though this area was so isolated, eventually it would become known to the general public. For our own sakes, we hoped this was something unimportant to the Russians; otherwise, they would never let any of us leave.

Freeing ourselves was out of the question, neither for the Russian exiles nor the prisoners of war. It rarely happened that anyone even tried. Fourteen days previously, two had attempted, only to be tracked down by dogs. They were shot. The soldier who gunned the escapees down was nevertheless punished. It turned out the two had voluntarily surrendered themselves to the guards in the woods, and in spite of this he fired into the group.

The guards, who were with us at the time, were anything but good to the people. How often it was that they kicked us with their feet and struck us in the face with their fist; on our backs or anywhere else, they hit us. The reason was always the same: the *desertnik* [*desjatnik*] could not report back until everyone had fulfilled their quota, even when it was eight or nine in the evening. The guard, however, wanted to go home. He would walk around the work site to see who wasn't finished. Then he would get his club. The platoon leader was powerless to do anything about it. If he tried to protect his people, the guard would strike him across the lower back.

It wasn't until the beginning of June that the snow was all gone. The woods were humid and wet. The felt boots were exchanged for well-worn shoes. The better footwear was taken from the *Schlappen*. They received a type of bast shoes [shoes from bast, a fibre made from the bark of certain trees], a few of which were woven by us out of birch bark. There were also wooden shoes with the top made out of sailcloth.

The humidity would last a minimum of a month. I knew this from the previous year. Thus, the woodcutters would stand the entire day with their worn shoes in the wet ground, and in the evening, they would march the way home in feet that were soaked. As a result, nearly all feet became raw from the chafing. But the doctor was not permitted to write anyone down as sick. It was said that we sometimes did this intentionally. Our toes would be wrapped in some bandagers – and the next day we would leave again – at least until the feet either healed or went septic, in which case he had to write us down as sick.

I continued to have duty with the *Schlapp* command and I saw the tired expressions each evening as they staggered through the door. Not one of them held his head high. Nevertheless, the commander required them to march in step, and to sing a marching song as they returned. If the company did not sing, then they had to go back out of the gate, and the officer on duty ordered them to goose-step. You couldn't look at them because it was torture. Wounded feet, exhausted from the demanding work, hungry, and hopelessly depressed, they marched as in a parade. At the same time, the Russians were laughing.

One day, all of a sudden and without warning, I received six hours in the *karzer*. Two Romanians went headfirst into the soup vat to scrape out the remaining scraps with their spoons. The old man saw it, screaming as he came towards me from across the yard, and he relieved me of my duty. That evening, however, a ruckus broke out in the barracks because no one was controlling the distribution of meals. Then I was hurriedly fetched out of my confinement. I then learned the reason I had been disciplined: *Eta nje Kulturrje* [This is not civilised] – 'that's not done here.' I had to take greater care that such things – like what had happened with the two Romanians, did not occur.

The detention cell was not exactly comfortable. The hut had a pungent, overpowering smell. With its very heavy wooden grating, the room was almost dark, and on the single bunk one could think about his sins. There was no toilet. In one of the corners was a bucket …

As the guard said to me, it was supposed to be better than the detention cell for officers.

Several in my *Schlappen* group developed jaundice. A few of them were even admitted to sickbay. As we were carrying one of them, I heard a dreadful shriek from the clinic.

As I came into the entranceway, I saw two Italians who appeared to be drunk. When I looked at them I broke out laughing, because the two friends were behaving as if they had had too much to drink. How was it that they could be intoxicated? One of them was completely smashed, and his words were so slurred they were unintelligible.

The doctor entered with a hose and a bowl in order to empty his stomach. He yelled at the man and slapped him across the face. The normally calm doctor was very agitated, and he did not hold himself back. But the two men did not react at all. The German doctors were summoned, because our doctor could not insert the tube by himself. Combining their strength, they finally managed to insert the tube.

I could not watch this procedure because the doctor handled these patients more roughly than any he had before.

I then learned that it was not alcohol which had caused this stupor, but that the Italians had eaten plants in the woods that poisoned them. The doctor did everything possible to treat them and to bring them around. But there is no question that the methods he used were rather unusual.

After an hour it could be said the operation was a success, the patients were only half dead. It took a few days before their health was restored.

As a result, the commander issued an order that it was strictly forbidden to eat any uncooked food or to bring anything into the camp. A good many had adopted the practice of enriching and thickening their soup with 'vegetables'.

The 'collection of vegetables' was organised. I was given permission to take ten men, without a guard, into a deforested area, where a particular type of rhubarb-like plants grew. They had long stalks and purple-coloured blossoms. In no time at all we filled five sacks which we carried into the kitchen. The plants were chopped up, and in the evening a thick, gelatinous, lilac-coloured soup was served. The wishes of many were fulfilled, the soup was thicker and it contained vitamins.

The people were kept busy planting potatoes. Here also there was a quota to fulfil. In this way, the *Schlappen* would receive more bread. My task was to walk about and make sure the *Schlappen* were not eating the seed potatoes they were given to plant.

We were ordered to cultivate a large perimeter all at once. The digging up of the terrain was done on our free days, because we were told all the rations concerned would be solely for our benefit. However, we would gladly have done it if it meant we would be sent home.

This *rasgartschovka*, or the cultivation of the soil, was very exhausting. Because wherever the soil was moist, there were also birch roots fanning out throughout the ground, and these were very difficult to remove. Each team had to – on their free days – clear a specific amount of rootstock. A fire was lit under the difficult roots so as to burn the main root, and only then would we dig up those that branched out.

Around the camp we tilled 2 to 3 hectares (approximately 7 to 7½ acres) of ground. The one free day was no longer sufficient to manage the amount of work. For this reason, everyone was placed onto a team which would work on construction. The 50-percenters, who were limited in how much they could do, were put to work clearing the soil as soon as they had finished their soup. The work was truly torture.

Behind every work was a quota; otherwise you would not get any bread, you could not return to the camp, you would not be dismissed, and all kinds of other threats.

From this predicament, the following scam developed that spread like a cancer. The 'digger' left the roots but concealed them in order to finish. The planter, equipped with nothing more than a Wehrmacht spade, which was limited in its use, would move beyond the 'digger'; otherwise, he would have had to dig up the roots and as a consequence he would be held back. He [the planter] would get even by going to where the ground was mostly even, and without working the garden he would simply toss dirt around. The seed planter, who was supposed to furrow the ground and sow the seeds, would pass by his predecessor when he discovered the ground was rock hard. In that way, he would help perpetuate this fraud in that he did not place any seeds in their holes.

This is a shining example of what I learned about coerced labour.

I hope that things were different among the renowned Stachanov workers [Alexei Stakhanov (1906–77) was a Soviet miner and hero of the Socialist Labour Movement].

The 'sabotage' that was practised here was not really all that terrible. As we heard, things were far worse among the Russians in the *SK* camps. In those camps, forced labour and the resulting work scams were already a tradition.

23

Release and Replacements

We were standing at roll call like we did every evening, waiting for the camp commander, who finally appeared swearing and agitated. Was it the vodka that made his voice so loud? No, he was pushing a prisoner in front of him. It was our little Romani, the fiddle player from the military hospital. '*Swinia, swinia*' ['Swine, swine' – worse than a pig], the commander said, insulting him again and again, and demanding he show what he had in his pockets. Then the Gypsy, quite dumbfounded and knees trembling, pulled the long tail of a big rat out of his pocket. The commander said he was trying to roast it when a guard caught him. He received a few days in the *karzer* as punishment.

We had to laugh, even though we felt sorry for the little Romani. He was certainly not the first to try cooking a rat. The Italians regretted what happened to him the most, because we knew they were the ones killing off the cats that were the *natschalnik magazina* [chief prosecutors] of the rats and mice. They never lived long.

For quite some time a rumour circulated that the Italians were supposed to be released to go home. It was actually true. These 130 men could hardly believe it. They were totally crazy with joy. I felt the same way. How wonderful to get out of this forest, and not be seen or heard from again!

We had our doubts, however, whether these wretched figures would actually be sent over the border. But it was really happening. One day after a short search they were gathered by the gate, hooting as they went forth in their tattered clothes. Great was the surprise when one day we heard they would be returning to forest work. But the cause for this was only due to the delay in transport, which would eventually take place. Two Italians who were very ill were taken along on a stretcher. Unfortunately, as we heard, one of them died before being loaded onto the train.

I was astonished, therefore, that a number of days later I saw several Italians in uniform through the fence, all our honourable old friends. I called to them and asked why they were returning. But they were unable to talk; they were completely despondent. I eventually learned they had been held back while loading. The NKVD had their obscure reasons to stop the journey home.

One could only imagine the kind of awful depression this caused, to have your hope shattered that you would leave this godforsaken region. They had already vested themselves emotionally in a reunion with their loved ones; they believed they had finally turned their backs and would never return to this land. With one blow this vision had been shattered, and they were worse off than before, because they did not know what would become of them. They felt forsaken, and for the most part, they were separated from their comrades.

They surely owed their thanks for this misfortune to one or another of their own comrades, who they denounced for having shamefully informed on them. As before, the Russians used every available means to track down any 'war criminals', and one of the most common methods consisted of offering bread and soup to the half-starved as an incentive to betray another comrade.

Shortly after the Italians were sent away, a new exciting rumour reached our ears. German National Socialists of the highest rank, *Gauleiter* and those of similar stature, were supposed to come to our camp in order to fill the gaps. [*Gau* was an old German name for a district, and *Leiter* is a leader. It was brought back into use under the Nazis. The *Gauleiter* was a high-ranking regional leader in the Nazi Party.] An additional 'cattle market' was conducted, and anyone who was *schlapp*, sick and unable to work, would immediately be deported to another camp. In this way, four barracks would be freed up. From this, we concluded that an impressive number would arrive. We looked forward to this transport with great anticipation, because we hoped to receive the latest news from home about the end of the war.

Personally, I was not pleased with these changes, because I feared losing my 'splendid position' overseeing the *Schlappen*. The commander, however, did not send me to work, but instead kept me back to serve as a translator.

The catchword on the coming transports was then revised: no party bigwigs or civilian prisoners of war; rather soldiers who were taken prisoner after the surrender.

One day the German-speaking company commanders and a few translators were called to appear before the camp commander.

'Tomorrow evening a 400-man *étape* [group of replacement troops] is coming. They will temporarily be housed in three empty barracks. The fourth will remain free. It is forbidden to speak a word to the new arrivals, except as required by your duties. Whoever is caught doing so will be severely punished. *Poniatna* – understood?'

He then divided us into teams of two sentries for each of the three barracks, emphatically forbidding us to allow any contact between the new arrivals and the older camp prisoners.

We knew there was something not quite right with this order. Perhaps there was something political behind it?

Around ten in the evening the first ones arrived. I had duty in the first barracks and saw how the camp commander, surrounded by guards and camp officers, assigned the first 130 men. Despite the darkness I was able to make out a well-equipped German company, only without weapons, marching in. It was so overcrowded that I had to pack them in like sardines. At the same time, they had a thousand questions for me, but I remained silent because the Russians were standing behind me. I couldn't risk it. I indicated I was not allowed to say anything and I only answered official questions. The new arrivals looked at me somewhat sceptically and they could not work out who it was who stood before them.

The overcrowding created an insane heat, and the bedbugs began a major offensive. The first screams and moans rang out, but there was nothing I could do to help.

At midnight I was able to get soup for the new *étape*. They received their little servings of soup with shiny mess tins and cutlery. The dim light was sufficient to see that they still had not been subjected to pillaging. Most of them were wearing wristwatches, and they had rucksacks, cloaks, boots and shoes.

Despite the ban on discourse, I now learned they were what remained of General Schnörner's forces, ending up in Czechoslovakia [General Ferdinand Schnörner was a commander on the Eastern Front in Russia; he served as the last Commander-in-Chief of the German Army during World War II]. In the tens of thousands, they arrived at transit camps in the vicinity of Kladno [central Bohemian region in the current Czech Republic], and from there they travelled by train directly here. They did not know where they were, and for the time being I did not say anything. They would learn soon enough.

It was probably two or three in the morning when the Russian sarge of the garrison called out to me. I knew him and I knew that he was not one of the worst. I also sensed that he wanted something. He came out with it pretty quickly.

'You know, this is a *novi* [new] *étape*, and they still have many *tschassi-uhra* [pocket watches] out of Germania. Get one for me. I will give *machorka* and *chleb*. An entire loaf for one watch.'

I understood him. But if the camp commander caught me, then my neck was on the line. I promised to take a look and I asked him to come back the next evening. However, he wouldn't leave me alone because he was now on duty, he said he would supervise everything, and now offered him the best chance.

So, I went back into the barracks and I attempted to initiate the deal. That's when the reason for all this secrecy became clear to me. The new ones had to be guarded and isolated so the camp commander could conduct the plundering all by himself. The clever sarge had anticipated this. At least he was offering bread in exchange.

Most of the new ones were awake. The poor accommodations, heat and bedbugs made it impossible for them to sleep. I began a conversation with one of them immediately. He had three watches on him and he gladly gave up two of them, because he had gone mostly hungry since he was captured, even though it was not that long ago.

I reported the agreement to the sarge. He exited the zone at once and returned shortly through the gate, two loaves of bread hidden under his coat. Bread and watches were exchanged. The *starschina* patted me happily on the shoulders and sent me a pouch of *machorka*.

Early in the morning, the camp commander appeared with two officers and guards and went into the barracks. Then the pilfering began. Although I was exhausted, I remained nonetheless so that I could watch the drama. One notices with the Russians how heartily they laugh as they gather 'trophies', especially when it is without a fight. Bags were filled with cigarette lighters, flashlights, leather trousers, spare shoes and boots, fountain pens, clothes brushes, mechanical pencils, billfolds, shoehorns, combs, etc. as they were snatched. The watches and other valuables were placed separately. I was amazed how these last of Hitler's soldiers still had everything on them. They were probably the ones behind the 'organising' in the last days of the war.

Now the commandant and his officers appeared entirely different. As if transfigured, they strutted through the camp. They now possessed things they could only dream about owning.

The camp commander availed himself of a gold Montblanc pen [Montblanc is a German manufacturer known for its quality pens and other luxury goods]. He also exhibited a superior mien as he looked periodically at his newly 'acquired' Swiss watch, and when he walked through the camp in the evening, he would constantly turn on his pocket dynamo as a source of light.

He thought nothing of it. These *nemtsy* were maleficent men who had everything, and despite this they had lost the war?

Despite all the precautions, rumours began to spread like wildfires in the barracks. The new men were trying to conceal things wherever possible. But the plundering was complete. Even though the watches were hidden in every nook and cranny, it didn't help. Boards were turned over, planks were lifted up off the floor, bunks were dismantled, and the Russians would smirk contentedly whenever a small ring or other valuable saw the light of day. They would exchange vodka with one another, and for some time the old man was not at all sober.

In my barracks the successful plunder was concluded with bartering, and they smartly handed over trifling objects to other camp inmates.

After the dismay of the new comrades over their treatment, it first occurred to them how badly our work details made us look. They could not believe that it was like this for prisoners of war. I just stood there and thought to myself, you poor men, it will not take long and you will look no different, and perhaps even worse, than us.

Out of their sheer joy and happiness, the camp leadership apparently forgot about the monthly plan, because it was three or four days before the new *étape* received their assignments.

After four days the new prisoners of war were just as poor as us. From toothbrushes to safety pins, they forfeited everything. The Russians thought they should not be burdened with such things when they went to work.

I was present when the assignments were made. It was a relief to see men before us again. Of the older camp inmates, not one of them would be considered a 100-percenter; they were working vegetables, a physical wreck. The difference was now readily apparent to me.

How long would the new ones endure? The commandant was extremely pleased with the physical condition of the new troops. The teams consisted of nothing but 100-percenters. I couldn't help but say to the commander – permit me to make an observation as an old camp member – it will not take two months before the majority of the *étape* will be useless in the forest.

'*Ti durak* – You idiot,' he called me. 'That's not going to happen.' I remained silent; he would see soon enough. The environment, rations and quarters would contribute to this. The new ones could not be compared to us, because we were already fully adapted.

The first week the quota was lowered in order for the new ones to get used to the work. That was something completely novel. Up to that point, nothing like that had happened.

With the regrouping I was moved to company commander. I had a lot to do, including seeing to and dealing with the worries and complaints of the new arrivals. The battalion and company commanders were now given permission to depart and enter the gate without an accompanying guard. That way, it was easier for us to help our teams.

So we went virtually every day, after the barracks were put in order, to the *proisvotsvo*, literally the 'operation', which was better understood as the work site. Our presence was supposed to direct the work. I spent most of my time where the need was the greatest and I could be of the most assistance, whether it was felling the trees, sawing the wood into logs, or stacking them.

We were finally able to convince the camp commander that the work could only be done right if the tools were intact. It did not serve our purpose that the prisoners of war had to give the *SK* who worked in the *instrumentalka* [equipment repair] a piece of bread in order to have the saws and axes sharpened for the next day.

As a result, prisoners of war began working in the *instrumentalka*. For every three work teams an *instrumentalnik* would accompany them into the woods, who would make repairs there and then. That support was key and it had a significant impact on the *kubatura* [cubage – unit of measurement for stacked wood – 1 cubic metre]. It was difficult for the camp commander to grasp that this had nothing to do with us being lazy workers, but instead was simply to increase our output, and that it was done in the best interests of the management and the commander.

In time, the woods were only damp in a few places. Along the train tracks it often occurred that sparks would ignite the dry grass, which would set fire to the stacked wood and tree trunks.

One day there was a major fire alarm. From our camp, we could see volumes of smoke that were moving quickly in our direction.

Everything in the camp that could be of use was assembled, and we were issued shovels, hoes and pickaxes to take to the source of the blaze a few kilometres away. The standing trees did not catch fire, but everything around them did: wood that had been left behind, tree trunks, branches and other kindling that had fallen during the summer was piled up and consumed by the fire. As far as the eye could see, smouldering and intense smoke from the burning tree trunks were visible. Fortunately, there was little wind.

In order to avert the peril to the camp, we dug metre-wide ditches and piled up dirt around them. Reinforced by returning work teams, we were able to localise the fire. In the locations where sparks from the fire were jumping the trench, we extinguished them with dirt. The firefighting brigades were continuously replenished. The fire just missed us.

The light railway, built by what prisoners called 'forest whores', which transported the cut wood, has its own story. One day I had the opportunity to see how they laid the track and the cross-ties. The work was only done by the *SK*s, and the pace of work was correspondingly slow and done carelessly. One had to wonder how the *SK* women were able to haul heavy wood, boards and blocks onto the foundation. The cross-ties were as round as the trees they were cut from, and they were laid on the damp, soft ground. Where the ground was too swampy, branches and beams and anything else lying around was placed underneath. Not a single rail was completely straight. For this reason, it was common to have a fully loaded train derail.

Very close to me was a train loaded with wood. The *SK* were heavily guarded. There was approximately one guard for every ten exiles – whereas I, as a prisoner of war and a foreigner, was able to move about freely and unguarded. We were probably seen as less dangerous than their own *SK*. I would like to have known how many cars they had to load in a day. Due to the guards, I could not find that out. I noticed that these lads were stronger than we were. To my knowledge, they received no more or no better food to eat than we did. The larger railcars held about 30 cubic metres of wood.

The train was just about to depart. All the cars were fully loaded.

Two shrill whistles, and eleven heavily loaded wagons pulled by one small locomotive started in motion. Since I was on my way home, and the train was travelling one stretch in the same direction, I ran after it and jumped onto the platform of the last wagon, even though this was forbidden. As I stood up and looked towards the front, I saw the locomotive and railcars moving up and down like they would in a mountain and glacier valley. I thought the locomotive or the railcars would jump the track any moment. The worst stretch was the one most recently laid. The sections of track that had been laid earlier had been repaired a number of times, and then the train could move at a somewhat faster speed. In the meantime, the time had come for me to jump off because my path diverged to the left.

So, I wandered early in the evening across the broad, barren landscape. The only things accompanying me on either side were tree stumps, roots and fallen trees. I had the desire to overcome the silence, so I began to sing as loud as I could, even though no one could hear me. That relaxed me somehow and made me happy. It was of no use to me to be sullen.

I stopped and looked behind me longingly towards the setting sun. How lovely it looked. It was certainly at present shining its warm light upon my homeland. At the time, it was the only connection I had with it. 'Tell them I'm alive!'

But I shouldn't have been sad. We had once again been promised that we were allowed to write home. Specifically, the government was supposed to make pre-printed postcards available. However, we had become great sceptics and we could not believe that the mail service to the homeland was functioning.

As I arrived at the gate, I reported as required. The *starschina*, who was always very friendly towards me, took me aside and whispered into my ear: 'Have you already heard? The first sick troops are being transported back to Germany, and in fact, to Frankfurt an der Oder [about 80 kilometres east of Berlin]. Psst! Don't say anything!'

I was completely beside myself with joy. Was it possible that some of us would be released, even if it was only the sick? It was a beginning, and at a minimum it was a chance to communicate verbally that we were alive.

When I arrived at the barracks, I had to go directly to the camp commander. He addressed me, saying, all those incapable of work were to go before a commission, most notably those with amputated hands and feet, as well as those with incurable scurvy and others who had severe battlefield injuries.

Late in the evening I brought all of those to the doctor, about twenty in number; there were only Germans and Austrians, much to the annoyance of the Romanians and the Hungarians. The men were placed on a separate list, sent to the *bania*, from head to foot – literally – shaved and washed, and were handed fresh underwear for the first time. At daybreak they were given rations for a day and then they left. '*Damoi*' – 'going home' – was the common expression.

The commander sensed my despondency, which I was incapable of hiding completely, and he said, 'Soon it will be your turn.'

If only he was right. I had the feeling, however, as long as a person was healthy and could stand on both feet, the Russians would not volunteer to let him go.

We heard that an entire camp of *Schlappen* were to be sent home. Could they release men in such a starved and emaciated condition? How would that affect Russia's reputation in our homeland? But Germany had lost the war, we were even the aggressor, and the Russians, confident from their victory, probably did not believe they were taking a risk. It did not seem wise to me, but what concern was it of mine? The main thing was we were going home.

Political propaganda was relatively unimportant here. It was even useless, because everything was so dependent upon our work that there was not time to do anything else. In many camps it was supposed to be different. In the view of our commander, the best antifascist was the one who did the most work. When I asked him during one of the recording days whether cooks and antifascists had to cut wood, he snapped at me: 'What is an antifascist here? Fascist or antifascist *seravno* – it does not matter. Everyone must work.'

Among each nationality there were one or two such antifascists, who we baptised *Kashisten* [those who received more porridge]. They were the ones who were supposed to urge us to work harder, and for this reason they received more *kasha*, which is why the name *Kashist* was justified.

Summer was very short here. Sadly, because the warmth did us good, and the onset of winter always frightened us. How many more would there be? I didn't want to think about it, not while the warm sun was shining.

I was spending a lot of time outdoors, helping whenever possible. Work was easier during the summer, as long as the weather was good. Still, our work teams had to go out regardless of the weather. Rain, even if it was raining cats and dogs, was no barrier. How often it happened that the people were completely drenched when they reported back in the evening.

I had noticed for some time that the *SK* brigades were coming into the woods less often. They were increasingly replaced by the prisoners. Only the *desertnik* and those used as foremen and supervisors remained behind. We even heard that they had been replaced as prisoner guards. That was a concern to us, because it appeared things were settling into a permanent state of affairs.

Even taking wood out of the forest and loading it onto the light railcars fell to our work teams. On this occasion, I found out that even the little horses that managed much of the heavy work were classified from one to four, according to their fitness. The horses were fed by the foreman himself; otherwise the oats, whether roasted or unroasted, would go into the bellies of the prisoners instead of the old nags. When the *SK* had them, the horses became weak and broken down before the *SK* did. This was because the horses were left almost without food, so that the *SK* could feed themselves.

24

Women Exiles

The camp commander summoned me about *proisvotsvo* [business]. I was supposed to go to *SK* Camp Z and deliver a letter to the *natschalnik lagera* [camp commandant]. He quickly scribbled a few lines on a little piece of paper, and then he skilfully folded it into a triangle shape – envelopes were unknown here – so that the contents could not be read.

After receiving basic directions, I started off. The commander told me that if I was lucky, I might find an empty car on the light railway line that would take me to the *SK* camp.

Apparently, the old man trusted me, at least more than his fellow countrymen, who never went anywhere without a guard.

After a good hour of walking I reached the light railway line, but I could not see a train for miles around. There was nothing for me to do but continue on my way.

Then suddenly, I heard a locomotive whistle behind me. Using long strides I ran back towards the stretch of railway, because at that moment the train had come to a stop. Another whistle indicated they were using the locomotive to connect another small car to the train. Two of the cars were occupied by *SK*.

Although there was nothing in my appearance that would differentiate me from them, one of them called to me, 'Come, Fritz, ride with us!'

At once, I swung onto one of the *Amerikaner*, which was what they called this wooden car. I was rather restrained in talking with this group who were opposite me. I had learned, just as they had, to be silent. One never knew who was before you, and denunciations were common and dangerous.

The little train moved at a relatively fast clip. Because the locomotive was pushing the cars from behind, there was a greater likelihood of derailment. No one was sitting, everyone stood, ready to jump if things went wrong.

We rode for over half an hour. Suddenly, what happened was as follows: there was a tremendous rumble, and I'm not quite sure how I reacted, but suddenly I landed in a bush. I did not suffer any injuries, but I heard shouts and calls for help. They began to drag a few men out from between the overturned, jammed cars.

But I had already become half Russian: I didn't take much notice; they would get the wagons back on the tracks soon enough. In going on I only thought to myself: once again, how lucky I was that something really bad hadn't happen to me.

The guard at the *SK* camp did not allow me into the zone until I showed him the letter. He showed me the way to the *natschalnik lagera*. On the way I had to go through one of the barracks. What a sight!

It was a women's barrack! How these females looked! It was probably a *Schlapp* brigade. Unkempt and emaciated, they wore grey-white shirts and men's underwear on their bodies, they were barefoot, either lying or sitting on the bunks. Some of them were busy looking for lice, in that they had placed their heads in the lap of another in order to be deloused. These hairstyles! I was already accustomed to many things, but I was appalled. Then one of them called to me from her bunk. More well-rounded, she was the lady of the barrack, and as the supervisor, she did not need to work. I waved politely and I left the room as quickly as I could. I had seen enough. The stench was dreadful.

Compared with that, our men's barracks were highly civilised.

I handed over the letter to a red-haired man with a broad face. He scribbled something in response, and handed me back the sealed letter. Almost hastily, I left the camp. I saw a few figures that looked like sticks crossing the *proverka-platz*. I did not need any further details about the equality of women in Russia; the visual impression alone spoke volumes.

Our doctor had always said that life in an *SK* camp was much, much bleaker than in a prisoner-of-war camp. For this reason, he had no desire to be transferred here. Now I understood what he meant.

My way home no longer led past the work site; instead I took the shortest route and headed directly for the camp.

As I was wandering along the tracks, lost in thought, I heard steps behind me.

Correct, a man was following me. He was surely going the same way. I deliberately slowed my pace, because it was more pleasant to have someone's company.

As he got closer, I asked him, '*Kuda vi* – where are you headed?'

'To the next camp, comrade. You can easily speak German with me. I am an Estonian, and I understand your mother-tongue well enough.'

As he opened his mouth, I saw that he could not be a Russian because his mouth was full of gold teeth. Something was wrong with this picture. I said something regarding my observation. He responded, 'This is also the only possession I have left, and I have often been in danger of having them knocked out.'

He was an electrician and he was working at the time on the telephone line that connected each camp. In his homeland he was the director of a wholesale company. He was shipped here for some obscure reasons.

After we had walked for an extended period of time next to one another without saying anything, he suddenly came to a standstill.

'My friend, do you see these many, countless tree stumps? In the years '41 and '42, everything around here was woods that we chopped down … At that time, so many of us died that today one of us could be lying behind every tree stump! Yes, the starvation was terrible after the war with Hitler began.'

25

Machorka and Bread as Incentives

'The Russians had their hands full on the front lines, and so they forgot about us. Every time we were supposed to get provisions, they failed to appear. Terrible scenes took place in the woods and in the barracks.'

I believed him [the Estonian]. I knew enough about how men behaved towards one another when there was no food. Then he continued. 'You know, I am a *pädiseat voassim* – a fifty-eighter. I will never go home.'

Astonished, I asked, 'What is a fifty-eighter?'

'Fifty-eighters are the political prisoners. Didn't you know that?'

To me, this description using articles and numbers was new.

He was, just the same, envious of me – me, a person to be envied! – because I had a legitimate hope of returning home.

'You must never forget: although you are here in the woods, you are not subject to the Sevurallag NKVD [Sevurallag was a site in the Urals where Estonians were imprisoned]; you only work for these 'firms'. Our headquarters were somewhere near Sverdlovsk [now Yekaterinburg, Sverdlovsk was an NKVD prison camp also located in the Urals; nearly 700 Estonians were executed there in 1942]; when all is said and done, you are subject to a military administration and your highest superiors are military officers. With us, most things were in the hands of civilians, though our guards were from a specially selected police task force. Incidentally, these policemen do not have it easy in the *SK* camps. The guards and the supervisors were repeatedly found dead in the woods. Mind you, there were occasionally rebellions, but they were brief and put down without mercy. Running away was next to impossible, even for the Russians. Many attempted this, but they were either picked up somewhere half-starved, or they were shot during the escape.

'Let me tell you something else. There were even people under us who would rather stay here than return home when they have finished serving their sentence. When it comes to politics, they have much less anxiety here. At home, however, the Sword of Damocles of political persecution is always hanging over them.

'For this reason, many of those in the camp never leave, because they get additional years added to their sentence for the most absurd reasons: insubordination, unsuccessful escapes, theft, sabotage or unauthorised sex extends the *SK* existence here by a decade.'

Meanwhile, we approached the camp and we said farewell to one another.

As I neared the gate there was a huge crowd. A covered stretcher was being brought inside. I asked the first person I saw.

'A Hungarian got caught. A tree hit him from behind right in the middle of the head.'

Yet another one. Unfortunately, it was not uncommon for a comrade to be killed by a falling tree. This was not surprising. Most of the time, the fault lay with the foreman because he did not have enough space between the people. To be sure, it was every person's duty to yell '*boissa*' [*boysya* – 'watch out'] every time a tree was felled, but the splitting of the tree often drowned out the cry, and the next man, who was at the same time busy sawing, unsuspectingly received the death blow from behind. The camp commander cursed like a coachman every time it occurred.

An *SK* called the *natschalnik besopassnesti* [safety observer] was added, whose job it was to prevent accidents. He was supposed to educate the people on the safety measures that were to be taken in forestry work.

Hardly six weeks had passed. Our strong German *étape*, who had been the pride of the commandant upon their arrival, were already showing the characteristics of these woods. As healthy men, each day they were drained of their strength. But now they were in the same category as all the other camp inmates in terms of their quotas. You could see traces of the wrinkles in their faces that resulted from the all-consuming forest work. Their demise was increasing by leaps and bounds.

The camp commandant sent the company commanders into the woods more frequently in order to better organise and encourage the workers. Specifically, he sent us out with 20 grams of *machorka* or two *piroshki*, cabbaged-filled bread rolls (instead of meat), to promise to anyone who cut 4 [cubic] metres of wood.

A new incentive, it could almost be labelled a trick, was introduced. Every morning the cook would come onto the *proverka-platz* with one or more large baked bread cakes. Those brigades which had cut, on average, 2 cubic metres or more per person were awarded them as 'a prize'. This ceremony was regarded as a solemn act by the Commissar. As a result, all the remaining hungry teams looked on with big eyes. It was a tantalising sight, even though these did not have chocolate or marmalade fillings, but simply bread and cabbage. Nevertheless, it did not fail to have an effect. It only made us drive them harder.

It appeared that cabbage was the main staple in Russia. Even when hunger was great, it was still possible to find cabbage.

26

Alexandrov in Frankfurt

One day, we were met in the woods with a particularly encouraging piece of news. American bacon was arriving and would be distributed in the evening.

For a large portion of us, however, this was met with disbelief. Experience had shown us these additional foods were distributed in such small quantities that instead of providing an incentive, it only produced greater hunger.

On a particular errand in my sector, I ran into a Russian guard who was drying tobacco and roasting a couple of potatoes. I took a seat by his small fire. I was very familiar with him, and so I wanted to chat a little.

'How's it going, Alexandrov? I haven't seen you in a long time. Where have you been?'

At this he smiled and said, '*Frankfurte Bill …*' [The meaning of this response is not clear. This was most likely Frankfurt an der Oder, because it was under Soviet administration and it is also mentioned in an earlier chapter.]

'What, you were in Frankfurt? How did you get there?'

'*S'transportem* – I went there with a train transporting the sick. Yes, yes, I was the escort. It took a long time to get there.'

Then he whispered into my ear: 'Over forty died during the transport, but – shush! – don't tell anyone.'

I explored further.

'In Frankfurt we handed over the sick to a Red Cross post. They all looked very bad. That's because the transport improvised too much. There were not enough medications, and the rations were poor.'

'And in Frankfurt?'

'Frankfurt is a beautiful city. There were so many restaurants and coffee houses, a tramway; no, they had everything there, everything.

It hasn't been damaged much.' [The Russian was certainly comparing the damage with what had occurred in Soviet cities. Frankfurt an der Oder was severely damaged during the Soviet advance.]

'Did you like it there?'

'Oh, yes, very much so. Do you know, the people there were all well clothed. All the men wore long trousers, jackets, hats and *Galstuck* (ties). The women all have fancy dresses and, do you know, whether man or woman, they all wear leather shoes!'

I could see he was very impressed.

'Too bad I was only there a short time, and now I am back in this accursed forest.'

Even though he was a soldier, Alexandrov had never been on the front before. He had only been in the forest. He poked the small fire with his stick and looked pensively at the embers.

'*Snaiesch schto* – do you know what?' he suddenly continued. 'Now I know, we are the poorest devils in the world.'

Thereupon, I could not help but saying, 'All the better for you that you have won the war. Now you are able to get whatever you are lacking.'

'Yes, yes.' He nodded approvingly.

There was one more thing I had to ask him. 'Tell me, Alexandrov, did you see other transports on the journey home?'

'Oh, yes, I saw several transports heading in the direction of Germania, but I also saw transports from Germania coming here, along with women. And many of the transports had trophies.'

I could imagine what these 'trophies' were. Among them were certainly sewing machines, which soon arrived at the camp. But even their best expert could not get it going, because the shuttle was missing.

'But there is one thing I noticed. There weren't any *kipitok* [tanks with boiling water] at the train stations, and I also didn't see any *bania*. Thereafter, I passed through Königsberg.'

You poor man, you cannot even imagine that there are places in the world where you don't need delousing stations, and in these places, there are better things to drink than hot water. I had such an answer on the tip of my tongue, but he provided me with such good information that I didn't want to vex him.

One day during the *proverka* there was a fuss. A rumour circulated that two men were missing. All the teams had to verify an exact count. In fact, they were two short – two Germans.

Had they actually thought they could escape? We considered that highly unlikely, because every previous attempt had failed.

Perhaps their hunger had driven them to seek out a village that was supposed to be some 20 kilometres from us. The village was apparently not inhabited by *SK*, but by Russians, who for years had been settling in isolated areas in this region.

The camp commander did not express himself on the matter, but he did admonish us to abandon any thoughts of escape.

At the time, we also thought it possible the men had gone out in search of berries, and got lost in the course of doing this. In some places there were a number of cranberries, not fully ripe, and to my amazement I found both red and black currants.

In the pitch black of night, I was suddenly and rudely awoken from sleep. The duty officer summoned me and four others to the gate. We were given a stretcher and, accompanied by a guard, we criss-crossed through the sea of tree stumps into the woods.

After approximately two hours, as dawn was already breaking, he stopped us. We were standing in front of one of the runaways, who was lying on the forest floor with a bullet hole through his head.

'Where is the other?' we asked.

'Already in the *karzer*.'

We carried the dead man back to the camp. Blood was still dripping from his fresh wound. We managed to arrive just as the work teams were assembling.

The camp commander ordered us to carry the dead man across the *proverka-platz*. The presence of the deceased was to warn us against attempting any kind of escape. As we laid him on the ground, I could ascertain that this fatal shot had been made at a very close range. The entry wound and the exit wound were noticeably large. It is likely they could have taken him alive.

During the interrogation of the other man we learned that they wanted to go to the village in order to get potatoes. Along the way they got into an argument and then were separated.

We buried the dead German the following night. Burials were always done at night. The company commander gathered together the sick or *Schlappe* to strip the dead of his clothes and to cover him with earth. These could hardly be called burials. There were no decorations, no flowers, only a simple wooden cross with his name. In winter the dead were simply left under the snow and they were not buried until spring arrived.

Sometime later, the camp was overcome with a jaundice epidemic [probably hepatitis A, which can be transmitted via faecal matter or orally]. The jaundice was so severe that in many cases the victims died despite medical help. With permission of the camp commandant, our doctor was allowed to prescribe double the rations of sugar and tea in addition to their diet.

The death of those dying from jaundice is rather unique and distinctive. As a result of the infection, they behave as if they are drunk, sometimes rising in jubilation, and then collapsing like an empty sack until they suffer the throes of death; afterwards, they lose consciousness and die.

The doctor believed that the large number of rats were to blame for the jaundice epidemic. We were so afraid of the rats that we were all stricken with fear.

This despondency was unexpectedly overcome with a piece of news. The commandant divided postcards in German, Russian and French among the company commanders. Unfortunately, there were not enough for everyone. What was the solution supposed to be? Each of us had a rightful claim to a card.

The best workers were supposed to receive one. Those who had been at one time a good worker, but had since become washed up, went empty-handed. There were more than a hundred men lying in the barracks, and I had fewer than twenty cards on hand.

Among the older camp inmates, however, there were many sceptics who had no interest in a card. They did not want to write.

'There is nothing for us to write, and even if we did, they would never leave this region. And what we want to write, they won't permit.'

Such were their responses.

I attempted to appease them and make it clear that now that the war had ended, the cards were certain to find their way home. The oldest prisoners should do everything possible to communicate with home – even if it was only the words 'I am alive.'

I wrote a card myself and tapped on it three times, '*Toi, toi, toi*,' in the hope it would certainly make it. ['*Toi, toi, toi*' is figuratively to 'knock on wood'; it is used in the performing arts, similar to 'break a leg', reflecting a superstition that wishing someone 'good luck' is in fact bad luck.] Mind you, I set more hope in word of mouth, which I sent along with an Italian who would, I hoped, travel through Austria on the way.

The camp number was on the card, which would provide the post office in Moscow the ability to send us an answer. An answer from home? I did not dare to think about that. It would be beautiful. A reply? How long would that take? By then, I hoped to be long gone. My release certainly would come before that.

Work on the Collective Farm

Harvest time had arrived!

The *Schlapp* command had to dig up and gather potatoes, heads of cabbage and beets. The potatoes were not quite ready to harvest, but it had to be done because there was a danger of freezing in the beginning of September.

Indeed, it actually snowed overnight. Two-thirds of the harvest surrounding the camp still had to be brought in. So, the best work teams were brought in and used to dig up the harvest, but only after they had cut their cubic metre of wood, when their work was completed, or on their free days.

For once we actually enjoyed doing the additional labour, because a substantial portion of the harvest was for our own consumption. The team leader made a small fire and was constantly laying the potatoes on the embers. A good many men, however, could not wait until they were spread out and they ate the green potatoes in their raw state. They had terrible diarrhoea as a result.

Several prisoners attempted to smuggle beets, cabbages and potatoes into the camp by stuffing them in their trousers or hiding them under their cap. It depended upon the guard whether they were successful. If he was hungry, he would frisk them for sure. In that case, he would either kick them or slap the side of their head, so that both the potatoes and the cap went flying. The guard would then gather the spoils and store them in the guardhouse for his own feast.

A small Hungarian went running right through the gate, his trousers so full they were ready to burst. He had the misfortune that the cord holding his trousers together came undone, and a shitload of *krumpli* [Hungarian potatoes] rolled across the ground. The guard had to be laughing to himself at the sight of this priceless Magyar, and on this occasion he let him go.

Our rations were enriched and made heartier with the harvested *produkti* [produce].

Winter had arrived. The German *étape* with which we had been replenished was a shell of its former self. At most, a third were still working in the woods. The remainder became either sick or *schlapp* – and they had the good fortune, provided they survived, to be transported home. And we, the old wrecks, still remained!

To our great dismay a civilian suddenly assumed control, which meant we were administered by the NKVD. In many ways, this change was to our detriment.

The supervisors were almost without exception *SK* who had recently finished serving their sentence, but who were still not allowed to leave. They wanted to receive a good report from 'on high' in the hope they would be released to return home. Because of this, they trampled all the more on the worker. For the most part, they understood the business better, and they were less likely to be deceived. The pressure on and exploitation of the worker increased under them, especially before the Russian national holidays.

Once again, on the day before the October Revolution, we had a recording day, in which not a soul could remain in the camp. If anyone tried to undermine work efforts in any way they would be immediately locked up. If anyone conducted self-mutilation, they were severely punished and then sent to a Russian *SK* camp.

Whereas the rations that we had been served earlier were augmented at least partially from our own inventory, now they would come only from the collective and they were supplemented with bran. And this bran was not in stock, but instead arrived at night in a sack, at which time it would be distributed.

All these events only strengthened the appalling belief that we would no longer be viewed as prisoners of war, but as *SK*. Along with this, our hopes for release only diminished, provided we were of use somehow.

This rumour generated such anxiety in the camp that it was even unpleasant for the Russians. They called for a *sobranje*, in which the commissar explained to us that these measures were simply organisational changes meant to simplify things, and that by no means would it affect our status as prisoners of war. The day we would be released was not far off.

I was cutting a large tree with a comrade. All of a sudden someone came to us. He was very excited, and he beckoned me to go with him. I asked him what he wanted, but he said nothing. Instead, he led me by the arm this way and that over the snow and fallen timber. Then he stopped.

I could hardly believe my eyes! There, one of our best buddies was dangling next to the saw in a fir tree, hanging by his braces. I went to him quickly and freed him from this position. He was already cold and dead.

'Can you tell me what happened?' I asked the other man. He shook his head and said, 'Ernstl's birthday was today. Earlier he requested a second serving of soup for the occasion.'

Naturally, I dropped the saw and ran to the forest master. I met him by the fire, and the camp commandant was also on hand.

As I reported the incident to them, they did not appear to be particularly surprised. They were certainly accustomed to such troubles, and having lived as slaves for fifteen to twenty years, they had seen a lot.

It was nothing new that once again a dead man was taken out of the woods on a sled, and then laid to rest under the snow.

The Russians made promises of flour and *machorka* in order to increase the work greatly. A man who met the quota was no longer special, and was even called lazy by the *politruk*. Teams that set records [for an explanation of 'record holders', see Chapter 18] were given additional flour and bran, even to the point where they could fill their cups in the morning, afternoon and evening. It was always the same porridge. The record holders also received a kilo of bread and 20 to 30 grams of *machorka*.

One morning the *politruk* formally announced that in the future, extra work would even be paid for in rubles. The payment of team and company leaders would be equal to what the average worker was entitled. Or so they said.

What were we to do with rubles to begin with? There was no canteen or store for miles around from which we could buy something.

The record holders worked more, first and foremost due to the additional rations, which this time was done without watering down the food. The rubles were indeed paid monthly. However, the only thing on the collective that one could buy was milk or bread from the *chlebareska* [bakery].

There was no gambling with this money. Every game of chance lost its appeal because the money was of almost no value to us.

Just before the holidays the guards began their usual pilfering. As always, all sharp objects were confiscated. No axes, saws, hoes or picks were allowed in the camp.

The police guards also tore my barracks apart. One of them called me over.

'What is this?' He rummaged with his hands through a satchel of unroasted coffee, which one of the last *étape* had concealed. I said to him that it was coffee. He looked at me in disbelief, and said '*Durak!*' ['Fool!'], flinging the satchel across the room so that the beans scattered all over the place. Obviously, he had never seen unroasted coffee beans.

It would have been better for him and for us had the owner of the beans acknowledged them sooner. When I reproached him, he said he just wanted to exchange them for something else.

So, all of us picked up the beans, each securing a few of them for himself. In the evening, a refined, unfamiliar aroma of coffee permeated the barracks.

Barter was a general characteristic of this camp. Bread for salt, salt for *kapusta*, *kapusta* for a mess tin, a mess tin for footwear, footwear for soup, and finally once again soup was exchanged for bread. It was a constant swapping of the most primitive items, which were either stolen or in some other way came into one's possession.

The latest change was that tables were brought into the woods on which the record-breaker was immortalised. A single labour commissar was employed who would deliver a speech to the prisoners every day before they began their march. The contents of this pathetic talk were always the same: 'Yesterday you worked, but today you must work harder. The quota must not only be met, it must be greatly exceeded. That is our primary objective.'

Just listening to it would put us to sleep.

As for world politics, we only heard rumours: a peace accord was imminent in San Francisco for the satellite countries. [This may have been the United Nations. At this point, he is describing events in the late autumn of 1945. The UN Charter was adopted in San Francisco on 25 June 1945, and it was ratified by the five permanent members of the Security Council on 24 October 1945.] We had concerns from the beginning about tensions between the West and the Soviet Union. We had always foreseen this and predicted it. Anyone who knew about this [the Soviet] system did not believe an understanding between the two was possible. The differences were too great.

We hoped we would not be casualties of this disagreement. We often heard, '*Amerikanzi, eti tschuliki* – the Americans, these criminals!'

As long as they were being sent weapons and provisions, they were good friends. Now the tables were beginning to turn.

December's brutal cold came upon us.

During one day, the temperature dropped from -25°C to -35°C. The current *natschalnik* of the camp, a real Asian with wide cheekbones who bore the marks of having lived in the forest for decades, allowed the work teams to be brought in at once.

However, it was already too late. The damage had been done. Many had already suffered second- and third-degree frostbite. In barrack number seven it was especially bad. More than two-thirds of them were casualties.

The *natschalnik* was foaming at the mouth. What did he do? The company commander was held totally responsible, he was relieved of his duties, and he was sent to the *karzer* for a day. He was accused of having done too little to look after his men, that he had sent them out to work in tattered boots, and so forth. The poor fellow did not say a word in his defence. The next day he marched back out to the woods again with a saw on his back.

When would it be my turn? All too easily, the company commander could find himself in a situation where a mistake was made and he would find himself accountable for things about which there was nothing he could do. It was to be expected.

28

Meeting the German Russians

The high snowdrifts whirled through the camp. The thermometer read -40°C. It was late in the evening. I stuffed the small iron stove full of wood and I divided up the night watch. I was the last one to go to bed.

The door was then ripped open, and a cold blast of wind whipped across the bunks. Those on duty told me to get up. All of the company leaders, the interpreters and the antifascists had to go immediately into the forest to load wood onto the small-gauge railcar.

Loading wood in the middle of the night in this nasty weather? Once again, it had to be done hastily.

Bundled up like an Eskimo, I exited the dwelling and trudged outside into the night. We assembled at the guardhouse, some cursing more than others. What were a few people supposed to be doing loading wood?

Out at the loading area, which we reached after an hour, we began to work. We loaded nothing but heavy timber. One of us made a fire, with which we could take turns thawing out.

Stacking wood on the wagon was not easy work. There was a lot of fumbling around in the dark that was only somewhat illuminated by the campfire. The higher the stack got on the wagon, the more difficult it became. One of us stood on top and pulled up the logs with clamps, and then placed them on the stack. The wood was so badly frozen and covered with ice that even hitting it hard with a pickaxe didn't work, and it was only with the utmost effort that we were able to load the logs.

Then reinforcements approached. Women! In fact, they were speaking a combination of German and Russian. Volga Germans [ethnic Germans who settled in the lower Volga region as part of a colonisation programme during the reign of Catherine the Great in the 1760s]. Not far from us, they were loading the same heavy logs as we were, with an agility and speed that simply amazed us. One of them would lug the logs on her shoulder and then toss them onto the wagon; something that required two of us to accomplish with some difficulty.

The last wagon was loaded. The Romanian commandant suggested we distribute the logs unevenly and at angles. If the load was on the one side, the wagon would derail, and then we would be able to rest for the night and sit by the fire.

The train departed and we sat by the fire. We threw large pieces of wood on top of it and we squeezed around it. In front it was hot while our backs were freezing.

The female work team leader approached us and asked in good German whether her people could also warm themselves until the next train was loaded. We secretly hoped that it wouldn't return at all, that things would go flying as it rounded the next curve.

About fifteen women sat around our fire. They were all dressed the same: black cotton blouses and pants, felt boots, gloves, dark scarves tied around their heads. They weren't wearing fur coats. We were very surprised that they were not cold.

'But we've already been working daytime and nighttime shifts for three years loading cars. We are the native *grusovtschiki* – the loaders. A few of us are sick. This may be why you were sent to reinforce us.'

Then they told us the same story we had heard about the German *normirovtschik* [standard setter – a person who organises labour and production processes] in construction. They came from various villages throughout the Soviet Union. It was only once they got here that they partly got to know each other. They knew nothing of their parents or their husbands. Poor creatures.

But they did not come across as poor; they were resigned to the situation. Despite the fierce cold, they began to sing beautiful German songs. The melodies sounded very much German, but they were entirely foreign to me. Their faces were hard and their hands worn. Nevertheless, they preserved a certain feminine nature. Our conversation with them was excellent.

When asked if they came out at night without supervision, they answered: 'We only have one female team leader in charge, this tall, slim woman. She is good to us. She is married to a Russian, which happens rarely among us. But even today, she doesn't know where he is.

'Several of us also work in the cellulose factory [pulp mill] which is here in the vicinity. By the way, a few of us are being sent to you shortly to serve as supervisors.'

To that, I said, 'That would not make us angry at all.' But, I thought, that might be easier said than done, because they would also be under pressure to push us to work harder in order to retain their positions.

The train must have derailed, because we heard nothing more the rest of the night. At dawn we started heading back.

As we arrived back at camp, the old man wanted us to head right back out again. We refused, and so we lay back down.

Approximately 100 Romanians were working with us. Because the Italians had been repatriated, they assumed it was now their turn. They refused any further work, preferring to be locked up and placed on half-rations. They insisted on being sent home.

One morning the following happened: two Romanian teams, who happened to be right in front of the gate, stepped out of their rows and stood there independent of the others. They refused to march to where the tools were passed out, but instead they goose-stepped in unison to the *karzer*. They did not look to the right or to the left, and they ignored the shouts of the astonished guards. All the screaming, cursing and yelling was to no avail.

After they recovered from their amazement, a few guards ran to those who were refusing to work, in order to bring them back. But the 'rucksacks' threw themselves in the snow and let themselves be kicked, because the blows from the felt boots were mitigated by their heavy fur coats and clothing, so they were able to endure them. Not one of them defended himself. They rolled up like hedgehogs.

Not until the Romanian company commander arrived did they stand back up. Nevertheless, they still refused to work. Their wish to go to the *karzer* was fulfilled.

But the camp authorities had ways of dealing with this. Over the next few days, a course of punishment was meted out. Anyone who was involved, regardless of the degree of culpability, was punished. Specifically, it was delivered as each one was led to and from the work site. His working hours began earlier and only stopped once the last person had fulfilled his quota.

Even in the event those under punishment fulfilled their usual quota, they did not receive their usual rations, i.e., not 800 grams, but 600 grams of bread. At the same time, if one of them did not cut his 3 metres of wood despite the prolonged working hours, instead of going back to the barracks, he would be stuck into the *karzer*. But several of the Romanians did not give in. They had had enough, and they wouldn't take it any more. They preferred to die, even if it meant slowly wasting away. A few of them endured this unrelenting pressure, literally, both emotionally and physically.

For anyone who continued to refuse to work despite this punishment, but somehow managed to survive, the Russians had another trump card in their hand. They immediately went before a summary court martial, and overnight they vanished to some other *SK* camp.

As a deterrent, it was announced that the *NN* [*Nomen Nescio* – Latin for 'name not known'] had been sentenced to ten or fifteen years in a 'camp' on account of consistent refusal to work …!

Even this failed to have an effect.

The joy was great when we were told one day that the *upravleniya* post office supposedly had mail from the homeland for prisoners of war. [This was the separate mail system for the Gulags. *Upravleniya* means 'management' or 'controls', and was part of the acronym for *glavnoe upravleniya lagerei* – 'gulag' – or 'main camp administration'.] We couldn't believe it, until a Hungarian and three Austrians actually had letters and postcards from their relatives in their hands. Even if we were not among the lucky few in that moment, it still caused a sensation for everyone. The slimmest hope grew into a belief in our hearts that we might also receive news from home.

Thus, the connection had been made. Perhaps my family too knew that I was alive.

At the same time, this knowledge also led to disappointment.

Our translator was sent to the headquarters to 'clear up a problem with the mail'. Although these few letters had been censored several times during the long way here, the commissar had not missed the opportunity to carefully examine the contents again. In the process, he had managed to make a complete mess in that the letters and the envelopes got separated, so that the contents no longer matched the addressee. Since the letters themselves did not contain the full name and the camp number, naturally, it was almost impossible to route them.

Our interpreter took great pains to try to match the script on the letters with the envelopes. 'Dear Hans, Dear Karl, etc.', was not enough. By so doing, they managed to deliver a large part of the letters. The remainder were undeliverable. But due to the shortage of paper, it did not take long before they were used as cigarette paper. They referred to them as '*nix gut*', as in not very good to smoke. Of course not, because the paper was gummy. But they knew nothing of that here. In Moscow, certainly!

It became increasingly obvious that our camp supervisors were making every effort to increase our capacity to work, even though they were lacking the most basic resources. For those who worked, there was bran and potatoes enough. However, for the many who could not meet expectations, hunger was a constant companion.

As far as 'hygiene' was concerned, there was a certain amount of progress. We had a regular supply of soap, and what was even more important, we received new underwear monthly. At our insistence, we were also given the razors, blades and brushes that the last *étape* had brought with them. With these, we finally had the ability to scrape off the last of the pesky stubble, giving us a degree of humanity.

We eventually came to a point where all the camps in the vicinity relied only upon prisoners of war, as a way for us to make restitution. The culture brigades were the only *SK* who visited us regularly. The presentations and the workers' assemblies alternated back and forth.

By handling us with these new methods, the Russians had success. They offered more food, even if it was daily the same poor, monotonous meal. The 'monthly *kubatura*' increased. The work teams, divided according to nationality, were cleverly pitted against each other. One time it would be the Hungarians, and then either the Germans or the Austrians who were portrayed as the model. Even *papirossi* with long tips were given out to good workers. When the best work teams maintained a good daily average, they were permitted to work without guards and they could return home earlier. The *vichatnoi* [*vyhodnoi* – day off], every ten days, was now actually work free, and no one was given additional duties.

Despite the improvement, losses remained high. The strength of the individual continued to be exploited, and the unbalanced rations took their toll. Frostbite was a continual problem. The camp only rarely received new felt boots, and the old ones had become worn out. When someone demanded redress, the response by our superiors was that we were not so sympathetic when we were on the front, setting Russian villages on fire despite the cold and snow, and similar things like that.

One time I had a related discussion with the forest master. When he became very coarse with me, I told him that he was in no position to judge a soldier. He, who had been expelled from his community for being a criminal, and who had never seen the front, would be better to keep his mouth shut.

That hit him deeply and he hurled the worst insults at me. He vowed that I would soon be putting the saw back in my hand because I would be earning Russian bread on my own.

He was soon proved right. For some time, we had started having 'antifascist' students (students who were required to attend an antifascist course) from Moscow in the camp. They did not have to work, but rather were trained to influence us. However, since they came directly from Moscow, they ended up giving speeches. It was their attempt to educate us politically.

Naturally, it broke the camp commandant's heart, when he had to look on as his manpower was turned over to the Antifa people, instead of being outside in the woods doing '*billi-billi*' (cutting wood). It therefore did not surprise us that all the translators and the company commanders and those in charge were dismissed and then replaced by the Antifa students.

So I took my saw on my back and I hauled it out into the woods. Cutting wood was no longer that difficult for me. I was able to cut my quota with little effort, but I did not cut one cubic centimetre more than was needed. I had no desire to deliberately ruin my health.

29

Serious Illness

In the meantime, a *Schlapp* transport departed once more. However, no one who was seriously ill was included. This time they had to stay back. The word that went round was that a large percentage of the transport did not make it to their destination.

My good doctor told me that the only way to be sent home was to be diagnosed with a permanent disability that prevented any further work. But who would risk such as an illness?

And once again – how many more times? – spring arrived in the Urals. I was tempted to work without wearing any clothing above the waist. That, however, would not have been a good idea. I developed a nasty cold that felt like a massive stabbing in the lungs. In spite of this I did not stay in the barracks, but instead went out into the woods.

After three days I couldn't go on any longer. What was wrong with me? The food no longer had any taste. The doctor wrote that I was sick.

In the barracks I lay my ragged body by the oven. It didn't help. I had no appetite, even smoking disgusted me. In the evening my temperature stood between 38 and 39°C. The stabbing in my lungs did not let up. They transferred me to sickbay.

Where had my doctor gone? Several days passed and I did not see him. The Russian doctor who served in his place made the well-known 'bars' sign with his fingers. Why? Ah, he happened to have had too much of a liking for one of the female members of the culture brigade. Illicit sexual intercourse got him another four years. He was transferred to an *SK* camp.

But Mischa, I thought. That was worth it. Compared to one night of lovemaking, locked up an additional four years!

My temperature continued to rise, and I completely lost any

appetite. The only thing that tasted good to me was American powdered milk, which was part of the treatment in sickbay. Unfortunately, I only received three very small glasses per day.

After a thorough examination, the doctor diagnosed me with pleurisy. Breathing became more difficult as each day passed, until one morning I was lying there bathed in sweat, grappling with the greatest difficulty to breathe.

The medic elevated my bed so I could sit upright. That made it easier to breathe. Every four hours I was prescribed powder, but because my stomach was empty, I could not tolerate it. I developed nausea and I had to vomit. The doctor became increasingly worried as he looked at me. I knew that it had to be very serious. I now had pneumonia in both lungs. The doctor tried to force me to eat. But I couldn't, not one bite. Perhaps if I'd had a piece of white bread and a soft-boiled egg or some food they could give to sick people … but I could not bring this harsh bran for prisoners to my lips. Now and then I would be given some cooked fish. It took everything I had to eat a few small pieces.

Several comrades came to my bed to comfort me. One even brought me a litre of milk that he had organised from the collective. It was touching that he had used his hard-earned rubles for me.

I was not about to die. Even if I had now reached rock bottom. I had been lying there over a month now. My temperature slowly went down, but then it rose again. The doctor consoled me and said it was better for the temperature to decrease slowly. He then added me to the list of those who had tuberculosis …!

He should have told me this. Certainly, I thought, the doctor was mistaken. The German doctor who sometimes treated me comforted me. He said I now stood a better chance of being sent home.

'Look, in this condition you at least have some possibility. When the commission comes around again, I will help you.'

Another week passed. Thanks be to God, my temperature dropped once again below 38 degrees. With the decrease in temperature, my appetite started to return.

Then Dr Frank, the German doctor, rushed through the room and reported: 'A commission!'

He bent down over me and said, 'It is enough to be transported!'

In fact, two doctors and officers entered our room. I did not know any of them. The medical history of each one of us was read. When it came to my turn, I heard the word: '*Tuberkulosnik*.'

I trembled with excitement under my covers – was I also included? My mind worked feverishly and envisioned going home in all kinds of ways. Then I thought it was inconceivable, and I was overcome with doubts. You, of all people, would be one of the luckiest people to get out of this shitty region. I didn't care, I only wanted to go home. It would never be so bad at home that I somehow couldn't recover.

I was on the list!

This was then forwarded to the NKVD. We heard that the Romanians, Austrians and Hungarians would go together.

Now came the big question, whether the NKVD would strike one of us off the list. Every now and then this happened. There was nothing on my conscience, but you never really knew for sure; they could find something wrong with anything, and all it took was a simple denunciation.

The days were full of anticipation. Nothing changed. I looked nervously at my temperature every evening, because anyone who had a temperature would not be allowed to go. I still had not reached the required 37 degrees. It had to go down a little more, otherwise I would remain here!

I worried too much about it. I had to avoid this, because doing so only caused the fever to go higher. These days seemed like an eternity. For hours I would stare at the whitewashed walls in front of me, and in my mind I was already far across the Russian border. I imagined a thousand images of a reunion with my wife and children, father and mother, and all my friends. Inwardly I would rejoice, and then in the same moment I would be seized with a feeling of uncertainty.

The day came when the doctor allowed me to attempt my first steps since I had been ordered to bed rest some time ago. I had to turn in my clothes, but I was happy to have the hospital coat and slippers that I was given for my departure. I should avoid the sun as much as possible, the doctor said.

Walking outside was very fatiguing. I noticed a strange sensation, as if my upper and lower jaws were dislocated, while the cheeks and the corner of my mouth were pulled tightly toward them. This realisation frightened me, because I had sometimes seen such a facial expression on people who were dying.

The next day, those who were confirmed to be on the transport were washed and shaved anywhere on the body where there was hair. They said we were supposed to leave that evening. We grabbed three days' worth of bread and fish.

I had large beads of sweat running down my forehead as I slipped on my clothes. Out of sheer weakness, I had to support myself and take a break.

The sheets were pulled from the mattress, and I was allowed to lie down again. In the afternoon we stepped out, taking it easy as we slowly went to the gate.

For the first time I realised what had become of me: I was incapable of working. As I approached the exit a few others recognised me and I spoke with them. I must have looked good, I thought. Supported by comrades, I sat down on a small bench and waited for the wagon that was supposed to take us along the wooden tracks to the nearest train station.

An hour passed. A few began to bite into their bread and fish. Personally, I was not that hungry. Unfortunately, I still didn't have much of an appetite; otherwise, I would have done so too.

All my friends, who I had spent such a long and difficult time with, were at work, so I was unable to say goodbye. A few of them had already made provisions for this, and had given me letters and the addresses to take home with me.

'Everyone back! It will not leave until tomorrow …'

After half an hour I was lying in bed, as I had for weeks beforehand. No one told us why or what was going on. That meant we simply had to wait once more. On the one hand, I was not that upset about it; the short trip to the gate was exhausting for me, and I was happy to be lying down again. On the other hand, I had this pressing concern that it meant I would perhaps not be leaving.

The strain had been so great for me that I fell asleep without having anything to eat, and I didn't wake until they took my temperature in the morning. An entire day passed and then another. The mood once again reached rock bottom.

Out of the blue, we were told to get ready. Once again, we stood before the gate. It was evening. Comrades who had already returned from work came up to me, shook my hand and wished me farewell. They all said to me, 'Tell them at home that we are alive, but tell them also what it is like for us in these cursed woods. Say to them that we look forward to coming home,' and many other ardent wishes they asked me to pass along.

'Yes, yes, I promise all of you I will do my best. But first, I must get home.'

Finally, the *vachorka* [guard] called us individually by name. We were not a little astonished when two Romanians had to remain behind the wire mesh. Their pleading and begging were of no use. They were not on the list, and it became obvious they had been struck from the manifest at the last minute.

Those of us who were fortunate sat down on the cart. An emaciated *panje* horse set us slowly in motion.

I looked back several times. Gradually, the last of the barrack gables and watchtowers disappeared in the distance.

I would not forget them, so I was determined to make it home alive. I would tell about their suffering. I would even, as long as I was strong enough, report what took place here to the world. I wanted to save all those who were ravaged and tormented here in these woods, regardless of whether they were prisoners of war or Russians.

30
On the Rail Transport

After a two- to three-hour evening ride we reached a main rail line. A sentry post and a few barracks were standing there. We lay down on the ground, chewed on our bread and, despite our poor physical condition, we were quite happy about things.

A Russian civilian then came past, who stuck a pair of worn-out canvas shoes in my face. He wanted me to remove my slippers and exchange them for his worn-out pair. He was very taken aback when I responded to him with the same foul language in Russian that I refused to do so. When he threatened to get violent, I called the guard who was accompanying us on the transport. He defended me, even though the civilian asserted repeatedly that I didn't need my shoes; in Germania they have plenty of shoes. He was furious, but being unsuccessful, he left.

Something else occurred that also caused me to be anxious. A few Russian officers passed by. One of them was familiar to me, a previous camp commandant who was with us for a little while. Before they had a chance to speak with us, I put my face in the grass and pretended to sleep.

'What is up with you, transport of the sick? *Damoi*? Going home?'

I didn't move, because I was afraid the former commandant would recognise me and would detain me. He had found me very useful before and had used me for various duties. I, however, preferred to go home and get better than to stay in the taiga under his care, where I would slowly but surely perish.

The train rolled up, one of the usual wood transports. It stopped. A few closed cars were attached in the rear.

The guard helped us onto the high steps. It took considerable effort to pull ourselves up, and we crawled into the interior of the car.

What was this? It looked like the inside of a cage that was used to transport wild animals. Above us and all around the inside of the car was a lattice of iron bars. Wood panelling was over them. There was hardly any air supply, and what bothered us most, the stench; there was no sanitary facility in the car.

This is what a Russian *SK* car looked like. It was well built for criminals.

We were assured the doors would be left open. None of us was going to try to escape. Mind you, this way of transporting us made me think it unlikely that we would travel to Frankfurt like this. Was it possible we were going somewhere else?

So passed a day and a night. As usual, there was bread and fish, and this time they even had rye bread and red salmon, which tasted excellent to us. We rode right across the taiga. Very early one morning our car was decoupled and we had to get out. The guard said we were going to a hospital.

We dragged ourselves along a wagon road that led us through open terrain. It was a long way. Mustering our last bit of strength, we arrived at an abandoned house. There we waited. We lay down on the floor and slept. The guard disappeared. There was no one for miles around. Naturally, there was also nothing to eat.

Then a man in a white coat appeared. He asked about our illnesses and our condition. 'First *bania*, then the hospital,' he said.

All our clothes were removed in the *bania*. We stood as we had before, in our underpants and undershirt, bucket in hand. In that moment, we abandoned all hope of a return home. Surely, they were going to try to nurse us back to health, so they could send us back to work. In short, we were finished.

We came to a barracks in which we encountered all nationalities, except German. German and Russian doctors were on duty, and the routine was as one would expect in a hospital. The German personnel reassured us that transports home were routinely organised from here. That calmed us a little.

Although the food and lodgings were not that unpleasant, the passing days were fraying on the nerves. We were examined and treated. On the one hand, we feared, in particular, that the X-ray examination would not show anything, and as a result we would be given a clean bill of health. On the other hand, we naturally did not wish for there to be some dire illness. We oscillated back and forth between Scylla and Charybdis [from Homer's *Odyssey* – between a rock and a hard place], a continuous pendulum of uncertainty and worry.

We also heard about the ever-increasing political differences between the Americans and the Russians. That might also create another obstacle for us.

The excitement came one afternoon. A Russki read the list of those who were being transported further. All those present were on the list, only I was not. I was almost speechless. With my knees shaking, I asked the Russian whether I was not also on the list.

'*Kak familia* – what is your name?'

I gave him my name. He searched for it.

'*Ja, sabil* – I missed it. It's good.'

I took a deep breath. A couple more shocks like that and I would have totally collapsed.

We received uniforms, certainly not those which we had worn previously, but instead some worn-out, torn pieces of clothing and footwear. That meant I could not keep the better pair of shoes I had arrived with. 'Move out, immediately,' came the command. Not to the train station, but to a meadow. Three chairs and a small table stood there.

Columns of men similar to ours came from every direction. We sat down in the vicinity.

Then the officers with the familiar caps and lapels appeared – NKVD. Each person was called individually, brought forward, and all sorts of papers compared and reviewed. Positive cases were gathered on one side and negative cases on the other. Roughly 300 men had to stay behind. In particular, former members of the military police were singled out.

Even then, we still didn't head towards the train station. We were detained in two large barracks for a few more days, where we were given plenty to eat.

All of a sudden, the strongest were selected and given scrubbing brushes and buckets to clean the cars at the train station. Upon their return we were met with another blow. There were not enough railcars. Some of us had to remain behind. Who would it be?

The next morning at dawn the NKVD returned and read out the names. A third of us had to remain behind. The others would have to wait, but they knew that 'next time' could also mean months.

Prior to leaving, we were able to stuff ourselves with soup. In columns of four we headed for the train station. Luckily, I was among them.

We stopped along the village road. The columns were turned over to the transport commandant of the train. Roll call was again conducted. The count did not match. Finally, the numbers agreed and the transfer was completed.

At the train station we were loaded onto the cars, which had been equipped with bunks. We also noticed a field kitchen, and an additional set of underwear was provided. Nurses, doctors and a *politruk* accompanied us. We also departed immediately.

It was an uplifting feeling. Now we genuinely believed that we were finally headed home. Our 'hospital train', which had cars loaded with wood in front, headed westwards nonstop.

In Sverdlovsk [an oblast (administrative region) east of the Ural mountains], it was rumoured that we were supposed to be connected to a main transport. When we reached Sverdlovsk, it turned out the train had already left. We were late.

Two days and nights we stood in one of the sidings. Neither the guards nor the officers knew what would happen next. Nevertheless, the Russians looked very much forward to the West and the eventual 'trophies', and they were very much in favour of continuing.

They finally managed to attach our cars to another train, and it even turned out to be an express train that was headed in the direction of Moscow. We were overjoyed.

We left several cities behind us at a rapid pace. We frequently saw piles of structural material, machines and vehicles exposed to the elements.

The oncoming trains were all heavily loaded. Anything that could not be nailed or screwed down was found on the cars.

The passenger trains especially attracted our attention, because the people were bunched together like grapes; men, women and children hanging outside, either on top, on the running boards, or even up forward on the side of the locomotive, whereas the interior of the cars were virtually empty. I learned that in this way, the people were allowed to ride for free. What would one of our train conductors have said about such unsafe operations? Time after time such trains would pass by, and whether rain or sunshine, the passengers continued to ride in this manner. Only coal trains, which came from Schlesien [Silesia, formerly a region of south-east Prussia located along the Oder River, ceded to Poland after World War II. It is known for being rich in deposits of coal, iron and other minerals], as the writing on the trains showed, were not fully occupied. Passengers were not permitted on these trains because too much of it was stolen.

Even though the war had long been over, the train stations were still heavily guarded, not for our sake, but to guard freight, and especially coal. When the coal cars were loaded they were sprayed with limestone, so that it could be determined immediately if some went missing.

The nurses and doctors inquired about our health at the places we stopped. So far, everyone was doing fine.

The trip to Moscow passed so quickly and pleasantly.

We did not see much of the capital city. We bypassed most of the city, and from Kiever train station [Kievsky] in Moscow we were transported towards the south.

From then on, the ride was unfortunately stop and go. We went from city to city, and each time we were coupled to another train headed in our direction.

We travelled through the former front lines that were still characterised by damaged rail lines, and burned villages and farmsteads. Many new wooden homes were under construction. Parked railcars served as train stations, equipped with the corresponding cables and tools.

In Gomel [a city in south-east Belarus along a tributary of the Dnieper River] the train stopped again for a long time. That meant we were supposed to take a bath. We appreciated that greatly, because we were indescribably dirty.

Despite the bustling traffic, we had to wash naked in the rail yard. In so doing, we once again were the target of ridicule by men, women and children. It was embarrassing to stand there naked. On the whole, we were not physically assaulted, even though an occasional drunken soldier grabbed his pistol and waved it around. Soldiers who were heading home on leave from their duties in occupied Austria or Hungary greeted us. They were even so friendly as to offer us cigarettes, and they told us their life was good in our homeland.

In Lemberg [Lviv – the largest city in western Ukraine] we stopped on the track next to a heavily guarded train of prisoners who were coming from Szopron [Sopron – a city in Hungary on the Austrian border]. The doors of this train were secured with barbed wire and even the small, high windows were wired shut. Outside a platform was erected, on which a guard was on duty with direct access to a telephone.

The occupants called out to us, and asked where we were coming from. We did not provide any precise information, because we preferred not to reveal to these poor devils what their future held. We heard that most of them were sentenced to ten to twenty years' hard labour for their activities as a Werwolf ['Werewolf' was a resistance plan organised by the Nazi SS to sow terror and demoralise occupying soldiers from 1944 to 1945], for political reasons, or more or less by chance.

I shuddered at the thought of what was in store for these people. They would not be classified as prisoners of war, but as *SK*!

Because we had been forewarned, we guarded against stepping outside the car. If for some reason someone went missing from one of these trains headed towards the east, then the Russians would simply pick up one of those returning home and place him in the ill-fated train, so that their count would again be correct.

In Tarnopol [now Ternopil, a city in western Ukraine] train station I had a minor disagreement with a Romanian who had an axe to grind. He had mistaken me for another man, with whom he apparently had a score to settle from his time in the camp. Unexpectedly, he threw a punch at me. I had enough presence of mind to fend it off, and the tall soldier fell onto the tracks. An interpreter resolved the argument. We concluded it was not worth attracting attention and putting our trip home in danger.

Over one of the passes in the Carpathian Mountains, we heard a peal of bells for the first time. We were on Hungarian soil. The Hungarians on our train knelt down and thanked the Lord God. The Romanians also shed tears and they made the sign of the cross. We Austrians also felt somewhat more secure. The situation at the border in this strip of land was very confused. Pretty soon we found ourselves in Hungarian, Romanian and Russian areas of influence. For the time being, our next destination was Marmorosz-Sziget. [Máramarossziget, today known as Sighetu Marmatiei, was a city in Transylvania, in the Kingdom of Hungary until the end of World War I. During the interwar period, Transylvania was ceded to Romania. It was annexed by Hungary during World War II, and then returned to Romania following the war.]

In the railway stations it turned out that these people were barter-happy. What kind of trade was there with people who were coming out of Siberia? They offered white bread, cigarettes and fruit for any kind of article of clothing or shoes.

31

Marmorosz-Sziget to Home

Early in the morning we arrived at Marmorosz-Sziget. Due to the early hour, very few people were on the station premises. Those who were had pity on us and distributed what they had at hand, a few apples or a piece of white bread. They asked whether we still had old Deutsche Marks. [This is in reference to the Reichsmark, as the Deutsche Mark was not introduced until 1948. The Reichsmark was in use from 1924 until 1945, and during the first few years of the military occupation.] It was likely they were still useful as a means of exchange.

Formed in rows of four, we went to a delousing station that was parked there. In an open square we undressed, we handed over our clothes, and we went into the car to be deloused. In the second car, warm showers were set up, which were powered by the locomotive. Mirrors were available, and there was plenty of soap and hand towels. This civilised bath made us feel respectable.

So, half a day passed. We waited for what would happen next in the shade of the few trees.

In the afternoon we marched through the city into a former Romanian base. We heard Romanian and Hungarian spoken, and almost everyone understood German. The city had experienced a very chequered past. One moment it belonged to the Romanians; the next moment to the Hungarians.

In the barracks square we were again processed through a medical commission. Naked, we anxiously imagined what might happen. Many of us had gained a decagram [i.e., their health had barely improved] and we feared being sent back.

Thank God the examination was easy. We then went to a place that was fenced off with barbed wire. It was located in the centre of the base and was guarded by sentries.

The food was good and there was plenty of it. The German prisoners of war who were on duty exchanged our shabby garments for something better. We spent the night on bunks in the barracks.

So, three days passed without any word about the continued transport. We waited eagerly for that moment.

We heard that a band accompanied every transport from here to the station. For this purpose, a separate German military band had been assembled which had been employed in this capacity since the end of the war.

They said they would prefer to be standing in ranks with us; let another group hail them home.

They also performed this service for us. With a *tschinta-rassa-bum* [an onomatopoeia for the sound of percussion instruments], a handful of Austrians and Hungarians marched out of the gate.

The train was standing in front of the base gate. Aha, pilfering! We hoped it would be the last one! Among others, I got kicked in the back because I had two letters that were found between my torn socks and the wooden clogs. The addresses which I had under my field cap remained undiscovered.

Then they started with the Radetzky March [composed by Johann Strauss to celebrate the Austrian victory against the Italians under Field Marshal Radetzky von Radetz in 1848] and other old Austro-Hungarian marches. In spite of the marching rhythm, we were far from the German goose-step. Each of us limped in his own way through the streets.

Only a few people were lured by the music. This ridiculous spectacle had already repeated itself too often.

The residents were not hostile towards us. Falling from windows, from hands unseen, they tossed us apples and bread.

When we reached the train station, a few civilians, more or less well dressed, approached us with some parcels which they wanted some of us to take. Before we could take them, the Russian guard intervened. He had a particular reason for doing so. An especially fashionable lady tried repeatedly to slip me a package, but the guard was too alert.

A train showed up earlier than expected. Great enthusiasm

ensued when we spotted the first Austrian railway official. We crowded around him full of joy, and we barraged the good fellow with a thousand questions. He provided us with cigarettes and gave us all sorts of information. The certainty increased further; hurrah, we were going home.

A few cattle cars were attached to the express train, and we were literally crammed inside. But this time, we didn't mind doing so.

I was in good enough shape that I was also able to bear another thirty-six hours.

A whistle – slowly, the train set in motion. I was emotionally overwhelmed. Although it certainly was not good for me, I smoked one cigarette after another. I had the jitters, and they visibly increased.

The train departed from Marmorosz-Sziget. As we were pulling away, a Russian officer jumped onto our car and sat next to me at the door. He offered me a cigarette and he was in good spirits.

'*Damoi jedisch* – are you headed home?'

A joyful Yes was my answer.

'Where are you from?'

'Vienna.'

'Oh, you are an Austrian. Oh, Austria is a fine land. I have a bride there, a blonde, in Gäserndorf [a city in Niederösterreich (Lower Austria), about 20 kilometres north-west of Vienna]. A lovely wife. And you have good wine. Everything is *karascho* – good!'

I asked him if much of it had been destroyed, how it looked in Vienna. He quickly strayed from the question, saying he had cancelled his furlough home because he wanted to return to his bride and it was far nicer in Austria than in Russia.

I preferred not to say anything, as I had become accustomed to doing. He began to speak bluntly about politics and he complained about the Russian system. Up until then, I had seldom heard someone talk in that fashion. Had his glimpse at conditions in the West really impressed him that much? Was it possible that because of the war, our country had been completely impoverished and destroyed?

Although he continued in this tone, I only nodded in silence. Then I asked him point blank: 'Do you think, Lieutenant, there is going to be another war? I mean between the Americans and Russia?'

'*No da*,' ['Yes'] he said. 'I think so, but not today and not tomorrow. But some day there will be a fight. But then, Russia will lose.'

The train drove slowly into a station and came to a stop. The officer shook my hand, jumped off, and said, '*Maltschi* – don't say anything!'

I thought about the incident. In the meantime, night was upon us and the train started rolling again. The consumption of all the fruit that we had received over the past few days from the local population made us noticeably unpleasant. Understandably, because our stomachs were clearly unaccustomed to the diet. Since no bathroom existed in the cattle car, there was nothing to do but to hang our rear ends outside the car.

In one large station, it got to the point that the stationmaster stopped the train until the area of 'discharge' was again clean. Aha, we finally realised that we were approaching the West, because as long as we were travelling on Russian territory, no one ever thought about preventing us from answering the call of nature anywhere in the station.

During the night we could barely catch any sleep. The cramped situation prevented this. There was no place to sit down or stretch out. Personally, I just talked to myself. Look, only a few more hours of discomfort! What is that compared to everything you have been through … I not only reassured myself, I also tried to calm my comrades. Unfortunately, I did not have much success. The people were too nervous and edgy. The ride had already lasted three weeks. Until this point, each of us had had the consuming fear that our journey wasn't really headed home; that one or the other of us would be held back, or that something else would get in the way, especially given the strained political situation, so we heard.

We had all become too sceptical. But now that we were travelling on an express train towards Budapest, there could be no doubt.

On the Hungarian–Romanian border we were fed by the Hungarian Red Cross. That was some soup! Our eyes were watering, partly due to our inner emotions and partly due to the spicy paprika pepper. It tasted so marvellous that I wanted to empty the entire bucket. How could one be so gluttonous?

The trip continued over a Hungarian plateau – the Puszta. The Hungarians in the car adjacent to mine went wild. They were singing as loudly as they could. Their journey ended in Budapest. That's where they would be handed over.

According to the timetable, we would arrive in the capital city around midnight. In the late evening, I somehow fell asleep in a squatting position. I woke up in the station concourse in Pest.

With 'Hope to meet again, but under different circumstances,' they said farewell. In six to eight hours, we were supposed to be in Vienna.

The time passed very slowly. We crossed the Austrian–Hungarian border at Szopron [Sopron]. When I heard the first Austrian words spoken on native soil, I was unable to respond to those shouting out. Something was stuck in my throat. My eyes were full of tears. I took a deep breath. The train came to a stop. I jumped to the ground, took dirt in my hands, and I was unspeakably overjoyed to be back home.

Well, I lived to see it! I thanked Heaven that I was permitted to make it home. Life in the homeland, after a war had been lost and with foreign soldiers occupying it, would certainly not be easy. All the same, I feared nothing more than going back [to Siberia], even if I had nothing and had to start from scratch.

They pushed newspapers into our hands. They were various party papers. But I couldn't read anything. I looked at the print, but I didn't process the contents. I was too excited.

As the train began to move again, I found myself. Slowly, I began to address my concerns. A huge question loomed before me. What would I do first when I arrived? What would the reunion look like? No one knew I was coming. Had my family even survived? Up until now, I had never thought about this, that in the end I might not be able to see my family again, that my parents or siblings might not still be alive …

These and other worries seized me for a moment. Do they even know I am alive? Was I perhaps even reported dead?

It just couldn't be like that. Remain confident, like you were up to now. You will find out that everything is okay.

The train sped across the fields.

The ruined farmsteads, bomb craters, remnants of walls, a picture that the landscape repeatedly showed, made it clear to me that the worst hostilities must have raged here. My homeland looked rather different to the last time I saw it.

Now, a new worry tormented me. Would I have a roof over my head? Perhaps my possessions were gone. It could be that I no longer had anything left to exchange except my shabby clothes. We knew that Vienna had been partially destroyed and plundered. All of this was possible.

Chin up, it wouldn't last much longer, and the Russians would restore your freedom. I could not even imagine this moment. What would it feel like to be free …?

The time came for the transfer. The Russians had given us hardly anything to eat since Sziget [a town near the Romanian–Hungarian border, about thirty-six hours earlier]. Apparently, they were keeping the remaining canned goods for the return trip. Our daily rations consisted of nothing more than a little blood sausage pudding for six people and some white bread. The transport commandant said laconically: '*Doma alles budjet* – it will all be available at home.' We just smiled, we knew them well, our 'Ivans'. Most certainly, everything would not be available at home. But what we did have would meet the Russian standard of living.

Then another said: 'Look, music and flags are certain to be at the train station.'

To which another replied, 'You idiot, do you think they will be playing music because of you? They might just take you straight to the Vienna Central Cemetery.'

At that, the man he addressed appeared to have had enough.

I also asked myself whether we would actually be welcomed, or whether things were in such a mess that we would be swept away in all the confusion.

We passed through the major outskirts of Vienna without stopping. The good train knew it could not hesitate. It had a precious cargo aboard, a cargo that wished to reach its destination at lightning speed.

Südbahnhof [Vienna's main railway terminus]. It had been badly damaged, I thought to myself. Everything had been destroyed, and there was no construction? It was probably because there was no money. Austria must have become impoverished.

The train came to a stop. A few people were standing and waiting there. So, they had heard that a prisoner-of-war transport was arriving.

Old men and women asked about their sons. But none of those they sought were among them.

A Red Cross office took care of us and distributed soup and street car tickets. The seriously ill aboard our transport, those suffering dystrophy and oedema, went immediately to the hospital.

In one of the rooms in the train station we were sprayed for lice, and we were given our papers certifying we had been deloused and discharged. From this bombed-out and makeshift office, I stepped out onto the street.

Across the way was a street car. Just like before. There were even some taxis. I chose to walk.

In my wooden clogs I stumbled across the Viennese cobblestones; in one hand were my constant companions, my mess tin and spoon, and in the other hand the haversack for bread and my discharge papers.

Looking joyfully ahead, I stepped in that direction.

A new life began.

Epilogue

The reader in the east will be interested to know who committed this story to paper.

I can assure you, it was not prompted by hatred towards the Russian people or their system. I would respond, they did not show me the same courtesy.

We know all too well what a high death toll the Russian people paid in this last war, what suffering and pain the people between Leningrad and Rostov, between Kyiv and Smolensk, must have endured. The enemy carried the war into their land.

A simple soldier of the last great war describes and tells of experiences from the moment when he was forced to throw his weapon away and put both hands up in the air, to show he was abandoning his role as a soldier and that he surrendered.

What is he trying to accomplish?

Is he trying to arouse the world? Is he trying to teach a lesson to sabre-rattlers in the West and East? – Absurd!

It is a simple observation. The prisoner of war is, in most cases, fair game; he is at the mercy and the favour or disfavours of the other side. He is subjected to the capriciousness of the other side, and hopes for a little mercy.

Should such an experience be silenced out of fear, powerlessness or other reasons? Is it not better to tell the truth and create clarity, than to allow blind conjecture, exaggerations or to disavow reports? What is written here is the truth.

The prisoner in war is a poor soul, and to survive, he must find a new courage to live.

I exhort those who might have something similar befall them: in this situation, don't expect sympathy. The other side is hard, cruel and often hideous.

And who is the other side?

Mankind.

Glossary

Antifa	Antifaschisten, Antifascists – an international Marxist–Leninist antifascist movement; the German Communist Party adopted it in 1932 in response to the rise of the Nazis, and both used similar tactics
bania	(Russian) bath or bathhouse
commissar	aka *politruk* – a Communist official in charge of political indoctrination and the enforcement of party loyalty
bistra	(Russian) quickly
chleb	(Russian) bread
davai	(Russian) move on, let's go
desjatnik	supervisor, foreman (Redler sometimes spells this *desertnik*)
étape	resupply troops
Freies Deutschland	Free Germany – a German anti-Nazi organisation (and its eponymous newsletter) operating out of the Soviet Union in World War II
HKL	*Hauptkampflinie* – main front lines
kapusta	a Polish dish of braised cabbage or sauerkraut
karascho	(Russian) good
karzer	punishment cell, detention cell
kasha	Russian porridge made with ground sorghum, fat and salt
kubatura	cubage – unit of measurement for stacked wood – 1 cubic metre
LKW	*Lastkraftwagen* – supply truck
machorka	Russian tobacco
MP	*Militarpolizei* – military police
natschalnik	commandant, chief duty officer

nemtsy — (Russian) mutes – a nickname for Germans, or often applied to any foreigner, because they did not speak Russian

njet — (Russian) no

NKVD — the People's Commissariat for Internal Affairs – the Interior Ministry, the Soviet secret police, formed in the 1930s and dissolved after World War II

oberrekordist — chief record holder

panje — small Polish or Russian draughthorse

papirossi — filterless Russian cigarette

proverka — (Russian) roll call

proverka-platz — literally 'verification place' – roll call or parade ground

Puszta — steppe grassland region extending from Hungary to the Burgenland in Austria

ruki verch — (Russian) hands up

saklutschoni — *SK* – an exile or banished person

schlapp — run-down, weak

Schlappkommando — literally, 'slack' or 'weak' command – light-duty brigade

Silvesternacht — New Year's Eve

sobranje — (Russian) meeting, gathering

Stalinorgeln — Stalin's 'organs' or instruments – Katyusha 13mm multiple rocket launchers, capable of firing as many as four dozen rockets more than 10 kilometres in a ten-second burst

starschina — (Russian) sergeant major; in the context of this text, it is better understood as the senior soldier in the room

T-34 — Soviet medium tank with a 76mm tank gun

taiga — a northern forest characterised by conifers

TB — tuberculosis

valenki — felt boots

Metric Conversion Table

The measurements Redler gives were likely very rough estimates, especially after he was captured.

1 kilometre = 0.62 miles
Redler's unit was about 390 kilometres from Stalingrad, which is about 240 miles.
During the march into Russia they covered about 30 kilometres each day, which is close to 20 miles.
The distance from the first holding facility to the first hospital was 800 metres or about 875 yards; when Redler suggested 800 metres might be more than a kilometre, the distance was probably closer to two-thirds of a mile.

1 metre = 39.4 inches or 3.3 feet
The ditch for the latrine they dug was 8 metres x 2 metres or 26 feet by 6½ feet.

1 centimetre = 0.39 inches
Tree trunks of 40–50 centimetres are approximately 15–20 inches in diameter.

1 cubic metre = 35 cubic feet
3 cubic metres, which was the daily quota of wood, is 106 cubic feet; in comparison, a cord of wood (4' high x 4' wide x 8' long) is 128 cubic feet.

1 litre = 0.9 quarts (Imperial) or 1.1 quarts (US)
Redler's comrades gave him 1 litre of milk when he developed TB.

1 kilogram = 2.2 pounds
The 80-kilogram sack of millet was just over 175 pounds.
Redler's body weight of 45.5 kilograms in the hospital is about 100 pounds.

1 gram = 0.035 ounces

300 to 400 grams (German field drinking cup) is about 10–14 ounces.

40 grams of sugar is about 3 tablespoons.

800 grams of bread is about 28 ounces; this amount of bread for meeting the daily work quota would be approximately 1 loaf of heavy bread; however, since the regulations required the content of bread to be 60 per cent water, the size of the piece of bread would be smaller than one might imagine, and at the least, difficult to compare with a normal portion of bread.

200 grams of *kasha* porridge is 7 ounces or slightly less than a cup.

Centigrade: (°C x 1.8) + 32 = °F

98.6°F, long considered the average body temperature, is 37°C; Redler's temperature spiked at 39.6°C when he had typhus, which is 103.3°F.

Winter temperatures in Russia were brutal; the prisoners stopped working at (minus) -40°C, which is where Centigrade (Celsius) and Fahrenheit meet.